T0306155

GOVERNMENT AND POLITICAL TRUST

If the government is a problem, what should be done about it? A new era of intervention has begun following a global pandemic, climate change and strategic rivalry – but will a *better* government emerge from this? Political turmoil and polarisation are causing people to question how well their societies are governed and how leaders conduct themselves, while urgent practical challenges are arising for public policy and administration. A deeper concern, then, is to re-examine the nature and problem of government itself.

This study covers historically enduring dilemmas that will persist, as well as emerging issues such as climate change and Artificial Intelligence. It sets out core concerns that systems of government, of all kinds, must address. The wide diversity of political beliefs and constitutions calls for toleration in order to foster effective collaboration across types and levels of government. Each country, community and individual follows their own path, but we can all do something to help restore political trust and to raise standards of public administration.

An essential guide for those seeking general and lasting principles of good government, including elected officials, civil servants, community leaders and students of politics and public policy.

Grant Duncan, PhD, is a scholar and author based in Auckland, New Zealand. Recent book titles include *The Problem of Political Trust* and *How to Rule?: The Arts of Government from Antiquity to the Present.*

GOVERNMENT AND POLITICAL TRUST

The Quest for Positive Public Administration

Grant Duncan

Routledge
Taylor & Francis Group

LONDON AND NEW YORK

Designed cover image: © Getty Images

First published 2024
by Routledge
4 Park Square, Milton Park, Abingdon, Oxon, OX14 4RN

and by Routledge
605 Third Avenue, New York, NY 10158

Routledge is an imprint of the Taylor & Francis Group, an informa business

British Library Cataloguing-in-Publication Data
A catalogue record for this book is available from the British Library

Library of Congress Cataloging-in-Publication Data
Names: Duncan, Grant, 1960- author.
Title: Government and political trust : the quest for positive public administration / Grant Duncan.
Description: First edition. | New York : Routledge, 2024. | Includes bibliographical references and index. | Identifiers: LCCN 2023041379 (print) | LCCN 2023041380 (ebook) | ISBN 9781032575278 (hbk) | ISBN 9781032575261 (pbk) | ISBN 9781003439783 (ebk)
Subjects: LCSH: Political science. | Public administration.
Classification: LCC JF51 .D86 2024 (print) | LCC JF51 (ebook) | DDC 320.4--dc23/eng/20230925
LC record available at https://lccn.loc.gov/2023041379
LC ebook record available at https://lccn.loc.gov/2023041380

ISBN: 978-1-032-57527-8 (hbk)
ISBN: 978-1-032-57526-1 (pbk)
ISBN: 978-1-003-43978-3 (ebk)

DOI: 10.4324/9781003439783

Typeset in Galliard
by SPi Technologies India Pvt Ltd (Straive)

This book is dedicated to those millions of people who undertake government as their steady and hard work.

CONTENTS

TABLES

PREFACE

I started planning this book in July 2021. As a snapshot, what was happening that month? Due to a series of dry summers and a heatwave, hundreds of thousands of hectares of Siberian forest were burning. The city of Yakutsk (population 280,000) was covered in a toxic smog, causing a severe health hazard. Similar forest fires burned out of control in western Canada and United States. Such fires had become an annual event caused by climate change, releasing large volumes of carbon compounds into the atmosphere, thus accelerating the problem. On the other side of the climate crisis, torrential rain and disastrous floods occurred in Europe, China, India and New Zealand.

The Covid-19 virus had thus far claimed over four million lives officially, which was probably an underestimate, and new, more infectious variants were emerging. Protests against health passes that would exclude the unvaccinated occurred in France, Italy, the UK and Australia. Many people were wary of vaccination, fearing that the shots represented a government plot or were unsafe, even though unvaccinated people were dying at a greater rate. Meanwhile in Brazil there were protests against then president Bolsonaro due to his minimisation of the coronavirus as 'a mild flu', his disdain for scientific advice and general mishandling of the pandemic response, as well as allegations of corruption. And, in the State of Florida, as thousands of new cases emerged daily, local officials imposed vaccine and mask requirements on government workers and some declared states of emergency, but the state governor, Ron DeSantis, opposed such measures. There was a lack of consensus about the disease and hence inconsistent policy. The issue had become mired in polarised politics across different levels of government and within communities, even though lives were at stake.

Half-way through the first year of his presidency, Joe Biden released his first budget, which the left-wing senator Bernie Sanders compared favourably to Roosevelt's New Deal. Meanwhile American troops were withdrawing from Afghanistan and the Taliban took over the capital Kabul on 15 August. After 20 years of military occupation, propping up an ineffective government, Afghanistan was back under conservative Islamist rule. This was an especially severe setback for women and girls. And then one of the world's wealthiest men, Jeff Bezos, was launched into space in a defiant act of egotism and conspicuous consumption.

1 July 2021 was the centenary of the founding of the Communist Party of China (CPC). President Xi Jinping marked the occasion by praising the party's role in national rejuvenation, reducing absolute poverty and building 'a moderately prosperous society'. Not everyone was celebrating this, however. Across the straits in Taiwan, the Chinese Nationalist Party, or Kuomintang (founded in 1894), pointed out that they have no tradition of congratulating the CPC.

My previous book, *How to Rule? The Arts of Government From Antiquity to the Present*, adopts a historical perspective on approaches that people have taken to running things, successfully and/or unsuccessfully. Having shown that 'the problem of government' is an ancient and enduring one, the next challenge was to ask, 'What do we do about it now?' This is an urgent question, just going by the number of books that have appeared lately about a putative crisis or demise of democracy, and the fact that the world faces survival risks, structural injustices, political polarisation and international conflict. None of these problems is effectively addressed without effective government, and yet confidence in government is at an all-time low. Government itself is a major problem. My aim, then, is to re-evaluate 'the problem of government' pragmatically from diverse angles, and then to show how government could become more trustworthy and better equipped for the future. But we shouldn't be looking for a quick fix; I have no new and improved formula to sell.

A person born in 2000 has grown up amid one global crisis after another, accompanied by waves of state intervention and underlying shifts in the aims and scope of government. Our children of the new millennium, then, may be more likely than their parents to accept public spending and progressive taxes. If they read political economy, they may agree more with J.M. Keynes than Milton Friedman, but they may justifiably feel that governments have failed them. From student debt to climate change to economic inequality to institutional racism, they see reasons for dissatisfaction and anger. Their generation – destined to hold the reins of governmental and economic power by mid-century – has had formative experiences, including disrupted education, that leave them with new outlooks on the problems discussed here. I can't predict what crises they'll face, nor how they'll deal with them, but this book is written with them in mind, in the hope that it may help a little in the difficult political choices and the hard work that lie ahead.

ACKNOWLEDGEMENTS

I'm especially grateful to my dear friends Parisa Kooshesh, Junjia Ye and Frankie Chu for many hours of conversation about politics and culture. Nigel Parsons sadly passed away following a long illness as I was completing this book. John Griffiths and I will help keep his memory alive. Elena from Luhansk must remain anonymous, but she taught me a lot about the real situation in Ukraine and stays in touch despite being displaced twice due to conflict in 2014 and 2022. I wish her peace and prosperity. Damien Rogers, Michael Fletcher, Simon Chapple, Jonathan Boston, James Liu and Sarah Choi are highly valued colleagues who've worked with me over recent years. I'd like to thank Ania Skrzypek and the Federation of European Progressive Studies in Brussels for including me in their programme and supporting my work. Finlay MacDonald and Susanna Andrew have been patient editors guiding me towards more readable non-academic writing – though I'm still struggling with that. Kai Jensen of Policy Train has been an invaluable editor and proof-reader for my books. Any grammatical infelicities the reader may notice, however, are my own last-minute meddling. Kai and Rajni are my constant friends. And I'm more than grateful to my daughter and academic colleague Pansy Duncan, her husband Tim van Dammen and their fabulous son Wolfgang, who make it all worthwhile.

1

INTRODUCTION

In December 2021, President Joe Biden hosted an online international summit meeting on democracy. Its themes included combating corruption, upholding human rights and protecting the integrity of elections. This was in part a response to crises within the United States: on 6 January 2021, the US Capitol had been stormed by a mob attempting to overturn Biden's election victory. But the conference was also an effort to re-establish the United States as putative 'leader of the free world' – despite its flawed elections and political polarisation.

Among those countries conspicuously not invited to Biden's meeting were the People's Republic of China and the Russian Federation. In response, China's State Council issued a document in English arguing that China practises a 'democracy that works' (see Chapter 6, 'One-party state') without mentioning either the suppression of pro-democracy protests in Hong Kong or the mass incarceration of Muslims in Xinjiang province. The term 'democracy' had become a weapon in the trans-Pacific propaganda war – although the Chinese *min zhu* and the English *democracy* have wide and differing connotations.[1] And only a couple of months after Biden's conference, the United States and its allies were supporting a war with Russia after the latter unlawfully invaded Ukraine. Would the corrupt government of Vladimir Putin (see Chapter 6, 'Neo-patrimonial state') get away with seizing more Ukrainian territory? If so, at what price? Or could Russian forces be expelled altogether? Biden's Summit for Democracy took place amid intense domestic and international rivalries, including stark differences in models of government and styles of leadership, and concerns about the future of liberal-democratic government. As the White House later put it: 'Democracies and autocracies are engaged in a contest to show which system of governance can best deliver for their people and the

DOI: 10.4324/9781003439783-1

world.'[2] This Manichean vision was, as this book will show, an over-simplification. Such rivalry is dangerous, although sadly all too familiar. The conflicts of the twentieth century were in part a gigantic contest over how best to govern industrialised societies: would the fascist, communist or liberal model prevail? So let's recall some of that history.

In the years following World War I and the Russian Revolution, it wasn't clear whether the capitalist economic system, offering freedom of choice for consumers and producers, would prevail over the international ambitions of socialists who wanted (in theory) to transfer the ownership and control of the means of production to workers' collectives. The challenge laid down in 1925 by the Soviet Union's war commissar Leon Trotsky (1879–1940) – who will overtake whom? capitalists or socialists?[3] – would remain for some time a moot point. Meanwhile a fascist regime had emerged in Italy – and later another in Germany – based on a corporatist (and anti-communist) model that would subordinate industries and workers to the aims of an all-pervasive militarised party-state with a dictatorial leader.

The fascist governments of Italy and Germany were defeated in 1945 and the constitutions of both countries were rewritten with American supervision. The subsequent Cold War rivalry was between the capitalist liberal-democratic and the communist models, especially after communists took control of China in 1949 under Mao Zedong. It was largely thanks to the enormous efforts and sacrifices of the Soviet Union that Hitler had been defeated, and the socialist command economy had worked for emergency wartime needs. But the Soviet regime was criminally inhumane and economically inefficient. By 1989 this oppressive system was not producing anything near the prosperity of the developed capitalist countries. Neither could it compete with the United States militarily. Ultimately the Soviet Union collapsed under its own weight, partly due to its failed invasion of Afghanistan and external pressure from America and its allies. The Berlin Wall was demolished in 1989, and the formerly communist regimes in eastern Europe transitioned to capitalism and adopted multi-party representative government. China meanwhile – though still under a nominally 'communist' one-party system – was undergoing a gradual opening up to the global economy, and hence embracing capitalism.

Once the fascist and communist forms of government were discredited, many Americans mistakenly thought that the next century belonged to them and that their values would prevail.[4] It looked as if a combination of free-market capitalism and competitive political representation (commonly called 'liberal democracy') had triumphed as the norm for all states. By 1999 President Bill Clinton was claiming that America's promotion of human rights and democracy around the world would be reciprocated with greater security and prosperity for Americans. President George W. Bush then asserted that prosperity would be enjoyed *only* by those countries that shared America's values of 'freedom, democracy and free enterprise'.[5] Confidence in America's leadership and moral authority was severely shaken, however, by the Bush administration's unjustifiable and destructive invasion of Iraq in 2003, and by its illegal detention and torture of 'foreign combatants'.

The accompanying economic model, which had favoured lightly regulated markets and open borders, also suffered setbacks. Following the 'stagflation' (economic stagnation accompanied by inflation) experienced in the capitalist world during the 1970s, there had been a shift towards smaller government, less regulation of industries, greater global mobility for goods, people and capital, and more competitive markets: an economic model commonly known as 'neoliberalism'. This was never a universally accepted package of ideas and policies, but it prevailed especially in the 1990s and at least until the global financial crisis (GFC) of 2008. The GFC originated in the US economy and raised doubts about the stability of its free-wheeling deregulated economic model. Massive government bailouts of large corporations and financial institutions were called for, but many working Americans suffered significant setbacks and losses during that time. Surveys revealed an ongoing loss of trust in government over the ensuing Obama and Trump years (2009–2021).[6] President Trump accused his domestic opponents of undermining Americans' self-confidence and pledged to put the American people and their sovereign interests first, and hence his 2017 National Security Strategy re-emphasised core values of liberty, opportunity, free enterprise and equality before the law (although his openly expressed prejudices against, for example, Mexicans and Muslims contradicted the latter principle).[7] Around that time, a populist push to put one's own folk first meant that America and Europe experienced increased intolerance of migrant labour and refugees, and this undermined otherwise accepted principles of universal human rights and economic integration.

By 2021, however, the world order was fundamentally changing – again. The pandemic of 2020 had necessitated border closures, economic shutdowns and massive borrowing and spending by governments. This caused a global supply-chain gridlock and inflation. In even the most capitalist of countries, governments were acting with much less restraint than before. In 2022, for instance, America's and Europe's punitive economic and financial sanctions against Russia (of a kind already familiar to Iranians) showed that, even in one of the G20 nations, sovereign funds and systems of international payments were not untouchable, and the supply of oil and gas could be used as a wartime bargaining chip – even though the consequences would be inflation and slower growth, if not recession. The neoliberal rules of the global financial system and energy economy had been set aside and there was a general resurgence of state intervention: renewed industrial policy (steering investment towards, for instance, climate-friendly technologies or 'strategic' products such as semiconductors), growing use of complex law and regulation, and higher taxes on corporates.[8] Moreover, governments were having to deal with complex new challenges, notably climate change, innovations in Artificial Intelligence (AI) and the Covid-19 pandemic.

Amid these events, an international survey had revealed a growing 'dissatisfaction with democracy'.[9] Now, 'democracy' can stand for many things: social values, open processes of decision-making (such as consultation or deliberation), a style of leadership, a shared participation in administration, a type of constitution and/or the election of representatives with a universal franchise. In response to some of the events alluded to above, many books were written about a 'crisis' or 'twilight' or even 'the end' of democracy. In such discussions 'democracy' often refers to little more than open competitive elections with a universal franchise, while an independent press and non-governmental organisations comment freely and critically on the sidelines. But because of the division of labour in representative government, the people, or the great majority thereof, don't actually rule or govern. Those important jobs are left to elected leaders and to hired experts with degrees in social science, economics and public health. Government *for* (or on behalf of) the people overshadows anything like a government *by* the people, even though it's still called 'democracy'.[10] Due to ambiguous uses of the word, 'democracy' sometimes obscures more than it illuminates, and, for the purposes of this book, I look at actual practices more than abstract ideals. This pragmatic approach to systems of government will give us a clearer picture of the rivalry between different models.

China meanwhile had been on a path of rapid economic growth since it opened up to global trade in 1978, while retaining its one-party, state-managed system. It was sometimes wrongly assumed that, as China became integrated into the world economy, and as the Chinese people grew wealthier, their government would become more liberal or 'western-ish'. Instead, China has consolidated its state-managed system, especially under President Xi Jinping, whose tenure was confirmed and extended in 2021. The official Chinese line is that they practise a 'whole-process democracy', led by the Communist Party, with elections by and consultation with the people. In a global survey of perceptions of democracy, 83 percent in China said that their country is democratic, but fewer than half of Americans said that the US is.[11] Admittedly, there is a problem of translation, as mentioned above. Regardless of which regime is democratic and which isn't, however, the coming century would not belong to America but would involve an 'inevitable' US–China rivalry.[12]

That rivalry is partly about what kind or form of *government* will predominate. Predictions are hazardous (see Chapter 2) so I won't guess whether it'll be Euro-American liberalism or Chinese-style paternalism or something else that prevails, or even whether there'll be a 'winner'. America's leading role in the world is assured for the time being, and yet it seems unlikely that China can lose. The most obvious reason for the latter supposition is the sheer size of

China's population. But it's not simply because China's 1.4 billion people are more than four times the population of the United States. The other factor is that more than a quarter of China's population is rural, and correspondingly more than a quarter of its workforce is in agriculture. China therefore has huge untapped potential for industrial workforce growth given its massive and (so far) underdeveloped agricultural base. Such potential is even greater in India. Between them, China and India seem set to return, sooner or later, to their past position as the world's two largest economies. Both already have commercial relationships all around the globe, supported by highly-skilled diasporas, and China's 'belt and road initiative' is a global infrastructural plan that will enable its growth. A comparative study by the Australian Strategic Policy Institute concluded that 'China has built the foundations to position itself as the world's leading science and technology superpower, by establishing a sometimes stunning lead [ahead of the US] in high-impact research across the majority of critical and emerging technology domains'.[13]

China has more than its growth and innovation potential to rely on, however. As its governing elite changes personnel only gradually – rather than through winner-take-all elections – they can play a long game. The Marxist-Leninist one-party model that Mao's government borrowed from the Soviet Union after the 1949 revolution was certainly a departure from China's traditional dynastic-bureaucratic model, but today's China inherits from its more distant past a paternalistic ethic of harmony and a dual character as a bounded nation and yet an unbounded imperial civilisation.[14] China's highly contested incorporations of Tibet, Xinjiang, Hong Kong and (if it gets its way) Taiwan, and the projection of its power into the South China Sea and South-East Asia, need to be understood against its long imperial history – quickly causing one to abandon ideas that China may 'westernise' in any fashion much deeper than business attire.[15] The Chinese view is that 'prosperity requires stability, and stability requires hierarchy'.[16] In a Sino-centric world, China would sit at the apex of a global hierarchy, somewhat like a patriarchal extended family, while distant relatives pay tribute and show deference to Chinese values and interests. Internally, Chinese authorities practise digital surveillance and disciplinary control over the people – to an extent that's unacceptable to liberal-democratic societies.

As we'll see in Chapter 6, there are more than two rival models of government discernible in the world at the moment: it's not a simple contest between democracies and autocracies. But surely we should learn to work collaboratively with different regimes, and avoid the kinds of conflicts witnessed in the twentieth century, and hence this book contributes to that aim. While cultures and governments differ significantly between countries, they all need some form of government, and they need ideas about how to improve their government. A good way to understand this issue is through the concept of political trust.

Political trust

> Tzu-kung asked about government. The Master said, 'Give them enough food, give them enough arms, and the common people will have trust in you.'
>
> Tzu-kung said, 'If one had to give up one of these three, which should one give up first?'
>
> 'Give up arms.'
>
> Tzu-kung said, 'If one had to give up one of the remaining two, which should one give up first?'
>
> 'Give up food. Death has always been with us since the beginning of time, but when there is no trust, the common people will have nothing to stand on.'[17]

But if the common people were dying for lack of food, wouldn't they already have *lost* trust in a ruler and a state that had failed to provide necessities of life? The logic of this verse in Confucius's *Analects* seems harsh, and hardly benevolent. Nonetheless, faith in rulers and governments, or political trust, is all about making and keeping a set of promises, including to protect lives. People lose hope and trust if such promises fail so badly that hunger strikes. No matter what kind of government it has, a country's success depends upon and reinforces political trust, but trust is a two-way street. It means reciprocation between rulers and ruled, and between diverse interest groups and classes, in ways that maintain adequate levels of wellbeing and a shared sense that justice will be done. Such political trust can't be a blind faith, for two reasons: the people's trust is conditional, depending on workable social compromises under changing circumstances, and we've learnt from history to trust no one unconditionally with unlimited powers. We've also learnt that, once it's lost, a formerly implicit or unspoken trust is hard to regain. Political trust is collective, not interpersonal, and restoring it takes a long time, partly because a complex broken system of government has somehow to fix itself. But it can be done, as states such as Germany have recovered from horrendous betrayals in the past.

Can we achieve political change and better public administration along with political trust? We can, I'll argue, and we aren't stuck with a single model of state and government. Nor need we buy into Manichaean visions about rival systems. The long historical pathways that humanity has taken through foraging, nomadism, agriculture, urbanisation and hierarchically governed states were never straight or clearly signposted, especially if we look around the different regions of the world.[18] Other than in versions invented retrospectively, there's no simple 'just-so' story of progress towards large-scale political order and civilisation, from which we could learn big lessons about our journey as a species, and from which we could discern an ideal outcome. Today's governments are diverse (see Chapter 6), and they're not inescapable products of historical political forces – so they can and will change. New forms of social reality *are* imaginable, and in fact they're being created all the time – although not always for the better.

We can ask for the new and different, but we need to be careful about what we're asking for. After all, Brexit was a major constitutional change authorised by a referendum, but it was poorly conceived and the process of getting there was (to put it kindly) farcical. In February 2017, the British politician and promoter of Brexit, Nigel Farage, addressed a conservative political conference in the United States and announced that Brexit and the election of Trump meant 'the beginning of a great global revolution'.[19] He may have been right, in a way. But Britons seem increasingly to be regretting the decision to leave the EU,[20] and Trump caused significant damage to America's political system. Since then, the Covid-19 virus drove even more profound practical changes in how all countries are governed. So, revolutions don't always end up where their instigators were aiming.

We can see other examples of people seeking structural changes in their systems of government. In Chile, a young left-wing president, Gabriel Boric, was elected in December 2021 in a second-round run-off against a far-right candidate. Although Boric disappointed many on the left, he declared that 'Chile was the birthplace of neoliberalism, and it shall also be its grave!'[21] Indeed, basic neoliberal principles had been entrenched in the Chilean constitution by the former military regime in 1980, and, following protests in October 2019, a plebiscite overwhelmingly approved the drafting of a new constitution. But the draft was later rejected by 62 percent in a referendum. This had looked like the biggest constitutional reform at the time, but the detailed proposal proved to be too progressive for the majority. Italians meanwhile had expressed their disapproval of politicians by reducing the number of elected representatives. And the island nation of Barbados ended its historical relationship with monarchy and appointed a new head of state. So changes in systems of government are sought after by people, and sometimes achieved, but not all changes work for the better. (I return to the Chilean and Italian examples in Chapter 8.)

A person may experience in daily life quite different forms of government (if broadly defined) as he or she fits into a bureaucratic, rule-bound workplace, a consensual community meeting and then a 'free-for-all' on Twitter. The kinds of rule-governed structures that we inhabit are diverse and changing, and to some extent we can vote with our feet and shift to an environment that's run in ways we regard as better. Social media, moreover, have wrought major changes in political communication and norms, to which we soon became accustomed. The Covid-19 pandemic necessitated significant shifts in thinking about what governments can and should do. Despite being something that no one wanted, the pandemic revealed the potential for political change and social adaptation. I suggest, then, that we needn't be pessimistic about the abilities of individuals and communities to change the ways they're governed. Thinking optimistically, future changes could even be made more deliberately and benevolently, if we're wise about it.

Since ancient times, however, there's been little improvement in the quality of political thought when compared with the huge advances in natural sciences and technology. As I'll show in Chapter 3, many ancient political ideas still resonate with us. We have much more sophisticated technologies today, but I see little evidence of greater sophistication of political and ethical thought. There's a huge body of literature from the past to inform and challenge our thinking, and it doesn't suggest that Bill Clinton or Angela Merkel, in terms of political acumen, rises above Thucydides or Anna Komnene.[22] We can still learn from the distant past, then. Indeed, one learns that competition between rival political systems has too often occurred with extreme violence and inhumanity rather than negotiation and wisdom.

The present book is written in the hope that progressive change can happen intelligently, and without resort to military or other coercive force. How can we achieve changes that people support and that restore trust, rather than causing further division in or between societies? How do we get the best leaders and deter the worst? How can we get a corrupt and untrustworthy system to develop into something transparent and trustworthy?

What is good government?

If we think of government in terms of purposeful actions, then we might judge how good it is by the results it achieves. What forms or qualities of government would maximise our chances to live in security and to improve the quality of life? Aristotle asked a similar question 23 centuries ago. We're still working on answers, in part because people differ over what constitutes a good quality of life, and in part because (as we'll see in Chapter 3) many problems of government keep recurring, even as they change in appearance. But historical experience and recent research can inform us about some essential qualities of 'good government'. It seems intuitively correct that the quality of government affects the quality of your life, without presuming or dictating what particular *way* of life you should follow. International league tables of wellbeing, prosperity and development can be accused of bias towards the values and priorities of wealthy developed 'western' countries, much of whose prosperity derives from a history of imperialism and exploitation. But, using those league tables as rough indicators, at the top we see countries that have stable, effective, fair and clean government and that respect human rights (see Table 1.1). They're also rich countries, so the table indicates some profound political and economic inequalities.

Economic efficiency and growth do correlate with people's sense of wellbeing, but they don't tell us all we need to know if we're asking about the best

TABLE 1.1 Global League Tables 'top 10'

World Happiness Index 2023[a]	Corruption Perceptions Index 2022[b]	Global Freedom Index 2023[c]	Human Development Index 2021[d]	Global Peace Index 2023[e]	Legatum Prosperity Index 2023[f]
Finland	Denmark	Norway	Switzerland	Iceland	Denmark
Denmark	Finland	Sweden	Norway	Denmark	Sweden
Iceland	New Zealand	Finland	Iceland	Ireland	Norway
Israel	Norway	New Zealand	Hong Kong	New Zealand	Finland
Netherlands	Singapore	Canada	Australia	Austria	Switzerland
Sweden	Sweden	Netherlands	Denmark	Singapore	Netherlands
Norway	Switzerland	Denmark	Sweden	Portugal	Luxembourg
Switzerland	Netherlands	Luxembourg	Ireland	Slovenia	Iceland
Luxembourg	Germany	Uruguay	Germany	Japan	Germany
New Zealand	Ireland	Japan	Netherlands	Switzerland	New Zealand

Notes

[a] World Happiness Report, URL: https://happiness-report.s3.amazonaws.com/2023/WHR+23.pdf (accessed 20 June 2023)

[b] Transparency International, URL: https://www.transparency.org/en/cpi/2022 (accessed 20 June 2023).

[c] Freedom House, URL: https://freedomhouse.org/explore-the-map?type=fiw&year=2023 (accessed 20 June 2023). Switzerland, Portugal and Belgium were tied with Japan and Uruguay on a score of 96/100.

[d] UNDP, URL: https://hdr.undp.org/sites/default/files/2021-22_HDR/HDR21-22_Statistical_Annex_HDI_Table.xlsx (accessed 20 June 2023).

[e] Vision of Humanity, URL: https://www.visionofhumanity.org/maps/#/ (accessed 25 July 2023).

[f] Legatum Institute, URL: https://docs.prosperity.com/2616/7736/3001/The_Prosperity_Index_Rankings_Table_2023.pdf (accessed 20 June 2023).

ways to govern. The materially richest countries (notably the USA) don't necessarily provide the best overall quality of life, in part due to inequalities, nor do they necessarily set the best examples of good government. Bearing that in mind, there's some evidence that good government in itself can increase people's wellbeing, especially through transparent and effective delivery of public services, and this in turn helps to build social trust and cohesion. So improvements in the quality of government and public administration can help to boost people's estimation of their own wellbeing.[23] But this effect may work differently in poorer nations than in wealthier ones. For countries that are struggling to deliver comprehensive, effective and transparent public services, improving these services' quality and availability may have a greater effect on how people rate their wellbeing than instituting free and fair elections.[24] There's been much international research and debate about which is the more important for a nation's development: electoral accountability to improve responsiveness to the people's needs, or transparent and capable public services that deliver basic goods. Do we begin with the high-level political regime or with the administration and delivery of public services by hired staff? It's complicated, of course, and it depends on the country you're looking at. Both dimensions are necessary; neither is sufficient on its own, however, and there's no technical or economic formula for policy success in all situations.[25]

Surveys in the Middle East and North Africa, for example, show majorities believe that democratically elected governments are indecisive and unstable, with weak economic performance, even though, paradoxically, most still agree that 'democracy' is best.[26] Those countries in the region that have a recent record of changes in governments following elections (Tunisia, Iraq, Lebanon) haven't fared well in social and economic terms, and scepticism about the benefits of democracy has grown since the Arab Spring of 2011. Indeed, that region-wide uprising often ended with more authoritarian government, as in Egypt. A referendum in Tunisia in July 2022 – boycotted by most of the people – authorised concentration of executive powers in the hands of the president, supposedly to end infighting and paralysis in government, and later that year a parliamentary election had a turnout below 9 percent. Genuinely representative and accountable government is preferable, but elections and referendums don't, on their own, always lead to that. 'Just add democracy' isn't necessarily the best recipe.

Among the wealthy OECD countries, in contrast, people rate their quality of life more highly if their system of government is a parliamentary one rather than presidential, if the electoral system is proportional rather than first-past-the-post, and if it's a unitary rather than federal state.[27] This implies that, if a higher quality of life was their aim, then America's founding fathers got it wrong when drafting the US Constitution – for which they could be excused, given scientific knowledge at the time. Nonetheless, no matter what the research tells them now, Americans are unlikely to demand (in sufficient numbers) an overhaul of their constitution to make it more like Sweden's. In any case, the statistical correlation between quality of life and constitutional design gets weaker when one takes account of a wider range of factors and countries (beyond just the OECD).[28] We shouldn't assume that there's a clear pathway from changing the constitution or the electoral system of a country to an improved quality of life for its people – although it could help in some cases, if changes can be achieved without too much strife.

It's safe to say, though, that the highest levels of prosperity and wellbeing are found in some smaller countries with government that's less corrupt, respects human rights and permits political freedoms. Looking at the top ten places on global indices of happiness (or subjective wellbeing), transparency (or low corruption levels), political rights, civil liberties, human development (including longevity, education and incomes), peace and prosperity, we find that a few names keep recurring. (See Table 1.1.) The fact that the highest performers tend to have smaller populations and use proportional representation in elections may indicate that people are better off with forms of government that give voice to diverse values, that are less remote from communities, and hence more accountable to the people. Among those listed in Table 1.1 more than once, moreover, Sweden, Norway, Finland, Denmark and New Zealand have taken steps towards self-determination for indigenous peoples; while Switzerland officially recognises four national languages, as does Singapore. Their political successes aren't premised on cultural homogeneity even though immigration has been controversial.

These 'top 10' lists are dominated, then, by countries with relatively small populations (some no more than a large city by global standards), by the Scandinavians, and by countries with proportional representation. Conversely, though, a country like Slovenia may also have a small population and proportional representation and yet still be rated relatively poorly in surveyed perceptions of corruption and political integrity, with attacks on independent institutions and political polarisation.[29] Moreover, countries that historically saw themselves as 'leader of the free world' (the United States)[30] or 'mother of parliaments' (the United Kingdom)[31] are conspicuously absent from Table 1.1, in spite of their economic and military might, their cultural capital and the sheer amount of 'noise' they make in global media. So this gives a hint about where to look, and where not to look, for leading examples of best practice in government. None, of course, is perfect; all are works in progress. Even in those countries that appear at the top of Table 1.1, there are still concerns about political integrity and hence there's a degree of distrust.[32] Although relatively successful, the best performers aren't problem-free.

There are things that can be done, then, to address public dissatisfaction and distrust, such as respecting the independent roles of media and courts and improving transparency around political donations and public spending. But now we must also ask: 'what form or qualities of government would maximise the chances of saving the planet?' The Happy Planet Index multiplies the people's average rating of life-satisfaction by their life-expectancy and then divides by the country's ecological footprint (global hectares used per capita). This gives an account of each country's wellbeing set against its consumption of the planet's limited resources. As shown in Table 1.2, it results in quite a different league table from those in Table 1.1.

Perhaps the countries in Table 1.1, other than Switzerland and Uruguay, have purchased their good fortune at the expense of poorer nations and of future generations who'll suffer the consequences of global warming and depletion of the planet's resources and biodiversity. It's great to have better government and better standards of living, but is 'the good life' attainable only for a minority in the right countries at the right time? Or can we learn to combine decent standards of living with sustainable levels of consumption? A search for better government now needs to take this question seriously.

TABLE 1.2 Happy Planet Index 'top 10'

HPI 2021[a]
Costa Rica
Vanuatu
Colombia
Switzerland
Ecuador
Panama
Jamaica
Guatemala
Honduras
Uruguay

Note
[a] Wellbeing Economy Alliance, URL: https://weall.org/the-latest-happy-planet-index-costa-rica-tops-the-list-beating-western-economies-on-sustainable-wellbeing (accessed 20 June 2023).

Where to from here?

One outstanding historical achievement of modern times is to have established that, in principle, the state exists neither for its own aggrandisement nor for that of its rulers. Modern government doesn't, or shouldn't, operate primarily for the benefit of the sovereign or a dynasty or their cronies. Instead the people who are governed give the state and its government their legitimacy. The aims of government should advance a publicly approved set of values, and leaders are accountable through the media and ultimately at elections, no matter what the exact constitutional arrangement. We know, however, that these principles aren't always respected, as there are corrupt authoritarian rulers even in some countries that hold elections for representative assemblies, notably Russia.

It's widely accepted, then, that the legitimacy of states is grounded in their people, and that their government should serve their common good. As the world's superpowers, the US and China have both claimed the mantle of democracy; they both claim to be acting in the interests of their people. They set very contrasting examples of how to do that, and neither sets the best example. What all countries do have in common, however, is the need for government. Some are certainly governed better than others – and the better ones deliver public services more effectively and equitably – but government always involves a common set of enduring and intractable problems, addressed differently in different systems. It's 'the problem of government', or that set of problems, that the present book examines. I don't follow the path of those contemporary authors who've warned of the end or twilight of democracy; instead, I ask, 'How can we get better government?'

The world's most powerful countries aren't setting the best examples of good government if the above league tables are any indication. Some leaders, and often their followers too, have simply disgraced themselves. We need to look more widely, then, for new ideas and to consider the great variety of forms of government around the world. This book goes back to basics and asks what government is, why we have it and why it's so perplexing. It surveys the historically enduring problems and dilemmas of government – those that are so ancient and recurring that they probably won't go away. It then asks what improvements have been made over the course of history nevertheless, and also what historically unprecedented crises now confront governments globally. Given humanity's cultural and ideological diversity, I then address the question of belief and fundamental political disagreement. There are profound differences of political belief within countries, but also between the differing models of government around the world, so we need to look at some of the main types. To clarify this task, I take the attention off the ideal of 'democracy' – not because one should overlook its values, but in order to take account of how government is done and what its consequences are. We don't have a 'crisis of democracy', for the purposes of this discussion; we do have a crisis of representative government. Having surveyed and cleared the ground, we can look at the elements of what government does, how its institutions change or resist change, and how people behave or misbehave within those institutions. We'll then be in a position to clarify what it takes to govern in a world of uncertainty and conflict, and how to do it better.

The early twenty-first century was marked by a series of shocks, beginning on 11 September 2001, which had consequences for the norms of government. The global financial crisis of 2008 undermined neoliberal policy orthodoxy, as governments intervened with large bailouts. Meanwhile, China's one-party state presided over an inexorable rise to superpower status. The Arab Spring of 2011 challenged authoritarian rule in that region, though not successfully. Syria, Yemen, Sudan and Libya declined into lengthy civil wars and humanitarian disasters. The displacement and migration of millions of people, especially from the Middle East, spurred anti-immigrant reactions in Europe and North America, where religion and race became divisive political issues. Possibly the most profound rebellion, however, came from Nature herself, at the levels of global climate and microbiology. The pandemic of 2020 changed not only the content of policymaking but also the perceived obligations, limits and methods of government itself. And for the longer term, climate-related disasters challenge us to rethink economic production and consumption, and will lead to further displacement and political upheaval. Digitisation and Artificial Intelligence, moreover, are creating new challenges for lawmakers and changing the means and scope of government, reaching deeper into private life and subjective experience on the one hand, and causing problems for law enforcement, defence and security on the other. Corrupt and authoritarian leaders are flourishing, surveyed trust in government and satisfaction with democracy have been declining in many nations, and yet government intervention is getting deeper and regulations more complex. Consequently, ethical leadership, effective policy-making and reliable public services are more essential than ever. It's timely, then, to reconsider what we mean by government and how we do it, and to ask how trustworthy leadership and competent administration could be restored. A contemporary movement for 'positive public administration' seeks to take us beyond negative discourses of policy failure and bureaucratic inefficiency, and asks instead 'what governments can do and how they can do this to the benefit of citizens and communities'.[33] This book contributes to that work.

Chapter 2 asks: what is government? Why do we need it? Why is it such a problem? How can we begin to define the problem? First I define government and administration in active terms, or 'what it means to govern and to administer'. This raises the old questions of why communities and nations need to be governed at all, and how and why the first states arose. But to govern well, and to be governed well, have entailed perpetual problems for diverse civilisations over history. These are primarily human, moral and political problems; they're not technical or scientific problems with indisputable solutions. They're also economic problems – but the economy is inherently political – and so the interrelationship between government and economy needs to be considered. Government is, moreover, a forward-looking and normative concern: what are we to do *next* in order to keep things running and meet threats in the face of uncertainty? So, what hazards are associated with making predictions and prescriptions?

Chapter 3 sets out the historically enduring or recurrent problems and dilemmas of government (i.e., those that will probably never go away). It cites cases from ancient and recent times to provide this historical perspective. Who should rule? What qualifies a person to rule? Who are 'the people'? What are the aims and limits of government? What resources can it command? Should we centralise or devolve powers? Should those who govern administer rewards and punishments or lead by example? How do we balance self-interest with the common good? How do we establish a basis of shared beliefs?

Aside from these enduring problems, we can see some long-term historical improvements in government. In particular, Chapter 4 cites the international outlawing of mass atrocities and slavery, the constraining of the arbitrary will of rulers, the subjection of rule-makers to the written rules they make, secularism and religious toleration, the progressive inclusion of women and ethno-religious minority-groups, and a better understanding of economic inequality. We also consider contemporary problems that are unprecedented in human history, notably climate change and the advance of AI. By contrast, the 2020 pandemic had precedents, and it was predicted. It revealed, however, that many people see the state as a source of protection, while others see it as a protection racket or a threat to freedom. It showed how new technologies have changed what governments can do, and hence what we think they should or shouldn't do.

A basic aim of government is to regulate events and make our social environment and conduct predictable – or less unpredictable. Another aim is to deal with adverse disturbances, pressures or threats. Social cohesion and commerce thrive on confidence that the future will be much like the past, if not better, and effective government fosters such confidence. It follows that systemic changes in the patterns of government tend to be resisted, and that, when they do occur, it's in the face of crisis and dissent. The aim in Chapter 5 is to understand why people disagree so vigorously, if not violently. This addresses the psychological nature of political belief and its role in social cohesion and division. Symbols and beliefs may be variable and controversial, but we can't govern without them, and hence we learn why the emperor actually *does* have clothes. The conclusion is that we should take political disagreement seriously as integral to political belief-formation, rather than strive for unity. The ethical test is less about what we agree on than about how well we *disagree*. Good government doesn't eliminate disagreement; it manages through and across disagreements.

What different kinds or styles of government – what different solutions to the problem of government – exist in the world today? Acknowledging the limitations of typologies – as they simplistically lump together diverse, complex and overlapping real-world arrangements – Chapter 6 studies the main rival models of government found in the contemporary world. With the defeat of fascism and the demise of Soviet communism, it was once thought that the Westphalian law of nations and Euro-American representative government (formed through free competitive elections) would prevail as the global norm. This general model was subject to its own rival interpretations, however: minimalist/neoliberal versus progressive/social-democratic versions; global integration versus protection of national sovereignty. We also see an illiberal authoritarian version of representative government. Coming from another civilisational background is the Sino-centric paternalistic model of government. And there are quasi-states that don't (or barely) meet the test for international recognition. Absolute monarchy and theocracy still exist, but are now exceptions. Could today's exceptions teach us something about the norms, however? Indigenous movements for self-determination produce innovative proposals for government too. The forms of government are diverse, but too often the practice of government becomes detached from people's needs, controlled by elites, and structurally violent and coercive – hence the growth of political distrust. This book takes a realistic, pragmatic and non-utopian approach; it doesn't prescribe one model of government for all. Instead, it recognises a diversity of models and hence sees the need for international toleration and collaboration.

Regardless of the particular model, what are the principal issues that successful government needs to comprehend and address? Chapter 7 doesn't aim for an exhaustive list, but basic concerns are:

• strategy
• power

- aims and scope of public policy
- changing institutions and constitutions
- personal conduct of leaders and followers
- people's participation and understanding
- governing diverse societies.

Good government constantly regulates, maintains and improves the conditions under which we live, but government itself needs constantly to be improved, in order to boost public confidence and political trust. Chapter 8 looks at some recent, but not altogether successful, efforts to change systems of government (Iran, Chile, Italy, the USA, the UK, Russia, China) and asks how it could be done better. It takes a closer look at matters needing urgent attention: leadership, ecological economics and new media. Leaders need to pay heed to people locally but also increasingly to think and operate globally; they need to embrace diversity in their own societies as well as diverse forms of government between societies. I conclude with basic principles and achievable aims for improving government and public administration.

Notes

1 Wei Lin. 2018. 'The Translated and Transformed Concept of Min Zhu (Democracy and Republic): A Political Cultural Influence on Translation'. *International Journal of Languages, Literature and Linguistics* 4 (4): 303–8.
2 The White House. 2022. *National Security Strategy*. Washington, DC. See p. 7.
3 Trotsky, Leon. 1925. 'Towards Capitalism or Towards Socialism? The Language of Figures'. *The Labour Monthly* 7 (11), URL: https://www.marxists.org/archive/trotsky/1925/11/towards.htm (accessed 8 February 2021).
4 Luce, Henry R. 1999 [1941]. 'The American Century'. *Diplomatic History* 23 (1): 159–71, URL: http://www.jstor.org/stable/24913736
5 The National Security Strategy of the United States of America, 2002, URL: https://georgewbush-whitehouse.archives.gov/nsc/nss/2002/ (accessed 9 November 2021).
6 Pew Research Center. 2021, URL: https://www.pewresearch.org/politics/2021/05/17/public-trust-in-government-1958-2021/ (accessed 11 November 2021).
7 US Secretary of Defense, URL: https://history.defense.gov/Historical-Sources/National-Security-Strategy/ (accessed 2 September 2022).
8 *The Economist* (15 January 2022) published a special report on these developments ('Beware the bossy state: Government, business and the new era of intervention').
9 Foa, R.S., A. Klassen, M. Slade, A. Rand & R. Williams. 2020. *The Global Satisfaction with Democracy Report 2020*. Cambridge UK: Centre for the Future of Democracy.
10 Mair, Peter. 2006. 'Ruling the Void? The Hollowing of Western Democracy'. *New Left Review* 42: 25–51.
11 Democracy Perception Index 2022. Latana, URL: https://latana.com/democracy-perception-index-report-2022/ (accessed 22 October 2022).
12 Mearsheimer, John J. 2021. 'The Inevitable Rivalry'. *Foreign Affairs* 100 (6): (e-version).

13 Gaida, Jamie, Jennifer Wong Leung, Stephan Robin & Danielle Cave. 2023. ASPI's Critical Technology Tracker – The global race for future power. Australian Strategic Policy Institute, URL: https://www.aspi.org.au/report/critical-technology-tracker (accessed 21 April 2023).

14 Ge, Zhaoguang. 2018. *What Is China? Territory, Ethnicity, Culture, and History*. Cambridge, MA: Harvard University Press.

15 Jacques, Martin. 2012. *When China Rules the World: The End of the Western World and the Birth of a New Global Order*. New York: Penguin.

16 Brook, Timothy. 2021. *Great State: China and the World*. London: Profile Books. See p. 389.

17 Confucius. 1979. *The Analects*. London: Penguin, trans. D.C. Lau. See p. 113, XII.7.

18 Graeber, David & David Wengrow. 2021. *The Dawn of Everything*. New York: Farrar, Straus & Giroux.

19 Owen, Paul & David Smith. 2017. 'Nigel Farage Says Brexit and Trump Win Are "Beginning of Global Revolution"'. *The Guardian*, URL: https://www.theguardian.com/us-news/2017/feb/24/nigel-farage-cpac-speech-trump-brexit-global-revolution (accessed 10 November 2022).

20 What UK Thinks, URL: https://whatukthinks.org/eu/questions/in-highsight-do-you-think-britain-was-right-or-wrong-to-vote-to-leave-the-eu/?removed (accessed 15 August 2022).

21 Bartlett, John. 2021. 'Who is Gabriel Boric?' *The Guardian*, URL: https://www.theguardian.com/world/2021/dec/20/who-is-gabriel-boric-the-radical-student-leader-who-will-be-chiles-next-president (accessed 10 November 2022).

22 Thucydides was an Athenian general of the fifth century BCE who wrote *The History of the Peloponnesian War*. Anna Komnene (1083–1153 CE) wrote *The Alexiad*, an account of the reign of her father, the Byzantine emperor Alexios I Komnenos. They're highly recommended reading.

23 I've been sceptical about this point in the past (Duncan, Grant. 2010. 'Should Happiness-Maximization Be the Goal of Government?' *Journal of Happiness Studies* 11 (2): 163–78), but evidence in its favour is gradually accumulating.

24 Helliwell, J., et al. 2014. 'Good Governance and National Well-being: What Are the Linkages?' *OECD Working Papers on Public Governance* No. 25. Paris: OECD Publishing, URL: https://doi.org/10.1787/5jxv9f651hvj-en (accessed 15 June, 2022).

25 Norris, Pippa. 2012. *Making Democratic Governance Work: How Regimes Shape Prosperity, Welfare, and Peace*. Cambridge: Cambridge University Press.

26 Robbins, Michael. July 2022. 'Democracy in the Middle East and North Africa'. *Arab Barometer*, URL: https://www.arabbarometer.org/wp-content/uploads/ABVII_Governance_Report-EN.pdf (accessed 7 July 2022).

27 Altman, David, Patrick Flavin & Benjamin Radcliff. 2017. 'Democratic Institutions and Subjective Well-Being'. *Political Studies* 65 (3): 685–704.

28 Helliwell, John. 2019. *Measuring and Using Happiness to Support Public Policies*. National Bureau of Economic Research, URL: https://www.nber.org/system/files/working_papers/w26529/w26529.pdf (accessed 16 June 2022).

29 Transparency International, URL: https://www.transparency.org/en/news/low-political-integrity-throughout-the-european-union-gcb-eu-2021 (accessed 9 July 2022).

30 'The free peoples of the world look to us for support in maintaining their freedoms.' Harry S. Truman. 12 March 1947. 'Address of the President to Congress, Recommending Assistance to Greece and Turkey', URL: https://www.trumanlibrary.gov/library/research-files/address-president-congress-recommending-assistance-greece-and-turkey?documentid=NA&pagenumber=5 (accessed 1 July 2022).

31 The idea that the British parliament was the 'mother' of colonial legislatures (the Westminster 'family') can be attributed to the MP John Bright (1811–1889) from a speech made in 1865.
32 Transparency International [note 29].
33 Douglas, S., T. Schillemans, P. 't Hart, C. Ansell, L. Bøgh Andersen, M. Flinders, B. Head, et al. 2021. 'Rising to Ostrom's Challenge: An Invitation to Walk on the Bright Side of Public Governance and Public Service'. *Policy Design and Practice* 4 (4): 441–51.

2

GOVERNMENT

Why is it a problem?

First of all, let's define *government* and *administration*. The word *governor* derives from the Latin *gubernātor*, or a person who directs, controls, pilots or steers. In English, a governor or governess may be responsible for the education of young people, and hence has a duty of care for their welfare and development. And in the Christian era, God is often described as supreme governor. In the age of the steam engine, a device that regulates the speed of a machine within a steady range came to be known as a governor. A human governor, however, mostly held a particular office in state, church or army, with recognised authority. So, as governors are persons, government is what they do. *Government* refers to sets of actions such as regulating people's conduct or setting rules (for minimising harm, providing care, etc.), ideally keeping things within predictable bounds, and responding to unexpected changes or needs. A president or prime minister has a leading responsibility in the government of his or her country. This sense of government as actions or rules was more common in the seventeenth and eighteenth centuries: for example, Daniel Defoe (1660–1731) set out verbatim the regulations 'for the Government of infected Families' laid down during London's 1665 plague.[1] The alternative sense of government as a body or bodies with institutionalised authority is an offshoot from its original meaning as activities that regulate what we do. For present purposes, we'll keep our eye on the actions or practices of governing, and not just the institutions established in capital cities. The contemporary custom of using the word *governance* to refer to processes and practices of government, especially at subordinate organisational levels, is thus unnecessary.

If we think of government as routine actions that sustain complex webs of relationships with mutual obligations, by which we achieve things of collective concern, then we can happily take our government for granted while it's

DOI: 10.4324/9781003439783-2

working well – but we become painfully aware of it when it fails. If a leader ignores past pledges, this may cause losses for many people; or a change of leadership may disappoint our expectations with new policies that adversely affect our interests. Such changes can create a sense that hopes have been dashed or promises broken. The word *government* includes the activities of such a vast array of persons (most of whom are anonymous to us) within such complex institutions and arrangements that, almost necessarily, it's failing to meet some of our expectations. When and how badly we perceive it to have failed will be conditioned by our values and interests, and by the people who most strongly influence us, so our assessment of success or failure isn't objective. By the same token, good government is working best when you don't notice it. For example, it takes a lot of intergovernmental collaboration, expertise and bureaucracy to ensure that global air travel is safe and efficient, but when you board a plane, luckily you don't need to think about the International Civil Aviation Organization, which coordinates the government of this complex set of tasks.

We often debate whether a problem calls for governmental action, or whether it's better left up to individuals or private enterprise. We can imagine a boundary between private and public spheres of responsibility and action, and the term government is nowadays mainly applied to the public realm. (In the seventeenth century, it still made sense to say that parents were responsible for the government of their children or that people should govern their own tongues.) But I'll shift attention away from the abstract noun government, as established hierarchical institutions, and towards the practical actions of governing. The job of government is to orchestrate *a complex web of activities and exchanges that aim to regulate matters of public concern and that, when necessary, restore regularity following disruption.* This may involve force, or threat of force, to limit what people can do, or promotion of well-being and prosperity, or maintenance of obligations between social groups such as employers and employees. It also entails responding to internal dissent and protest.

The English words *minister* (both noun and verb), *administer* and *administration* were borrowed from French and Latin in the fourteenth century. Their original uses were mainly in the church, such as in the administration or dispensing of a sacrament, or for members of the clergy known as ministers. To minister to someone may mean to care for or to serve, and one may administer a medical treatment. *Administration* in the sense of the performance of public duties, or the actions required to organise and implement political decisions, arises in the sixteenth century. Later still, 'an administration' could be the body of people who, for a certain time, govern by making and implementing decisions. A minister is someone appointed to advise and act for the head of state or government, or to oversee a public organisation or an area of public policy. We sometimes distinguish 'the government', or the higher-level authorities and policymakers, from 'the administration', or the agencies that implement policy. But, if we speak of 'Mrs Thatcher's government' and 'Mrs Thatcher's administration', there's no clear line dividing the people and actions belonging to each. A change of leadership following an election may mean the replacement of many subordinate unelected administrators, especially in Washington DC where a presidential transition involves around 4,000 appointments.

Sometimes, confusingly, we use the word 'government' to refer to the whole set of public institutions including the elected leaders, the legislature and the administrative bureaucracies. So we need at times to distinguish between the permanent system and the people in charge for the time being. Australians, for example, may distinguish between the Commonwealth Government in general, the Labor government that's in office (at the time of writing) and the hired public servants who are politically neutral and whose positions don't depend on elections. Despite overlapping uses of words, public administration normally refers to the *practical actions taken, by various agencies and officers, to execute law, implement policies and deliver services mandated by a government*. Following Woodrow Wilson's 1887 essay on administration,[2] academic specialists often make a distinction between politics and administration: the political decision-makers are elected and hence accountable to the people; the hired administrators or managers serve the government of the day and implement its decisions for the public good.

Belgium is a case that helps us to see the distinction. It's culturally and politically divided between Dutch-speaking and French-speaking regions, and elections have led to fragmentation as radical left and right-wing parties grow, causing difficulties in negotiations to form majority governments. In 2010–11 Belgium went for 589 days 'without a government', and in September 2020 a seven-party coalition agreement ended a record 652 days of caretaker and minority governments. In spite of this, life went on and public administration continued under existing norms and laws. The administrative branches of government didn't stop working.

Bureaucracy is a form of organisation that has a hierarchy of offices governed impartially by rules, rather than arbitrarily by the will of its leaders. Setting aside negative connotations for the moment, bureaucracy has traditionally suited the purposes of modern professional public administration. This was an improvement on older systems in which decisions could be arbitrary and offices sold or inherited. Bureaucratic paper-based organisations evolved to deliver public services impartially and in accordance with law, with civil servants employed to perform duties of office diligently and impersonally. But the digital era has further transformed organisational structures and capabilities, and Artificial Intelligence (AI) is causing yet another wave of changes. Even the idea of what's 'public' is changeable. Over the course of history, and across cultures, there are significantly different values and beliefs about what should be open for all to view and share, what belongs to all the people to enjoy, or what obligations should be shouldered by all.

This defines our terms, but let's consider an example that shows how complex, multi-levelled and changeable the real-world problems of government and administration – or politics and regulation – can be.

Basic problems

Mark Zuckerberg realised early in his career that making Facebook openly available meant 'free' social interaction (for those with a device and internet access) *and* massive data collection about people and their likes and dislikes – data that's of great value for advertising and selling products. But this calls for means to keep people active on the platform and recruit new users. The greatest growth potential is in countries with the lowest rates of membership, especially where there's less regulation – and where Facebook isn't blocked, as in China and Iran. A good target is Kenya, for example, but the problems there are a low rate of internet penetration and the cost of internet services. So why not use Facebook as a vehicle for free access to low-data, text-only versions of selected websites on cheap mobile devices? That was Facebook's proposition. It sounded almost philanthropic, as more people in poorer parts of the world could get basic services online. But they also got Facebook as a default provider, and were fed into its marketing machine. In Africa, Facebook became more than just a frequently used social media platform: it evolved into a provider of service infrastructure while gaining a goldmine of metadata about users.

That was the logic behind Facebook's 'Free Basics' push into Africa. Free Basics makes Facebook the internet service provider and default page for users – and not just an optional app – in return for free access to low-data versions of selected websites. Free Basics had been ejected from India in 2016 as it violated the principle of net neutrality: that internet service providers should treat all sources and traffic equally. By favouring certain key sites for free text-only access, Free Basics created a quasi-monopoly for preselected content providers in markets with new customers. The policy dilemma was that, while 'zero-rating' gave poorer consumers more affordable access to the internet (by not counting against data caps), it violated net neutrality by favouring certain websites, and it gave Facebook an unprecedented opportunity to harvest personal data. Any regulatory crackdown on zero-rating, however, would inequitably disadvantage poorer consumers.[3] And this raised wider political issues. Since the Arab Spring uprisings of 2011, social media has played significant roles in movements for democratic change. In response, many states used digital surveillance and censorship to counteract these movements, so the technology cut both ways: it opened up potential for emancipation and yet was also used for oppression. In Egypt, for example, the state responded by banning Free Basics, blocking many news sites and monitoring social media, as well as old-fashioned detention of dissidents. Amid such volatile politics, the big Silicon Valley tech companies sought to exploit Africa's new and growing markets. By 2019 Free Basics was live in most countries on the African continent – but those countries lacked regulations on data protection and privacy as effective as the European Union's General Data Protection Regulation (GDPR), and many have oppressive and corrupt government.

The global south offers growth markets for Facebook and for its advertisers. With fewer privacy regulations and weaker enforcement, the opportunities for data extraction and exploitation are greater. But Facebook and others use social connection to justify, in effect, a contemporary digital colonialism by the world's wealthiest corporations in the world's poorest countries. A digital 'cannibalisation' of developing countries gets under way well before the affected publics and non-governmental organisations can even debate data privacy and protection, let alone seek effectively and transparently to govern the matter.[4]

This reveals an emerging problem in how to govern. It's an especially complex and self-perpetuating problem, as the rapid uptake of social media changes the economic and political landscape by changing the speed, volume and type of information available to individuals – and to those who police them. Social media companies naturally wish to present themselves positively as platforms that support social connection, communication and debate. But their basic motive is private profit, not the public good. Furthermore, they create outlets for vitriolic attacks, hate speech and misinformation,[5] and they're used for covert interference in elections.[6] But the political problem goes further than just propaganda and the control or censorship of falsehoods and extreme opinions. Drawing on Marshall McLuhan's maxim that the medium is the message, social media have changed the structure of awareness and opinion formation. For example, a lot (if not most) political dialogue now occurs online, often without one needing to leave the privacy of the home, and often anonymously. But we need also to ask: to what extent have tech companies become political entities, seeking to shape (or avoid) regulation? Their monopolistic behaviour has stimulated a renewed interest in antitrust law, for instance, and so, how should they be governed?

The tech giants form and dominate digital spaces, plunder private data for commercial gain, compete with existing local businesses and become, in effect, corporate colonial actors. They aren't simply extracting data from communities; they're actively building and shaping the informational environment in which the exploited people live in order to create the 'data wealth' that they need. They aren't 'mining' existing private information, but creating a new form of persona (the online profile) with new forms of consumption – factors that didn't exist before the online world. There's a feedback loop between social media platforms and consumers in which each supplies information to the other. Facebook supplies mobile access to its own data-rich virtual world, which in turn creates imagery and structures desire in new ways. Facebook then harvests the data that users supply voluntarily and repackages them for sale to advertisers. The users' choices are formed and conditioned by the online market that's presented to them; Facebook and its clients profit from their users' online activities.

A prominent example of Facebook's concern for profits over human rights occurred in Myanmar when it hosted anti-Rohingya messages that were connected with genocidal violence and ethnic cleansing in 2017.[7] Lawyers speaking for the Rohingya accused Facebook of greed, negligence and callousness, as the platform had been warned about this hate speech.[8] Big tech companies have become political actors and targets, whether they're being used to publish propaganda or to censor it. They're creating new exploitable spaces for digital capitalism, reshaping political dialogue and setting the agenda for government, often by taking advantage of a lack of regulation and enforcement. Their effects are sometimes comparable to those of a hostile state or colonial trading enterprise. While instant access to information is beneficial, the new media platforms aren't always promoting the common good, and the extremely wealthy companies who profit from them operate in a borderless world with ineffective regulation.

Then there's the Chinese model. Just as American companies have moved into Africa's growing markets, so the Chinese tech company Huawei, backed by state capital, has built data centres (for governments and private companies) and telecommunications infrastructure, including participation in a submarine cable surrounding the continent to provide 5G and broadband. This requires all servers to be located within a country's own borders, for the sake of 'cyber-sovereignty', unlike the open, competitive American model. There are suspicions that Huawei products have built-in back doors for espionage: for example, it's alleged that large quantities of data were harvested from the African Union headquarters in Addis Ababa.[9] But the US National Security Agency (and allies) also conduct global data capture and surveillance.[10] Facial recognition technologies are increasingly used for government services and law enforcement in Australia, for instance.[11] The Chinese and American models are both enabling and exploiting massive data gathering and targeted surveillance. The Chinese approach is more state-centred, and its 'social credit' system openly aims to maximise trustworthy, obedient behaviour by rating individuals who are monitored through technologies such as CCTV and facial recognition.[12] The American model favours private enterprise and is more about commercial surveillance or 'platform capitalism',[13] but state surveillance operates covertly in the background. The pace of innovation is rapid and the international competition is intense. Chinese-owned social media app TikTok came under scrutiny by the US Congress in 2023, amid calls to ban it on national security and wellbeing grounds. This rivalry isn't only about who has the most advanced gadgets and algorithms; it's also about the rules that will govern the political and military uses of new technologies: will they enable an open and free or a controlled and authoritarian form of government?

The problems here are enormous, but not unfamiliar: there are competing models of government, multiple levels of administration (from the individual to the global), borderless operations, and conflicts between private profit and public good, security and freedom, social benefits and commercial exploitation. It sounds like a job for some kind of super-government, but there isn't one, and international agencies lack the powers to intervene. Where are the state and its government when we need them? Can we go back to the start and rethink the whole thing?

What is a state?

The earliest states can be identified by archaeological remains that point to the existence of a ruler (or ruling family, council or assembly) and hence hierarchical power relations and social distinctions or classes, including a spatial distinction between a prominent seat of government with large structures surrounded by smaller households and settlements. Civil, military and devotional labour that supported the system from below was reciprocated by obligations to protect and care, and to defend by force when necessary. But the boundary between what was a state and what wasn't, or when growing communities attained the form of a state, isn't at all clear. Max Weber's concise definition of the state as 'a human community that (successfully) claims the *monopoly of the legitimate use of physical force* within a given territory'[14] is handy, but, while a Seljuk sultan or a Ming emperor, with their soldiers and tax collectors, might have claimed such a monopoly, their claims might not have been successful in all corners of their realms, given their imprecise maps, contestable boundaries and slow communications. Many of history's feudal fiefdoms, nomadic hordes, colonial settlements and self-declared republics wouldn't qualify as states by any strict definition, but they did govern their own affairs.

The state-based form of government, as we now know it, and as found in most of the inhabited world, includes: a supreme authority (backed by force and with a duty of care) across a territory and a population; apparatuses for exerting force, discharging obligations, regulating public affairs and executing decisions; and recognised classes of persons who exercise the state's obligations. The definition of a state in international law is in the Montevideo Convention on the Rights and Duties of States (1933): 'The state as a person of international law should possess the following qualifications: (a) a permanent population; (b) a defined territory; (c) government; and (d) capacity to enter into relations with the other states.' It's assumed that each state is an independent sovereign political entity with inviolable borders – norms that are all too often violated. This legal model was consolidated in Europe following the Napoleonic wars, but it harks back to the Peace of Westphalia in 1648 at the conclusion of the Thirty Years' War. Precipitated by numerous postcolonial independence struggles, by the dismemberment of the Ottoman and Austro-Hungarian empires after World War I and by the collapse of the Soviet Union, the numbers of internationally recognised states grew dramatically over the course of the twentieth century. Westphalian-style states now represent the norm across most of the globe's habitable surface – plus their adjacent territorial waters. But to labour an old metaphor, the ship of state has never been fully seaworthy, it was never officially launched, and different kinds of vessel have appeared. The state isn't a completable project; it's always changing and needing repairs and modifications. There's no uniform origin story, historical trajectory or future of the state. There isn't a standard model by which states are governed, and there are many territories that may claim independent statehood but that fail to govern effectively or to establish diplomatic relations with others.[15] States are now diversified and complex arrays of public institutions with legitimate authority, administered by cohorts of people with specialised skills and tasks. But they're more than that too, because by right every person is (or should be) a legally recognised member or citizen of a state. No one should be stateless, and no state exists without its people. Hence a state and its members are mutually constitutive. (In Chapter 3 we consider 'the people'.)

Having defined 'state', we can ask how it arose historically, and whether this was beneficial for the people. States have adopted diverse means of government (see Chapter 6), but we'll also ask: why did we even need government in the first place?

Origins of the state

We're still learning about (but will probably never fully understand) just how politically astute and well organised prehistoric human communities really were. We shouldn't think of them as simple or static groups. They adapted to changing environments as they foraged, hunted and migrated, and they self-consciously changed and varied their social and political arrangements, including periodically dismantling and remaking institutions.[16] To assume, for example, that a Palaeolithic way of life was 'closer to nature' than today's may well underestimate its cultural and political sophistication and the ingenuity needed for collective action. Recent archaeological discoveries make us abandon ideas about a Neolithic or agricultural 'revolution' and developmental stages – bands, tribes, chiefdoms, states and (at last!) civilisation – and hence to suspend ideas such as 'primitive' or 'simple' in contrast to 'civilised' or 'complex'. Some hunter-gatherer societies built significant sites that evidently required complex organisation of labour for their construction and that were centres of long-distance trade and interactions between diverse social groups. The domestication of plants and animals and the adoption of farming were uneven developments occurring over thousands of years and were sometimes rejected or resisted in favour of foraging or nomadism. Farming and city-dwelling weren't adopted by all those who became acquainted with them. There was no 'linear trajectory' from agricultural food production to storage of surpluses and then to the formation of the first states.[17]

Nonetheless, urbanised and stratified societies that qualify as states did appear (and sometimes disappeared) in various forms around the globe, especially around large rivers and deltas. Ever since the earliest-known states in Egypt, Mesopotamia and the Indus Valley, rulers began to be served by people who would record events, write down laws, keep archives, collect taxes, organise and pay armies and spy on people – although we shouldn't assume such figures were just like officials of modern times, as religious and administrative affairs were often indistinguishable. Unfortunately there are huge gaps in our knowledge of the earliest city-states and empires. We're limited to information recorded in forms (such as stone or pottery) that were hard enough to survive the centuries, leaving uncertainties about unrecorded customs of everyday life and their complex settings. And practices undoubtedly differed greatly from region to region. So we shouldn't settle for one orthodox origin story, and there are differing schools of thought about how and why hierarchical state-based government got under way.

One version holds that there was a very gradual and uneven movement, in a few parts of the inhabited world, from foraging or nomadism to more settled agriculture, and eventually there appeared some walled cities with rulers, priests and centralised government. But urbanisation required top-down coercion and wasn't good for human wellbeing overall, it's argued. People were forced into fixed-field agriculture, their diets became more limited, and their lives were more likely to be shortened by crop failure, unsanitary conditions and infectious diseases. A minority ruling class was the beneficiary, however, and oppressive arms, laws and taxes were needed to keep them on top. Government was thus despotic and monarchic, slavery was common, and, it's been argued, humans may have been better off in small relatively egalitarian bands of hunters and gatherers. Indeed, most people avoided living in or around the walled city-states, preferring mobile foraging or pastoral nomadism in less accessible mountain, desert, forest or steppe country, and many centuries passed before the majority of humans lived regulated ways of life governed by states, let alone residing in urban spaces. People didn't all flock to inhabit cities at the earliest opportunity. Communities often retreated into hill and forest country in order to 'remain stateless'.[18] Historical records show that the Roman, Chinese and Persian empires were, for many centuries, fighting off (and often defeated by) nomads of the Eurasian steppe who tended to avoid settling down.

Other authors give a more optimistic view of early states and empires. In the mid-fourth millennium BCE, the Mesopotamian city of Uruk was, according to archaeological evidence, 'a well-run place and people lived there not under duress but voluntarily'. The surrounding regions were more dangerous places to be.[19] Much later, the large peasant workforces that were mustered to build Egypt's pyramids, for example, may have seen the great occasion more as collective security, festivity and devotion than enforced drudgery. During the months when the Nile River inundated the land, people could be put to work and paid in kind with food. Accommodation was built for them in townships that in turn required management and policing. This monumental work reinforced mutual obligations between the people and their political-religious institutions; the 'labourers and craftsmen sought to ensure their own eternity through service in constructing the royal tomb'.[20] Their labour may not have been entirely voluntary, but neither was it slavery, as the wealthy could pay their way out and workers sometimes went on strike.[21] But the collective activity of construction may have been more important for their social cohesion than the final product.

Some ancient concepts of justice were more holistic than today's codes of written law (which are applied through institutionalised bureaucracies and courts), and they involved divine authority, legally recognised rights, social and family cohesion, and the protection and equitable treatment of the vulnerable, all of which contributed to the legitimacy of rulers. The best-known (though not oldest) ancient law code is inscribed on the stele of Hammurabi who reigned in Babylon, Mesopotamia (1792–50 BCE). Although referred to as a 'law code', it wasn't a set of statutes directly applied by judges, as it's not mentioned in records of trials. This stele is perhaps better seen as a monumental public expression of regal legitimacy, showing key principles of Hammurabi's reign. The frieze at the top depicts the king standing before the god Shamash, and the preamble evokes divine legitimation for Hammurabi as righteous lawmaker – in terms that seem overblown to us today – suggesting a 'relationship between the king's divinely mandated obligation to provide just ways for his people and the opportunity of his people to have access to the written and public account of what constituted those just ways'.[22] Its edicts range from criminal to civil and family law, and are generally framed as: 'if a person does that, then this is the consequence.' It espouses broad principles of divinely inspired justice, truth and wellbeing. While women were treated differently from men, they did have rights and protections, including property and inheritance. Going by surviving correspondence between king and officials, Hammurabi 'seems to have cared a great deal about the welfare of his subjects, and, in many instances, he protected them against the loss of their land or livelihood'.[23]

There was 'an emerging idea of a rule of law in the legal thought of ancient Mesopotamia and Egypt [including] separation of powers between assembly and king, fairness of legal process [and] the use of written law'.[24] There were assemblies and juries, and principles of justice and equity. Contracts could be verbal (oaths) or written, and were legally binding, so people could appeal to courts or monarchs for redress. Protection of the weak, especially widows and orphans, was expected of the rich and powerful.[25] We may ask whether the poor and the weak were actually protected and cared for very well, as the preserved documents were written by and for the elite. But principles of justice, care and due process were announced: the ruler should not oppress subjects; predictable law and fair treatment were normative. There were laws about victim compensation, inheritance, debt forgiveness and time limits on debt peonage. The laws of Moses in the Old Testament bear strong similarities to earlier law codes from the ancient Near East. The early states weren't necessarily despotic, then. The city-states of Southern Mesopotamia in the mid-first millennium BC, for example, had formalised administration, the citizens' assemblies exercised wide-ranging executive powers, and the authority of city governors was constrained by popular consent.[26]

The fact that there was slavery in ancient city-states gives us pause, of course. Slavery could take diverse forms including temporary debt peonage or indentured labour, as well as chattel slavery. Slaves had fewer rights and suffered harsher punishments, but they did have rights and protections under law, and there were legal conditions under which they could be freed.[27] Furthermore, recalling that ancient Athens also had slaves, it's been argued that the institutions (such as assemblies, juries and legal rights) that led Athenians to call their system *demokratia* can be found in earlier states around the Near East.[28] The Athenians didn't invent democracy out of nowhere, but they did give it the name we've adopted.

The earliest states evolved gradually, then, over many centuries: there was no moment that we know of when a multitude of ungoverned people who lacked laws got together and decided, or were told, that they needed them – along with a government to enforce and administer them. Preliterate societies are governed in the broader sense, often quite strictly by unwritten lore and custom, regardless of the size of community or the extent of hierarchical authority. Across the Eurasian continent, non-literate nomadic peoples and literate urban peoples continued to live side by side, trading and fighting with one another for many centuries, and so urban civilisation didn't appeal to all who came into contact with it. Nomads thought it dishonourable to leave the saddle and settle for urban life. It's not the case, moreover, that civil government is something that advanced (mainly European) states 'gave' to the peoples in distant colonies. In Africa, for instance, systems of government with kingship, hierarchical administration, international relations and processes for popular participation and consensus had developed long before the arrival of colonial powers.[29] We're still left to ponder, though, whether the development of the earliest city-states in the Middle East more than five millennia ago was beneficial or not – or, if it was beneficial only for some, then for whom, and at what cost to others?

Is the state a good thing?

Let's review some contrasting ideas about this. A pessimistic account of the state was given by Friedrich Engels (1820–95) in *Origin of the Family, Private Property and the State*. The state arises, he said, at a stage of economic development at which commodity production for exchange has become the norm. This leads to the exchange of persons as slaves, and then the accumulation of wealth in the hands of a few increases the demand for slaves, making them a primary labour force. Communal ownership, especially of land, is replaced by private ownership; belonging through kinship is replaced by membership based on residence in a bounded territory. And wealth becomes concentrated in male hands, leading to smaller patriarchal family units with monogamous marriage, and relegating women to 'domestic slavery' – while prostitution flourishes. A division of labour arises between crafts and agriculture. A class of merchants also appears, exchanging commodities that others produce. Frequent wars of plunder and conquest consolidate military command structures, and hereditary monarchy is modelled on the patriarchal family. Forms of currency and capital develop, resulting in moneylending, interest and hence debt slavery. Such a society is divided into classes with irreconcilable differences between freemen and slaves, and between rich and poor freemen. So the state evolves to deal with these internal social contradictions and to keep class antagonism in check. This growing state apparatus requires military organisation for defence, and courts, juries and prisons for internal order, and hence a workforce that collects taxes and records debts. The state also contracts debt on behalf of its taxpaying members. But the basic job of the state, according to Engels, is not just the containment of class antagonism for the sake of order, but also the oppression of an exploited class by an economically dominant ruling class. This changes in form over the course of history.

> Thus, the state of antiquity was above all the state of the slave owners for the purpose of holding down the slaves, as the feudal state was the organ of the nobility for holding down the peasant serfs and bondsmen, and the modern representative state is an instrument of exploitation of wage labour by capital.[30]

There may be times, he accepts, when the conflicting classes balance each other out and the state gains some independence as a mediator between them. But Marx and Engels predicted the obsolescence and eventual demise of the state once society reorganised material production 'on the basis of a free and equal association of the producers'.[31] Marxism in its original form regards the origins and purposes of the state as oppressive, and it's doomed to 'wither away'.

An alternative tradition treats the state positively, as an outcome of our natural need for association and cooperation, first for survival and self-sufficiency, but ideally to achieve the highest possible quality of life. We can call this the Aristotelean model – with the reservation that Aristotle regarded slavery as 'natural' and implied that the best life would be enjoyed by well-off educated free men only. We now reject his exclusions of slaves and women from political participation and fulfilment in life, but Aristotle's more optimistic view that the state arises by nature for positive ends left a long trail, east and west. Islamic philosophers such as Abū Nasr al-Fārābī (ca. 870–950 CE) and Ibn Sina (Avicenna) (980–1037 CE) developed and adapted the Aristotelian approach. Commentaries on Aristotle and on Plato's *Republic* were produced by Ibn Rushd (Averroes) (1126–98 CE), who was born in Córdoba. At the other end of the Islamic world in thirteenth-century Persia, Nasir ad-Din al-Tusi (1201–74 CE) took a distinctly Aristotelean approach to ethics, economics and politics and outlined a model of the Virtuous City akin to al Farabi's. These ideas were transmitted from Persia to the Mughal empire in India in the sixteenth century. In Catholic Europe, the theologian St Thomas Aquinas (1225–74 CE) adapted Aristotelean philosophy to the Christian context, including the ideas that the state arises naturally and that good government is important for improvement of society and for people's chances of perfect happiness in the afterlife. We also see an Aristotelean approach to rulership in the work of Niccolò Machiavelli (1469–1527 CE), especially in his *Discourses on Livy*, in which he asks why the Roman republic was relatively stable and successful for four centuries.

A positive consensual view of the state was fostered by the social contract tradition. In an effort to demolish the idea of inherited kingship by divine right, John Locke (1632–1704) imagined that political leadership had evolved from the family's innate trust in their protective father into a larger community's trust in its bravest men who led them in their defence, and thence to the eventual establishment of kingship.[32] This political trust that was given to princes (at first implicitly) had established, he thought, a right to rule by popular consent, strictly for the benefit of the people. Too often, however, trust had been abused by rulers: in such cases, consent may be withdrawn and a new form of government instituted by the people to better serve their needs. Today, many of us may prefer Locke's idea of popular consent, in principle, as it's an improvement on absolute monarchy and divine right. The Lockean idea of natural rights (ordained by God) has no basis in biology or history, but social contract theory was progressive for its time, as it grounded the right to govern on the consent of the governed. Locke saw all political power as originally a trust granted by the people; hence it was up to the people to judge if that political trust had been broken. These ideas were directly relevant to the English and Scots in 1688 and to the Americans in 1776.

States and their diverse modes of government are mutable and contestable; they're sometimes trusted and sometimes not. Even within a state, an individual may experience differing, and even competing, styles and forms of government, depending on the locality and the activity concerned. One might engage in employer–employee workplace negotiation during the day, then a face-to-face meeting regarding local government after work, and then go home to hear about national politics on the nightly news. How we participate in (or endure) our government differs markedly across time and place. There are also different ways in which people acquire an authoritative role in the duties and privileges of government, at any level, ranging from birthright to competitive examinations. (See Chapter 3.) In some historical cases a state may appear to be personified and led by one supreme person, but it must (conceptually and practically) outlive that mortal. It's self-evident, moreover, that you can't be a ruler without subjects. But why do subjects have to suffer such rulers and these governed entities called states? Do subjected peoples really need rulers, administrators, judges, armies, tax-collectors and spies? Or, to ask the question another way: if they weren't governed from above at all, would people have seen a need to invent a state and then have gotten together and formed one? Modern advocates for anarchism say no: the state is unnatural and oppressive; we'd be better off without government and law. Humans are naturally self-responsible and possess an innate sense of justice, and hence with no top-down government we'd be free to govern ourselves and to associate cooperatively with others as we choose. In the proper sense, anarchism doesn't mean chaos; it does suppose that humans are spontaneously self-ordering and self-directed. It denies the necessity and legitimacy of the state and its laws.[33]

Did we need government?

Archaeological investigation of some (but not all) of the earliest urban sites reveals little or no evidence of hierarchical government. There may be no remains of a ruling household, palace or temple, or other traces of social stratification or political division of labour. As communities occupying relatively large built spaces, such early townships could have been self-governing in their own ways, but without monarchs or elite families.[34] Urbanisation could therefore have preceded the socially stratified state, at least in some parts of the world, and their government may have been non-hierarchical, consensual and guided by shared norms. A lack of evidence of a centralised state may not signify that they were anarchic; there could have been a more fluid, but nonetheless well-regulated, form of government. There's something appealing, I find, about the idea of an urban community that's organised with little social hierarchy, or one in which people at large gather periodically and then disperse. But that model was eclipsed as urban societies grew. The first Mesopotamian cities that formed during the Uruk period (4000–3100 BCE) had rulers, or priest-kings, by the time of the earliest written records, around 3300 BCE, if not earlier. They ruled on behalf of the gods; they performed rites that ensured divine goodwill; they exercised military leadership and judicial authority.[35] 'The origins of [early Mesopotamian] kingship are unclear but, once invented, monarchy clung on tenaciously'[36] – but it wasn't absolute monarchy, as kings were surrounded by queens, priests, priestesses and councillors.

Today, five millennia or more later, it seems we're stuck with hierarchical states and local authorities. In countries with competitive representative systems, people collectively choose between potential leaders and parties at big rituals called elections, but there isn't an option on the ballot paper saying, 'No government at all, thanks.' And you can't emigrate or escape to a place devoid of government, or one in which you're fully free to govern yourself, because there isn't one. You could withdraw into a wilderness, declare yourself exempt from the law or sovereign of yourself, or form your own micronation,[37] but the forces of the state will impose themselves anyway when necessary. This doesn't mean, however, that there's only one version of state-based government today; nor does it mean we can't imagine and produce change for the better. There's scope for self-governing autonomous groups to form in those spaces left open by institutions of state and market, for example. And given the challenges that the world faces today, we do need to revisit and rethink how we're governed.

Generally it's been assumed by political historians and theorists that the state – with its institutionalised government and law – is necessary for (at least) our defence and safety, and some say that, if run well, it enables us to enjoy a better quality of life than we would otherwise. Most philosophers in the Christian and Islamic worlds stuck (more or less) with Aristotle's view that the human being is a political animal, destined to belong to a community or state in which justice and its administration are at issue. St Augustine took a more pessimistic view that government – no matter how bad it might be – was God's punishment for our original sin, inherited from Adam and Eve, and insisted that we obey rulers even though they too are sinners. Other thinkers asked us what life would be like without government, law or leadership. Indeed, such questions arose early on in China and India. For example, the fifth-century BCE Chinese philosopher Mo Zi argued that, when there was no government, everyone acted on their own principles, differing from one another, leading to accusations, hostilities, wastage of crops and general disorder – hence people needed to be unified.[38] Indeed, the quest for, or maintenance of, harmony through unity is an enduring theme in Chinese civilisation. In ancient India it was often said that, without a king who enforces just laws, the weak would have no protection from the strong; there would only be 'the law of the fish' where the large devour the small.[39] Government, or *dandaniti*, meant literally the administration of the rod. Punishment was its overriding principle, and was necessary for good order and prosperity.

The political philosophers whose work is standard reading for students – Confucius, Aristotle, Thomas Hobbes and so on – were highly literate individuals who lived and worked within states under written law and whose lives were affected by war. They assumed that sovereign power, civil government and law were natural and/or necessary, while any situation in which they failed or were absent looked dangerous. Early modern European thinkers, including Hobbes, called a hypothetical condition without law or government a 'state of nature'. This was the premise of social contract theory, and the more pessimistic one was about such circumstances, the stronger the form of government one was likely then to recommend. Hobbes inferred that life in a state of nature would be 'solitary, poor, nasty, brutish and short', and so an unimpeachable and indivisible sovereign person or assembly assumed ultimate power, as if the people had authorised it. In contrast, Jean-Jacques Rousseau painted a more sympathetic (but still imaginary) picture of early humans roaming freely in a state of nature, entirely lacking society and language, and only eventually forming small communities.[40] He launched a critique of social inequality and dependency, and then called for a social contract in which all citizens would relinquish their possessions in return for renewed law and government that would express and execute the general will.

The state of nature was a stimulating thought experiment, but had no basis in any general prehistoric situation that we know of. On the contrary, humans have always lived in organised communities, and anthropologists show us the endless diversity in how communities have been led and how they've upheld customs and norms. Societies that lack writing self-evidently don't produce written laws and archives, but their government (in the broader sense of the term) entails considerable political acumen, oratorical skill, customary norms, economic collaboration and military capability. In a small community, people regulate their own conduct for fear of disrupting significant relationships, and an offence is not against a state or a sovereign, but against the web of relationships that comprise the community. Disputes over aberrant or untrustworthy behaviour may be settled by reference to commonly understood values, possibly with payment of a fine or a ceremonial offering by way of reconciliation.[41] Prehistoric humans never lived in an ungoverned state of nature, although in smaller communities political structures and practices must have been much less hierarchical and rule-bound than the state institutions that we endure today.

It may still be the case that the state, from the outset, was a massive confidence trick or protection racket. Anarchism, by definition, may never rule, but we needn't dismiss the idea that people may have been better off as foragers or nomads, without formalised law and government. For most authors down the ages, however, successful statecraft and rulership were seen as necessary for good order and justice, and social contract theory was one way in which some tried to justify it. This book belongs, then, to a long history of people thinking about the most effective and just forms of government. I won't propose that we dismantle the modern state and eliminate government. But, if we do need to be governed, then how should we do it? How do we train leaders to be trustworthy and ethical? How should a ruler organise and relate to advisers, ministers and lower officers? What moral principles constrain the behaviour of leaders and officials? How do those who govern make people comply? – by setting a morally good example or by imposing penalties? These are some of the basic questions people have posed over the centuries.

For example, Machiavelli's infamous text *The Prince* (written in 1513) is a scandalous adaptation of an ancient genre called 'the mirror of princes'. A classic mirror of princes such as Christine de Pizan's *The Book of the Body Politic* (1407) offered moral education, guidance and exhortation to an heir to the throne. Al-Ghazali's *The Counsel of Kings* (c. 1105 CE) instructed the Seljuk sultans on their duties and on righteous conduct. Such texts have been written since ancient times, but they flourished in the Christian and Islamic realms. There have also been more pragmatic manuals on how to rule and to govern. Texts such as *The Book of Lord Shang* (fourth-century BCE China) and the *Arthashastra* of Kautilya (c. first-century BCE India) are manuals of statecraft that are amoral in tone, sometimes brutally so. These texts show us how people through the ages have been thinking – and disagreeing – about how best to rule and to govern a society.

Founding principles

We learn from history, then, that there've been widely diverging theories about state and government, about why we have them, what's good or bad about them, and how they should work. It's natural to think that, if we could only rediscover how and why the state emerged in the first place, we could draw some definitive conclusions. But it's not that easy. Origin stories rely on scant and partial evidence, and so the narrative gets slanted by our present-day ideological purposes: if we want to reject state-based government, then we argue that it was created through oppression; if we accept it, then we tell a story about collective security and popular consent. As there's no single agreed narrative about the birth of the state, then perhaps we could at least settle on one set of principles, now that we're in it. But that's not so easy either. In spite of their efforts (whether appealing to the will of God or to *The Communist Manifesto* or to any other set of doctrines) rulers could never do away with dissent and opposition over what's just and beneficial, and, when they tried to do so, the consequences were often inhumane and disastrous. Empires have always been culturally and religiously diverse, and the best (or least bad) rulers accepted this fact; but this also meant profound political differences around questions of equity and administration. This goes deeper than disagreement over the rights and wrongs of particular laws, policies or public services. People disagree on fundamental principles: for example, whether the individual or the collective should be our basis for defining rights and punishing wrongs, or what kinds of claims a person can make on public resources, or why we should pay taxes.

Could we find a way, then, to identify fundamental principles that would allow societies to arrive at particular policies without persistent dissent? Accepting that people have differing needs and beliefs, can we all stand on the same platform? How does a pluralistic and tolerant society freely agree on one set of basic rules? Philosophers have explored ways of doing this through public deliberation and consensus, and the most influential was John Rawls (1921–2002). Assuming people regard one another as free, equal and rational, he wondered what basic rules of justice a community would willingly adopt. He asked us to imagine that those tasked with negotiating these rules do so from behind a 'veil of ignorance' that makes them temporarily unaware of their identity or role in society; hence they don't know for the time being what their gender, colour, class, abilities and wealth are in real life. Each person is represented as a free and equal citizen but, removed from partial considerations of status and competition, they reach conclusions from a disinterested position with mutual respect. As they wouldn't know whether they may be one of society's worst off, Rawls argued that these representatives would conceive justice as *fairness*, in two main ways. First, each person must enjoy basic liberties (such as freedoms of speech and religion) to an extent that's consistent with all others having the same. Second, economic institutions should meet two criteria: that positions are open to all on the grounds of equality of opportunity (thus prohibiting discrimination and requiring fair access to education and training) and that any unequal distribution of economic goods would work for the benefit of all, especially of those who are least advantaged ('the difference principle'). This would mean making the worst off as well off as possible. Rawls argued that justice as fairness would result in a greater sense of mutual obligation and shared social commitment, and that it was superior to rival principles that seek to maximise utility or liberty.

Rawls's proposal requires redistribution, which is always politically controversial, and rival schools of thought continued. Not long after his *Theory of Justice* was published in 1971, Robert Nozick (1938–2002) replied with *Anarchy, State and Utopia* (1974), which argued for a minimal state that protects only the basic individual rights (to life, liberty, property and contract) and that doesn't impose redistribution of incomes. Individuals could, if they choose, join a socialist community, for example, with protection of their basic rights guaranteed by an overarching minimal state – but socialism shouldn't be forced on everyone.

Neither Rawls nor Nozick favoured utilitarianism, or the principle that the best kind of government has the effect of maximising the aggregate – or alternatively the average – level of happiness in the community. Capitalist economic thought is basically utilitarian, although it gave up on the idea that we could measure utility (happiness, satisfaction or wellbeing) as this is subjective, and most economists have settled instead for 'revealed preference': the idea that people's freely chosen exchanges in a market must be making the parties better off, in their own estimation.[42] Doubts arose about this approach, however, when it was found that, in spite of decades of strong growth in the postwar economy, surveys were revealing that Americans on average weren't getting any happier.[43] Indeed, unrestrained consumerism and materialism could be sources of misery![44] Some economists (but by no means all) drew the conclusion that, where markets had failed to maximise happiness, the state should step in and do things such as encouraging stable family life and voluntary contribution to communities, rather than a relentless pursuit of higher incomes and more consumer goods. The growing practice of surveying people's subjective wellbeing has resulted in the UN endorsing an annual *World Happiness Report*. This has asserted that happiness is 'the proper measure of social progress and the goal of public policy',[45] advancing a new kind of utilitarianism.

In addition to those mainstream theories, there are social movements that attack historical subordination of women within a patriarchal society, racial discrimination and the legacies of slavery and colonisation. They have questioned, for example, the blindness to these issues within Rawls's theory. While there has been progress, such as the removal of discriminatory laws, political controversies continue around principles of justice and equality, including calls for reparations in some cases, and people still need to combat racism and sexism. The economic debate about the balance between individual liberty (or free markets) and distributional fairness (or welfare states) is also ongoing and unresolved, and this cuts across contemporary struggles (sometimes described as 'culture wars') over gender and race.

Often missing from such debates, however, is close consideration of 'our inevitable dependency on others and the web of caring relationships that sustains us',[46] and hence we need also to ask what care and support we deserve from and/or owe to others in our communities, beyond our family. No one will survive and thrive from infancy to childhood to adulthood without the concerted work of professional carers and educators and the caring work of family members – most of which labour is performed by women and is unpaid, notably pregnancy, giving birth, breastfeeding and parenting. There can be no economic, social or human capital 'without the vital reproductive work that men cannot perform'.[47] For significant periods of our lives (or for most of many people's lives), we're neither free nor equal, but dependent and vulnerable, and at any stage in life we may need support in misfortune and suffering. We aren't always the free, autonomous, responsible person who embodies liberal-democratic citizenship. In Chapter 8 I'll return to the 'ethic of care' in relation to government, as it provides an important corrective to ideas about impartial application of rules.

If the reader is feeling a little confused by now about basic principles of justice, then I've achieved my aim. We don't have a single unimpeachable set of values to start from; but we do have an ongoing debate. This includes, for example, an ethical dilemma over whether to consider mainly the *consequences* of our actions (such as minimising suffering or promoting wellbeing) or to stick to inherently right or necessary *duties* even when the consequences may be unpleasant. Most models of government and economics in modern times adopt the consequentialist approach, but the ends don't always justify the means, especially if the means trample on fundamental rights. Finding the balance in particular circumstances is a matter of judgement, not scientific measurement. There won't ever be a commonly accepted or indisputable set of fundamental values or principles that can guide everyone, without dispute, in making such judgements. Rather than worry about this lack, we could accept that *political diversity, difference and negotiation constitute the field of government itself.* If we accept that government means working with and through our differences, then we can tease out some enduring features of a long civilisational debate, with philosophical speculation, practical advice and experience handed down to us from the past. So, what is this enduring debate about? It comprises a number of questions and controversies, and I summarise them in the next chapter, with historical examples. In the meantime, we should consider the relationships between government and economy.

Political economy

Much of the technical data that guides decision-makers is economic. The state and its mix of industries and consumers are thought of as an economy. Economic success is critical for people's livelihoods and state revenues, and hence for political success. So problems of government have always been economic problems. Moreover, local and global economies never achieve a stable equilibrium; they're constantly evolving, often unpredictably. In turn, the economy is inherently political: it produces inequalities; it's riven with competing interests, values and priorities. Economic struggles – between, say, employers and employees, or creditors and debtors – pose challenges for public policy and for political leaders. But the way that 'the economy' is represented in the media often gives an impression that it's an impersonal set of statistics. Instead, I think of an economy as a vast and complex web of activities and exchanges undertaken – through deals made and promises fulfilled – by living people in real time. This means making, trucking, selling and buying: the kinds of things people like you and me do daily. Cooking dinner for the kids may not be counted in official economic statistics, but it's as much a part of the economy as growing the food that they eat. To facilitate this economic activity, we have institutions such as firms, banks and regulators, and we write laws governing commerce, property, competition, taxation, redistribution, inheritance, copyright, international trade and so on.

For present purposes, such matters of political economy are viewed in terms of their government. And as discussed in Chapter 1, the violent world events of the twentieth century can be seen in part as a contest over how industrial economies would be governed. The three main rival models back then were: liberal-democratic capitalism, fascist corporatism and the socialist command-economy. We now see a contest between China and the USA,[48] and China's rapid economic growth has occurred despite (or is it because of?) its one-party politics and state-managed economic development. China's growth meant a reduction in poverty levels, but also a steep rise in income inequality.[49] While China has nominally 'socialist' policies, it still has relatively weak systems of redistribution and social security,[50] and it plays an increasingly competitive role in the global capitalist economy. The Chinese model looks anomalous, as it challenges the idea that success in the capitalist world goes hand in hand with liberal-democratic representative government. So we need to take a broader look at government and political economy.

First, socialism isn't necessarily inimical to democracy and need not equate with authoritarian government. Joseph Schumpeter (1883–1950), writing in the midst of World War II, saw in capitalism 'a tendency toward self-destruction' (for example through corporate monopolisation) and this could lead to 'the emergence of a socialist civilization'.[51] This wasn't a firm prediction, but neither was he warning that socialism necessarily spelt the end of democratic politics. A fully socialist society, he said, may be 'led by an absolute ruler or be organized in the most democratic of all possible ways; it may be aristocratic or proletarian'.[52] Since Schumpeter's time, it's become too easy for opponents of socialism to accuse it of being undemocratic. But this reflects historical contingencies, especially the USSR and Maoist China, rather than anything like an invariant law. Equality is a core principle of democracy, and many socialists call for political equality (which could include 'one person one vote') as well as a more profound social and economic equality. Socialists may argue that their vision is more democratic than what we see in a market society, especially given the grotesque inequalities of income and wealth that have emerged under contemporary capitalism. For a socialist, genuine freedom and personal autonomy can only be enjoyed by all members of society if all are prepared to aid and support one another through public education, housing and distribution of basic goods. A radical socialist, it might be conceded, envisages the end of private property, and that may not be achievable without coercion – which hardly sounds democratic. Socialism under Stalin and Mao was certainly inhumane and authoritarian. Nonetheless, even Marx and Engels in their revolutionary text of 1848, *The Communist Manifesto*, were demanding policies that are now regarded as normative for democracies, such as progressive income tax, a state-owned central bank, free public education and abolition of child labour. And in those countries that had regular free and fair competitive elections during the twentieth century, socialist and labour parties often won majorities and implemented policies that redistributed income, provided public services and regulated private enterprise. In Scandinavia and Australasia, it was not unheard of for people to vote for socialist policies. Indeed, democratic socialists hoped that this popular support would grow to such an extent that, gradually, countries would become more socialist and less capitalist. But that historical trend was disrupted by the neoliberal turn that commenced in the 1970s.

Second, a capitalist economy can be *un*democratic, as lightly regulated markets produce widening inequalities of wealth and income, and unemployment and precarious employment are treated as if they were natural or necessary in a thriving economy. Even though every adult citizen – rich or poor – may be entitled to a vote, the wealthiest individuals and corporations have the resources to lobby and influence elected representatives, particularly through campaign donations. The poor are less likely to vote at all, and have little voice in public debates about policy. They're the objects of public policy, not the initiators, and are alienated from the system of political representation. In North America and Europe, policymaking is largely carried out by bargaining among elites. Hence, political parties' social and economic policies are less likely to take account of the needs and interests of the least well off. And the wealthy gain more political power in an economy that has few brakes on private enterprise and low levels of redistribution. Economic inequality 'undermines the quality of democracy' because a small but very rich minority 'get disproportionate control over the political process as a result of their wealth'.[53]

Third, just as socialist economics can be compatible with democratic politics, so capitalist economics can be compatible with authoritarian politics. For instance, in a violent US-backed *coup d'état* in 1973, a military junta deposed an elected socialist government in Chile and then implemented neoliberal economic policies, following advice from the Chicago School of Economics. The main aims of these reforms were described by one of the ministers in that government, José Piñera: 'cut the fiscal deficit to reduce inflation and stabilize the economy, free prices to be set by the market, sell off the state-owned enterprises, open the economy to trade with the rest of the world'.[54] The ideas of free enterprise and freedom of choice contradicted (in principle) the violent political oppression, as noted by one of victims of that regime, Orlando Letelier[55] (assassinated in 1976). Although the neoliberal school, which was born in post-World War I Vienna, had unequivocally opposed the totalitarian regimes that dominated Italy, Germany and Russia in the 1930s, the later implementation of neoliberal policies was often done – unapologetically – through undemocratic or oppressive means. By the 1990s, it was suggested that, if faced by opposition, even elected political leaders might override democratic processes and proceed by 'deliberately provoking a crisis so as to remove the political logjam to reform', and that '[neoliberal] reform will be easier where the opposition is discredited and disorganized (or repressed)'.[56]

Furthermore, the People's Republic of China is a counterexample to the claim that capitalist prosperity accompanies liberal democracy. China hasn't followed the neoliberal pathway, but has shown how economic success in a capitalist world can be achieved by an authoritarian regime. While it may be the case that most of the world's most economically prosperous countries have multi-party representative governments, we shouldn't assume that authoritarian governments are never economically successful.

We shouldn't separate or abstract the economy from state and government; neither should we assume any straightforward relationship between one type of economy and one type of government. The relationship is central, but it needs to be considered within changing historical contexts. A failure to appreciate this historical contingency in political economy has led to disastrous errors. An example was the false and dangerous idea of 'spreading democracy', or remaking distant countries in the image of the world's superpower, as part of a flawed case for invasions of Afghanistan and Iraq in the early 2000s.[57] Economic prosperity, let alone peace, doesn't follow elections in the manner that night follows day.

Learning from history

'Those who cannot remember the past are condemned to repeat it.' Those words of George Santayana (1863–1952) are often taken out of their original context.[58] He wasn't making a grand statement about learning from history; rather, he meant that, in order to develop, a creature needs memory. Anyway, I much prefer Hegel's view that history teaches us

> that nations and governments have never learned anything from history or acted upon any lessons they might have drawn from it. Each age and each nation finds itself in such peculiar circumstances, in such a unique situation, that it can and must make decisions with respect to itself alone.[59]

On any given day, a nation is embroiled in complex and contradictory circumstances; events develop quickly and unpredictably, even as we strive to regulate things. Of course we should understand the past, but that won't prevent our falling over an unexpected obstacle. History isn't repetitive; each day sees a unique series of events. So, unlike algebra, history lessons don't teach us how to solve previously unseen problems using familiar techniques. In the next chapter, I set out some basic problems of government that have endured over the long course of history. But the fact that they reappear in differing guises over time doesn't mean that we find enduring solutions. Instead, I present them as problems that will probably endure into the future precisely because there's been no solution to them. We shouldn't assume that the future will be like the past, but it may be safe to assume that problems of government that have bothered the best of minds for centuries without resolution are probably here to stay.

Books about world politics are all too often written as if the author can tell us where things are heading or, even more boldly, what ought to be done and how we ought to think. And naturally, many readers are looking for solutions or guidance. What trends should we be aware of? Are things going to get worse or better? How should we solve major global problems? Writers often oblige with answers, but their predictions often turn out to be mistaken due to misplaced optimism or pessimism, or because they were looking in the wrong direction for clues as to trends – and hence their prescriptions turn out to be weak or even worthless. Some authors fall back on the values that they learned from the past, without critical appraisal, for example concluding (or exhorting) that we just need a better democracy or a better political culture, as if broken things could fix themselves. So we should pause to consider how we view historical events and how we look to the future.

History is punctuated by events that 'changed everything' – events of such magnitude and consequence that, from then on, all things look different, our lives are changed and later events are narrated in reference to them. The terrorist attacks on New York's Twin Towers and the Pentagon on 11 September 2001 are a prime example. Another way of considering such events, however, is that they puncture a collective *lack* of consciousness and make us aware of things we had failed to notice. Rather than 'changing everything', they may be seen as symptoms that bring to awareness the way things had already changed. They wake us from a kind of sleep and force us to deal with reality. The basic elements behind the 9/11 attack were not unfamiliar: the bombing of the World Trade Centre by terrorists in 1993 has been described by the FBI as 'something of a deadly dress rehearsal for 9/11';[60] the use of aircraft as weapons wasn't new; American facilities around the world had already been targets for Islamic extremists. And indeed, Islamic and Christian societies had been clashing from time to time since the first wave of Muslim conquests in the seventh century. While the surprise attacks of 9/11 did change world history, they were also a symptom of pre-existing conditions. This is not to claim that the attacks ought to have been foreseen and hence prevented – although in hindsight prevention was possible. It's only to say that one's present world view has blind spots. All too often it takes a disaster to make us look directly at something, and even then governments may misperceive the significance of events and make poor decisions – for example, a futile and destructive 20-year occupation of Afghanistan.

The significance of the fall of the Berlin Wall in 1989 was misunderstood due to a similar kind of blind spot. Yes, it did presage the end of the unsustainable communist command economy and the end of the Cold War. But it was followed by severe recession and corruption in the former Soviet republics as a new class of oligarchs raided state-owned assets. Multi-party elections did become the norm in the formerly Soviet-dominated eastern European countries. After an initial burst, however, voter turnouts in these newly independent countries dropped, and then anti-liberal populist parties began to prevail, most notably in Poland and Hungary. Russia's rigged elections perpetuated an autocracy under Vladimir Putin, and his opponents were systematically crushed. With the benefit of hindsight, it's not surprising that the demise of atheistic, internationalist socialism was replaced by religious, pro-family nationalism, and not by globalist neoliberalism, especially given the major economic collapse. An adversary of the United States and its NATO allies did indeed fall in 1991, but it was evidently naïve to think that the nations that emerged from its collapse would unquestioningly adopt free and fair competition in markets and elections. The saddest case is Ukraine, which found itself caught between the eastward advance of NATO and the EU on one side and corrupt Russian government on the other, resulting in devastation and dismemberment as the Kremlin grabbed territory.

Mainland China's integration into the global economy was smoother than Russia's. The Communist Party decided in 1978 to modernise and open up and, by the mid-1990s, China was on a trajectory to return to its former status as the world's largest economy. China had suffered greatly during its 'century of humiliation' (from the opium wars in the 1840s to the Japanese invasion in the 1930s), but there was now a clear determination – and ability – to keep foreign imperialists at bay. Western observers who thought that economic integration and reform would mean that China would also adopt political liberalism or economic neoliberalism had failed to take account of the country's history and civilisation.[61] 'Socialism with Chinese characteristics' turned into a distinctive blend of state management and private enterprise, all under the guidance of Communist Party officials who exercise 'long-term governance'.[62] To regard China's opening up as progress towards western liberalism was ethnocentric,[63] as it relied on lessons from European and American history rather than looking realistically at China's own history. (See Chapter 6, 'One-party state'.)

People naturally want to draw lessons from recent major events in order to reveal 'where things are heading'. But this often goes awry due to ethnocentric assumptions or unwillingness to look at the facts. If it's easy to mischaracterise the nature of 'what's happened', then predicting what's to come is surely even more hazardous.

Making predictions

A fair criticism of this book would be that it's replete with problems of government but has too few solutions. Naturally people want solutions to the world's most pressing problems, and an important part of that project is to improve the quality and effectiveness of government. Good solutions imply at least a

fair degree of confidence that a certain action taken today will have the consequences that are expected tomorrow and thereafter, and that this will be better
than any other option for change, and better than doing nothing. A political
solution requires a plan and hence a prediction of where things are heading
under present conditions, and where our proposed option would lead instead.
But historical experiences show that predictions – let alone prescriptions – are
hazardous. Some of the most eminent minds have failed Futurology 101.

A famous example is John Maynard Keynes's prediction in 1930 of the
economic standard of living in advanced capitalist economies 100 years on.
His forecast for long-run income growth was conservative but reasonable, at
around 2 percent per annum, leading to a predicted standard of living in 2030
between four and eight times what it was in 1930. This turned out to be an
underestimate, as there was a fourfold increase within just 50 years. But Keynes
predicted that such growth would mean that his grandchildren's generation
would have solved the basic problem of economics (that is, the problem of
scarcity), they would choose leisure over employment, and they would only
work about fifteen hours per week. He was thinking only of the wealthy economies, and didn't account for inequalities between countries, let alone the
distributional problems within countries. He didn't anticipate the present
day's highly unequal distribution of income between wage-earners and capi-
tal-owners. Nor did he anticipate how consumption preferences would change
and grow along with innovations in manufacturing and leisure-time technologies. And he underestimated the psychological and social benefits of work. Far
from working fewer hours, a greater proportion of people are now in paid
employment, and the highest paid are working longer hours, especially in the
United States with its high per capita incomes and flexible labour market.[64]
But we needn't be harsh on Keynes, as a recent study shows that economists
aren't very good at predicting recessions – or their depth – even one year
ahead,[65] let alone making predictions one century ahead.

A common misprediction in the 1990s was that globalisation and democratisation would prevail and would lead to the demise of nationalist ideology
and the nation-state.[66] But nationalism and national borders instead became
stronger, not weaker, due to the populist surge two decades later. President
Donald Trump, for example, swearing to put Americans first, wanted to
ban Muslim immigrants and launched a quixotic trade war with China. The
Covid-19 pandemic of 2020 necessitated a previously unthinkable closure of
borders and caused a global supply-chain crisis – all of which was the exact
opposite of the supposedly inexorable force of globalisation. Covid-19 raises
another example of misprediction: only a few years before the pandemic, we
were assured by a best-selling author that pandemics were a thing of the past
because, 'in the arms race between doctors and germs, doctors run faster'.[67]
Although a combination of public health restrictions and rapid innovation in

vaccines and antiviral drugs to combat Covid-19 showed that there are now far more effective responses than ever to disease, this particular virus appeared at times to run faster than the doctors. Such examples suggest exercising more caution before making predictions.

This doesn't mean forecasting is entirely a waste of time. Take for example the Club of Rome's 1972 report *The Limits to Growth*.[68] Some of its projections turned out to be fairly accurate – others not. It estimated the world's population at 3.6 billion in 1970 and projected that to rise to 7 billion within 30 years. That figure was reached in 2011, just over a decade late. The report also studied the growth of energy consumption per capita, the corresponding rise in the combustion of fossil fuels, and hence an exponential increase in the concentration of carbon dioxide (CO_2) in the atmosphere. The report projected this to reach 380 parts per million by 2000 – although that didn't occur until 2006.[69] It was unable to estimate how much CO_2 could be released into the atmosphere 'without causing irreversible changes in the earth's climate',[70] and it placed this issue alongside other forms of pollution from substances such as lead and pesticides. It didn't anticipate how emission of carbon compounds would become a cause of catastrophic changes in climate, and hence become the leading environmental issue. The great achievement of this 1972 report, however, was its model of a complex world system, accounting for the likely changes in and interrelationships between quantitative variables (of population, capital, food, non-renewable resources and pollution), and to simulate how this system would tend to behave in future as it reached carrying capacity, or the limits to its growth, under different sets of assumptions. This was a significant step forward in efforts to model humanity's unsustainable demographic and economic growth and resource usage – despite shortcomings to which the report itself admitted, and others we now see in hindsight. It recognised that our planet is a finite system, that unchecked growth is unsustainable, and that technological solutions alone won't suffice. The best way to avoid population collapse at some point during the twenty-first century, it forecast, would be to achieve an 'equilibrium' or steady state in population and capital, supported by innovations in recycling, solar power and so on. Societies would have to set clear short- and long-term goals, with future generations in mind, requiring a significant shift in our values – and hence political change and effort. The measurements and forecasts in *The Limits to Growth* have been revised since its publication,[71] and climate change is now paramount, but the general message remains relevant: shift social and economic values, set growth-limiting targets, and switch to renewable resources, or face a global catastrophe that will force change upon us anyway. In the meantime, however, population more than doubled since 1972 and world economic output increased (in real terms) more than fourfold, so the message wasn't heeded.

Conclusion

Government is inherently a forward-looking and normative set of activities. As well as responding to events that have occurred, those who govern must anticipate what could happen and decide what should be done next. Policymaking and political success entail promises about future security, prosperity and well-being. Projections and prescriptions are integral to the job, but they're also prone to errors caused by sheer unpredictability or by self-interested and wishful thinking. Given the unpredictability of events and consequences, the probability of failures of government are high, and such failures are costly. Having governments do less and leaving things more to private enterprise has its own risks, however, as competitive markets widen inequalities and are prone to cycles of boom and bust that can destroy people's wealth and careers. We may be stuck with government, but there are many ways of imagining and practising the arts of government, as we learn from past and present. We've looked critically at the origins and benefits of the state and we've asked (not for the first time in history!) why we should be governed at all. But, from here on, I'll assume that membership of a state is a necessity and not an option born of consent. A basic human right is the right to a nationality, and to be stateless is to be cast out into a dangerous and ill-defined zone. The critical questions, then, are how best to govern a state, and what conditions should come with our membership. The next chapter maps out the range of historically enduring problems of government.

Notes

1 Defoe, Daniel. 2003 [1722]. *A Journal of the Plague Year*. London: Penguin. See p. 37.

2 Wilson, Woodrow. 1887. 'The Study of Administration'. *Political Science Quarterly* 2 (2): 197–222.

3 Nothias, Toussaint. 2020. 'Access Granted: Facebook's Free Basics in Africa'. *Media, Culture & Society* 42 (3): 329–48, RUL: https://doi.org/10.1177/0163443719 890530 (accessed 5 September 2022).

4 Gehl Sampath, Padmashree. 2021. 'Governing Artificial Intelligence in an Age of Inequality'. *Global Policy* 12 (Suppl. 6): 21–31, URL: https://doi.org/ 10.1111/1758-5899.12940 (accessed 5 September 2022).

5 Banaji, Shakuntala & Ramnath Bhat. 2021. *Social Media and Hate*. London: Routledge, URL: https://doi.org/10.4324/9781003083078 (accessed 10 November 2022).

6 Persily, Nathaniel. 2017. 'The 2016 U.S. Election: Can Democracy Survive the Internet?' *Journal of Democracy* 28 (2): 63–76, URL: https://muse.jhu.edu/ article/653377 (accessed 5 September 2022).

7 Banaji, Shakuntala & Ramnath Bhat. 2021. *Social Media and Hate*. London: Routledge, URL: https://doi.org/10.4324/9781003083078

8 McCue, Jason & James Libson. 14 December 2021. 'Facebook Put Profit before Rohingya Lives'. *The Guardian*, URL: https://www.theguardian.com/ commentisfree/2021/dec/14/facebook-profits-rohingya-lives-courts-myanmar (accessed 5 September 2022).

9 Van der Made, Jan. 2021. 'Chinese Tech, Ignored by the West, is Taking over Africa's Cyberspace'. *RFI*, URL: https://www.rfi.fr/en/science-and-technology/20210722-chinese-tech-ignored-by-the-west-is-taking-over-africa-s-cyberspace (accessed 5 September 2022).

10 Greenwald, Glenn. 2014. *No Place to Hide: Edward Snowden, the NSA, and the U.S. Surveillance State.* New York: Metropolitan Books.

11 Mudditt, J. 24 June 2022. 'The Nation Where Your "Faceprint" is Already Being Tracked'. BBC, URL: https://www.bbc.com/future/article/20220616-the-nation-where-your-faceprint-is-already-being-tracked (accessed 1 July 2022).

12 Liang, Fan, Vishnupriya Das, Nadiya Kostyuk & Muzammil M. Hussain. 2018. 'Constructing a Data-Driven Society: China's Social Credit System as a State Surveillance Infrastructure'. *Policy & Internet* 10 (4): 415–53.

13 Srnicek, Nick. 2017. *Platform Capitalism.* Cambridge: Polity Press.

14 Weber, Max [1919] in: Gerth, H., W. Mills & M. Weber. 2009. *From Max Weber.* London: Routledge. See p. 78.

15 For a survey of various recent concepts of the state, see: Raadschelders, Jos C.N. 2020. *The Three Ages of Government.* Ann Arbor: University of Michigan Press. On the past and future of states, especially the four 'superstates', see: Roberts, Alisdair. 2023. *Superstates: Empires of the Twenty-First Century.* Cambridge: Polity Press.

16 Graeber, David & David Wengrow. 2021. *The Dawn of Everything.* New York: Farrar, Straus & Giroux.

17 Ibid. See p. 252. Examples of archaeological sites that have challenged the traditional narrative about human progress towards state-based urban civilisation are Göbekli Tepe in Turkey and Poverty Point in the State of Louisiana.

18 Scott, James C. 2017. *Against the Grain: A Deep History of the Earliest States.* New Haven, NJ: Yale University Press; Scott, James C. 2009. *The Art of Not Being Governed: An Anarchist History of Upland Southeast Asia.* New Haven, NJ: Yale University Press.

19 Podany, Amanda H. 2022. *Weavers, Scribes, and Kings: A New History of the Ancient Near East.* Oxford: Oxford University Press. See p. 19.

20 David, Rosalie. 1997. *The Pyramid Builders of Ancient Egypt: A Modern Investigation of Pharaoh's Workforce.* London: Routledge. See p. 58.

21 Cromwell, Jenny. 2022. 'The First Recorded Strike in History'. *Papyrus Stories,* URL: https://papyrus-stories.com/2022/03/15/the-first-recorded-strike-in-history/ (accessed 24 November 2022).

22 Slanski, Kathryn E. 2012. 'The Law of Hammurabi and Its Audience'. *Yale Journal of Law & Humanities* 24 (1): 97–110. See p. 109.

23 Podany [note 19]. See p. 282.

24 May, Larry. 2019. *Ancient Legal Thought: Equity, Justice, and Humaneness from Hammurabi and the Pharaohs to Justinian and the Talmud.* Cambridge: Cambridge University Press. See p. 23. Abridged.

25 Mirakhor, Abbas & Hossein Askari. 2019. *Conceptions of Justice from Earliest History to Islam.* New York: Palgrave Macmillan.

26 Barjamovic, Gojko. 2003. 'Civic Institutions and Selfgovernment in Southern Mesopotamia in the Mid-First Millennium BC'. In *Assyria and Beyond*, ed. J.G. Dercksen, 47–98. Leiden: NINO. See also Graeber & Wengrow [note 16].

27 May [note 24].

28 Isakhan, Benjamin. 2011. 'What Is So "Primitive" About "Primitive Democracy"? Comparing the Ancient Middle East and Classical Athens'. In *The Secret History of Democracy*, ed. B. Isakhan & S. Stockwell, 19–34. Houndmills: Palgrave Macmillan.

29 Gomez, Michael A. 2019. *African Dominion: A New History of Empire in Early and Medieval West Africa.* Princeton, NJ: Princeton University Press; Kizza, Immaculate. 2011. 'Africa's Indigenous Democracies: The Baganda of Uganda'.

In *The Secret History of Democracy*, ed. B. Isakhan & S. Stockwell, 123–35. Houndmills: Palgrave Macmillan.

30 Engels, Frederick. 1972 [1891]. *The Origin of the Family, Private Property, and the State*. New York: Pathfinder Press. See p. 160.

31 Ibid., p. 162. Marx and Engels predicted that the propertyless proletariat would collectively sweep away the capitalist mode of production and form a temporary ruling class. By abolishing itself as a class, the proletariat would eliminate the causes of class conflict, and the state would wither away. Marx, Karl & Friedrich Engels. 2008 [1848]. *The Communist Manifesto*. London: Pluto Press.

32 Locke, John. 1980 [1690]. *Second Treatise of Government*. Indianapolis: Hackett.

33 Kinna, Ruth. 2020. *The Government of No One: The Theory and Practice of Anarchism*. UK: Penguin.

34 Graeber & Wengrow [note 16].

35 Emberling, Geoff. 2015. 'Mesopotamian Cities and Urban Process, 3500–1600BCE'. In *The Cambridge World History, Vol. 3*, ed. Norman Yoffee, 253–78. Cambridge: Cambridge University Press; Nissen, Hans J. 2015. 'Urbanization and the Techniques of Communication: The Mesopotamian City of Uruk during the Fourth Millennium BCE'. In *The Cambridge World History, Vol 3*, ed. Norman Yoffee, 113–30. Cambridge: Cambridge University Press.

36 Podany [note 19]. See p. 81.

37 Forming your own country is apparently a popular option in Australia. Hobbs, Harry & George Williams. 22 October 2022. 'Raising the Drawbridge: Why Are So Many Australians Creating Their Own Countries?' *The Guardian*, URL: https://www.theguardian.com/books/2022/oct/23/raising-the-drawbridge-why-are-so-many-australians-creating-their-own-countries (accessed 24 October 2022). Or there's the 'sovereign citizens movement', as described by the Southern Poverty Law Center, URL: https://www.splcenter.org/fighting-hate/extremist-files/ideology/sovereign-citizens-movement (accessed 16 May 2023).

38 MoDi. 2010. *The Mozi: A Complete Translation*. Hong Kong: The Chinese University of Hong Kong Press, trans. Ian Johnston. See p. 91.

39 Olivelle, Patrick. 2016. *A Dharma Reader: Classical Indian Law*. New York: Columbia University Press. See p. 10.

40 Rousseau said we needn't take literally his depiction of innocent humans in a state of nature.

41 Pirie, Fernanda. 2014. *The Anthropology of Law*. Oxford: Oxford University Press.

42 Samuelson, Paul A. 1948. 'Consumption Theory in Terms of Revealed Preference'. *Economica* 15 (60): 243–53.

43 Easterlin, Richard A. 1974. 'Does Economic Growth Improve the Human Lot? Some Empirical Evidence'. In *Nations and Households in Economic Growth*, ed. I.P.A. David & M.W. Reder, 89–125. New York: Academic Press.

44 Kasser, T. 2002. *The High Price of Materialism*. Cambridge, MA: MIT Press.

45 Helliwell, John, Richard Layard & Jeffrey Sachs. 2017. *World Happiness Report 2017*. New York: Sustainable Development Solutions Network. See p. 3.

46 Engster, Daniel. 2007. *The Heart of Justice*. Oxford: Oxford University Press. See p. 12.

47 Waring, Marilyn. 2018. *Still Counting: Wellbeing, Women's Work and Policy-Making*. Wellington, NZ: Bridget Williams Books. See p. 114.

48 Mearsheimer, John J. 2021. 'The Inevitable Rivalry'. *Foreign Affairs* 100 (6): (e-version).

49 Luo, Chuliang, Shi Li & Terry Sicular. 2020. 'The Long-Term Evolution of National Income Inequality and Rural Poverty in China'. *China Economic Review* 62: 101465.

50 It does at least include pension schemes, medical insurance and a minimum living standard guarantee. Cai, Meng & Ximing Yue. 2020. 'The Redistributive Role of

Government Social Security Transfers on Inequality in China'. *China Economic Review* 62: 101512.

51 Schumpeter, Joseph A. 2008 [1942]. *Capitalism, Socialism and Democracy*. New York: HarperCollins. See p. 162.

52 Ibid., p. 170.

53 Dahl, Robert A. & Ian Shapiro. 2015. *On Democracy*. New Haven: Yale University Press. See p. 200.

54 José Piñera in: Williamson, John. 1994. *The Political Economy of Policy Reform*. Washington, DC: Institute for International Economics. See p. 225.

55 Letelier, Orlando. 28 August 1976. 'Economic "Freedom's" Awful Toll'. *The Nation*: 137–42.

56 Williamson [note J. 54]. See pp. 20–21.

57 Hobsbawm, Eric J. 1 September 2004. 'Spreading Democracy'. *Foreign Policy* 144: 40–41.

58 'Progress, far from consisting in change, depends on retentiveness. When change is absolute there remains no being to improve and no direction is set for possible improvement: and when experience is not retained, as among savages, infancy is perpetual. Those who cannot remember the past are condemned to repeat it. In the first stage of life the mind is frivolous and easily distracted; it misses progress by failing in consecutiveness and persistence. This is the condition of children and barbarians, in whom instinct has learned nothing from experience.' Santayana, George. 1905. *The Life of Reason*. Indianapolis, IN: IUPUI, URL: https://santayana. iupui.edu/wp-content/uploads/2019/01/Common-Sense-ebook.pdf (accessed 5 September 2022). See p. 172.

59 Hegel, G.W.F. 1975 [1828]. *Lectures on the Philosophy of World History*. Cambridge: Cambridge University Press. See p. 21.

60 FBI, URL: https://www.fbi.gov/history/famous-cases/world-trade-center-bombing-1993 (accessed 17 July 2023).

61 Harvey's 'neoliberalism with Chinese characteristics' was misguided. Harvey, David. 2007. *A Brief History of Neo-Liberalism*. Oxford: Oxford University Press.

62 Communist Party of China. 2021. 'Resolution of the CPC Central Committee on the Major Achievements and Historical Experience of the Party over the Past Century, 11 November 2021', URL: http://english.www.gov.cn/policies/latest releases/202111/16/content_WS6193a935c6d0df57f98e50b0.html (accessed 5 September 2022).

63 Jacques, Martin. 2012. *When China Rules the World: The End of the Western World and the Birth of a New Global Order*. New York: Penguin.

64 Keynes's 1931 essay 'Economic Possibilities for our Grandchildren' is republished with expert commentaries in: Pecchi, Lorenzo & Gustavo Piga. 2008. *Revisiting Keynes: Economic Possibilities for Our Grandchildren*. Cambridge, MA: MIT Press.

65 An, Zidong, João Tovar Jalles & Prakash Loungani. 2018. 'How Well Do Economists Forecast Recessions?' *International Finance* 21 (2): 100–21.

66 Fukuyama, Francis. 1992. *The End of History and the Last Man*. New York: Maxwell Macmillan International; Ohmae, Kenichi. 1996. *The End of the Nation State: The Rise of Regional Economies*. New York: Free Press.

67 Harari, Yuval Noah. 2017. *Homo Deus: A Brief History of Tomorrow*. London: Vintage. See p. 14.

68 Meadows, D.H., D.L. Meadows, J. Randers & W.W. Behrens. 1972. *The Limits to Growth*. New York: Universe Books.

69 Our World in Data, URL: https://ourworldindata.org/ (accessed 16 November 2021).

70 Meadows et al. [note 68]. See p. 81.

71 Herrington, Gaya. 2021. 'Update to Limits to Growth: Comparing the World3 Model with Empirical Data'. *Journal of Industrial Ecology* 25 (3): 614–26, URL: https://doi.org/10.1111/jiec.13084 (accessed 5 September 2022).

3
ENDURING DILEMMAS OF GOVERNMENT

One general purpose of government is to prevent, minimise or solve collective problems, but government itself is a perpetual problem that no society has ever really solved, despite reforms and revolutions. And the problem of government is more than a technical one that could be fixed by carefully crafted constitutions and policies. It's a complex human problem, and it changes and varies through history and across cultures. This chapter and the next map out important features of this set of problems. First, we can discern some commonly shared and historically enduring concerns. What have been the main themes and dilemmas in this intractable problem of government?

By the rod or by example?

By 256 BCE, at the end of the Chinese Zhou dynasty, the number of warring states had been reduced to seven. It was widely thought that imperial unification was desirable for the sake of harmony, but the question of which state would lead this was to be settled violently. It was the western state of Qin's King Zheng (259–210 BCE) who came out on top in 221 BCE, to become Shi Huangdi, or First August Emperor – best known today for the terracotta warriors. His mode of government placed merit above inheritance, centralisation and standardisation of administration (including standardisation of the Chinese characters) above local customs, and strict adherence to punitive laws above benevolence. Pragmatic legalism was preferred over the virtuous examples set by past kings; many books were burned and scholars executed.[1] The first emperor's reign was brief, however, and his successors were soon overthrown, to be followed by the much longer-lived Han dynasty. Opponents attributed the downfall of the Qin dynasty to its refusal to follow the noble

DOI: 10.4324/9781003439783-3

traditions of the ancient Shang and Zhou dynasties. This heritage had upheld faithful and correct observance of rites, filial piety, reverence for ancestors and benevolence towards subjects. It had been preserved by revered philosophers, notably Confucius (c. 551–479 BCE) and Mencius (c. 372–289 BCE), who held that strict punitive law would not be needed if members of the ruling class kept high standards of conduct and led by benevolent moral example. Confucius is recorded as having said:

> In administering your government, what need is there for you to kill? Just desire the good yourself and the common people will be good. The virtue of the gentleman is like wind; the virtue of the small man is like grass. Let the wind blow over the grass and it is sure to bend.[2]

Legalism was quite the opposite approach, however. It went back to political advisers Shang Yang (c. 390–338 BCE) and Han Fei (c. 280–233 BCE) who influenced the rulers of Qin and the first emperor. *The Book of Lord Shang* states that the ruler should (without exceptions) punish all transgressions, even those that are yet to be committed, and encourage informers. The aim was to increase the efficiency of the population in farming and in fighting, to conquer more arable land, and hence to preserve and strengthen the state and its ruler.[3]

The Chinese civilisation-state, which originated many centuries before the first emperor and survives up to the present, has shown a remarkable continuity. While dynasties rose and fell, its bureaucratic model of government survived. Its governing systems combined legalist administration with an ideal of virtuous rule from above, along with cultural norms of loyalty to family that, in turn, modelled loyalty to provincial and imperial rulers from below. Its enduring concerns were 'regulating the household, governing the state, and bringing peace to the world under heaven'.[4] Its institutional binding was a civil administration run by scholars drawn from all provinces and versed in Confucian thought. It was not based on open forums or representative assemblies. The Chinese sought a synthesis of government by the rod and by virtuous example.

Today, every country needs some combination of exemplary ethical leadership and compliance with law. Maintaining complex systems such as airlines and telecommunications – and hence the freedoms that they give us – requires legalistic regulation to make them reliable and safe. This calls for some bureaucratic organisation – much of which is automated and digitised nowadays. Furthermore, people want an open and predictable rule of law that should apply equally to all, including to those who make the law. The consistent application of laws and regulations, and hence penalties for breaking them, are as important as ever. But the personal qualities and ethical conduct of political leaders still matter a great deal too. The wish to be led by example persists, and this becomes painfully apparent when a political leader causes scandal due to misconduct or sleaze.

Let's look at a recent example. In 2010 the people of Toronto, Ontario, elected as mayor Rob Ford, then a 41-year-old who had previously served three terms as a city councillor. Ford was a fiscal conservative who wanted to lighten the load of government and to build subways instead of a planned light rail. He was known for bluntness, which his supporters took to represent honesty and authenticity, while his opponents found him erratic, abrasive and offensive. Amid numerous controversies, it became apparent that Mr Ford had a substance abuse problem and was sometimes intoxicated. Indeed, he had been surreptitiously videoed while smoking crack cocaine. After many denials, in November 2013 he admitted in public that he had smoked crack. There were sincere apologies and pledges to clean himself up and get on with the job of leading the city. But further revelations of intoxication and abusive behaviour emerged. Ford registered as a candidate for the 2014 mayoral election, but later withdrew and stood only for a seat on council. A new mayor, John Tory, was elected, while Rob Ford won back his local ward with 58 percent of votes. He had withdrawn from the mayoral contest due to the discovery of a tumour; he died of a rare form of cancer in March 2016. In the meantime, however, he had made global headlines for his extraordinary behaviour, especially his drug use.

Ford's story could be retold as a tragedy of an outspoken civic leader who was brought down by addictions and defeated by cancer. However, his conduct was sometimes abusive, and drug and alcohol dependency is incompatible with mayoral responsibilities. These flaws brought into question the soundness of his judgement and his trustworthiness. He wasn't setting a good example for others. In reply to an interviewer's suggestion that, *if* he were an alcoholic, he might want to seek help, Ford may have been right to say, 'I wasn't elected to be perfect.'[5] But he was dodging the question about alcoholism – and hence about his fitness for office – on the self-evident premise that there's no morally flawless leader. The Rob Ford story highlights, in a negative way, the general – and ancient – need for ethically sound leadership. We can't rely on constitutions, laws and technical regulation to govern everything. The human factor still matters; leaders should set us good examples. Even so, Mr Ford won his council seat back after his poor conduct had been widely exposed.

The law doesn't sanction the best conduct; it does sanction the least desirable. One of the achievements of modern government is an impersonal rule of law, requiring the lawmakers to abide by the laws they make, and preventing any individual from dictating or suspending the law arbitrarily. But the concern with the moral qualities of leadership – above what's prescribed by law – is still very strong, and with good reason. I'll return to this theme through the coming chapters.

Self-interest or the common good?

A related question concerns whether rulers make laws and govern in their own interests or in the interests of the people over whom they rule. It may seem self-evident that government ought to be for the common good. If not, it's simply not legitimate. I agree in principle, but the matter has never been that easily settled. For example, in Book 1 of Plato's *Republic*, Socrates gets into an argument with the sophist Thrasymachus, who asserts that justice is whatever serves the interests of the strong. Regardless of who they are, those who make the laws are, almost by definition, the strong; so whatever's deemed to be just in a society is what the strong have decided it is, which will be the kind of justice that suits them. Furthermore, if you do what's right and fair all of the time, you'll never get ahead. People who play by the rules lose to those who bend them. Thrasymachus seems to want it both ways: that rules of justice are made in the interests of the powerful, and yet the strongest players win by ignoring the rules anyway. The winners make the rules to suit themselves, and follow them only when it suits them. But Socrates is having none of it, counter-arguing that good rulers act in the interests of their subjects, not themselves, and that the very best rulers would be philosophers who know – and are ruled by – the abstract and universal source of justice, or Form of the Good.

It sounds grand, but Socrates doesn't convince me that there's one (and only one) underlying form of justice, or doing right, applicable to all peoples. Nor am I convinced that those who do what's right will always prosper, while those who don't will necessarily suffer for it. He claims, but can't prove, that tyrants are all leading miserable lives. And he doesn't account for, say, slaves who strove to do what's right, and yet could never enjoy the freedom and prosperity of aristocrats like Plato. Being a morally good slave wouldn't have earned you the fullest and happiest life, surely. A slave does make a brief appearance at the start of *The Republic*, following an order to run ahead and ask Socrates to wait for the others, but Socrates doesn't suggest freeing him. Later on, Plato has Thrasymachus storm out of the party, so Thrasymachus doesn't stay to hear Socrates out; nor does he get a right of reply. So Plato doesn't do Thrasymachus justice, and by the end of the dialogue Socrates hasn't satisfactorily rebutted Thrasymachus's sceptical realism, even though we may not like the idea that justice serves the interests of the strong. Thrasymachus may be morally wrong in our eyes, and yet be factually right.

Nonetheless, most political philosophers agree that government is intended for a common good, meaning at least our common defence and security, but ideally the promotion of a higher quality of life. Under the monotheistic religions, this included the improvement of people's chances of salvation and eternal happiness in the afterlife.[6] Nonetheless, since ancient times there've been opposing schools of thought, such as Chinese legalism, that insisted that the aim of government was to preserve and strengthen the state, especially the person who ruled it.

Today, we still struggle to balance self-interest and the common good. On one hand, people say that the test of a well-governed society is how well its most disadvantaged members are faring, and that law and administration should aim to eliminate discrimination and to promote the wellbeing of all. On the other hand, we often hear accusations that leaders, being merely human, are self-interested, and that any ideas about serving the common good that they once had get cast aside as political advantage and personal ambition take over. How else does one get to the top in the competitive world of politics? Moreover, key assumptions underlying neoliberal reforms were that 'public good' is an incoherent notion, and that 'interests' pertain only to individuals, not to communities. Politicians and public servants were all presumed to be acting in self-interest, and hence law and policy should be redesigned to make it in their interests to serve a primary goal of maximising economic growth – assuming that rising national income would 'trickle down' and make everyone better off. If humans are essentially 'rational utility maximisers', then the self-interested conduct of public officials leads logically to wasteful administration and corruption, unless the right incentives are in place. Or better still, let private enterprise do as much as possible, and then government's job is to cut public spending, reduce taxes, return budget surpluses and punish criminals. With the right incentives and rewards in place, the 'natural' self-interest of public servants would make them act in line with efficiency goals and curb their empire-building habits.

When self-interest really takes over, on the other hand, we see autocratic leaders who amass power and wealth for themselves while they watch their own countries get ruined and their people impoverished and imperilled – and then they punish those who complain about it. When those countries that uphold human rights object to what they're doing and impose sanctions on them, they simply turn to other autocratic regimes for support.[7] Sadly, not all leaders today are putting the common good first.

Even if we agree that the common good should be the aim of government, however, we run into disagreements about what the common good actually is and how best to achieve it. It's hard to disentangle 'what's in the interests of the whole of society' from 'what's best for people like me'. It's not easy to set aside our own interests when judging public policy. Humans can be both selfish and altruistic; neither kind of motive is necessarily more natural or more efficacious than the other.[8] And, if we choose to be altruistic, then there are differing liberal-progressive and conservative-religious versions of 'the common good'.[9] We need, though, to make it worthwhile for people to act collectively for a common good, whatever we judge that to be. We don't all believe in and value the same ends, but political leaders should state what they believe 'the common good' means in practice. In a diverse society, though, is there a set of beliefs that's shared widely enough to form the foundations of a consensus?

A shared belief system?

Religions

Abū Nasr al-Fārābī (ca. 870–950 CE) was one of the greatest philosophers of medieval times. He came from the eastern provinces of Persia, ruled by the Abbasid caliphs in Baghdad since 750. The caliphs had sponsored the translation into Arabic of important works from Greek. Despite religious qualms about pagan philosophers, the rationalism of Plato and Aristotle thus had a major influence on Islamic thinkers, including al-Fārābī. By the tenth century, however, the caliphate was gradually disintegrating. Despite its universal claims, the Islamic faith hadn't preserved imperial unity. Instead, differences over religious doctrine had caused dissension, including rivalry over who should succeed as leader of the Muslims and whether one ruler (or caliph) should embody the supreme religious and secular political authority. The Prophet Muhammad (d. 632 CE) had been the source of divine revelation as well as a successful military and political leader. But by the tenth century his successors were viewed by many as impious usurpers and they were losing their grip on power; their empire was divided among rival dynasties, and religious authority had passed into the hands of a wider community of preachers, scholars and jurists. Al-Fārābī could see a decline from the once-ideal city of Medina, when ruled by the Prophet, and he explained how philosophy and religion helped to keep communities together after those golden times. Philosophy, he said, seeks universal principles, discovered by reason, but few people (especially in his time) have the literacy and time to study it. Religions use the less precise means of likenesses and symbols to convey such truths, and this suffices for the uneducated masses. All religions, al-Fārābī said, seek ultimate happiness for the people. He respected religions but considered them second best to the true philosophy.

Religious beliefs caused division and conflict as well as harmony, however. The political uses of religion, both Christian and Islamic, often meant enforced adherence to an orthodox belief system, and this resulted in a long history of oppression and sectarian strife. Islam was divided between Sunni and Shia and other minor sects, each with its own view about political and religious authority. In Christendom, emperors from Constantine onwards failed to get all bishops to agree to a single set of doctrines. The Goths who sacked Rome in the fifth century had adopted the heretical Arian doctrines, and other non-orthodox sects flourished in Persia. In the eleventh century, the Greek- and Latin-speaking sides of Christendom parted ways irrevocably. The western

European religious wars of the sixteenth and seventeenth centuries caused massive destruction and death, ending in a compromise in 1648 that allowed each sovereign nation to observe its own version of the faith, be it Catholic, Lutheran or Calvinist. Efforts to make all subjects conform to one belief system have caused more harm than good, then, as enforcement of orthodoxy created resistance and division. Inasmuch as it may succeed, strict orthodoxy is inimical to creativity and intellectual progress. Indeed, the eras of greatest cultural and intellectual creativity have tended also to be times of political disunity and interstate rivalry – for example, the Warring States period in ancient China, the competing city-states of ancient Greece and the political disunity of the Italian Renaissance. And yet a complete lack of common belief and common cause isn't helpful either, especially in a time of emergency when concerted action may be a matter of survival.

Nations

The modern era has largely permitted religious diversity (see Chapter 4, 'Secularism and toleration'), so where do countries now find sources of shared beliefs? One option has been to promote belief in and deference to a supposedly benevolent ruling class. Confucius and Plato both tried that, and the monotheistic religions often sought to justify political hierarchies ('the powers that be are ordained of God'[10]). In reaction against such conservative ideas, many socialists, and especially Marxists, believed in the inevitability of the defeat of an economically dominant ruling class by the proletariat, once the latter realised its alienation and its collective potential. Millions of people have been killed in the service of imposing religious beliefs and atheistic communism, however.

A belief in the nation itself became an alternative. The cultural belief in a 'people' who share a common heritage or origins became a political belief that 'we' have a right to form an independent state that's recognised as sovereign by us and by all others. The idea that a people who occupy a territory have a right to their own state, governed according to their own will, gained strength from the American and French revolutions. It found a clear statement in the nationalism of Giuseppe Mazzini (1805–72) who called for the unification of Italy. An independent nation-state would uphold the rights of its members, who in turn would have duties to the state. Mutual recognition among nation-states should foster international cooperation and peace. Things didn't work out so well in practice, unfortunately. Political unification didn't overcome internal strife within the new Italian state. Many believed war would inspire people to rise above their sectional interests, but Italy emerged from World War I still divided internally between radical workers' movements and their bourgeois enemies. The extreme nationalism of Mussolini's fascist regime (1922–45) was certainly no solution. In recent times, secessionist movements have sought independent nationhood for regions within Italy, and, in the opposite direction, far-right nationalist parties, such as Brothers of Italy, have emerged.

In contrast to Italy's unification in the 1860s, the Austro-Hungarian Empire broke up into smaller states after its defeat in World War I. The dual monarchy of Austria and Hungary had encompassed ten major language groups and numerous faiths, including Lutheran, Calvinist, Latin Catholic, Eastern Catholic, Orthodox, Jewish and Islamic. But the 'culture wars' that began to divide the empire were caused by ethno-religious group identification that fuelled numerous nationalist movements, and these political conflicts further reinforced their perceived differences.[11] In the 1867 'compromise', the Habsburg emperor was crowned King of Hungary, appointing a government in Budapest that was responsible to an elected bicameral parliament. The end of World War I, however, brought about the demise of imperial Austria-Hungary through recognition of the nationalist movements. The postwar treaties separated Austria and Hungary and reduced them to small landlocked countries, alongside the newly formed states of Czechoslovakia and the Kingdom of Serbs, Croats and Slovenes. Large territories were ceded to Romania and to the second republic of Poland. The new postwar Hungary had lost two-thirds of the territory of the prewar kingdom, while about a third of Hungarian-speaking people found themselves in neighbouring countries, and so a new set of political problems was created. The complex real-world tapestry of nations didn't fit neatly into the nation-state borders drawn up in treaties at Versailles. With the fall of the Austro-Hungarian, Russian and Ottoman empires after the war, millions of people left their homes to settle elsewhere. Minority groups were often poorly protected and many people were made stateless. The cause of nationalism didn't work as well as Mazzini had hoped.

Nations created from colonial conquest were often left with profound internal divisions. Nigeria, formed in 1914, is a case in point. Direct British colonial rule began with the annexation of Lagos in 1861. British policy was driven by competition with French and German colonial ambitions and by commercial interests, especially around the big river systems. The subsequent forty years saw increasing involvement of indigenous communities, who had their own rivalries, with Christian missionaries and chartered trading companies. Political subjugation occurred through treaties, sometimes willingly, but often at gunpoint, and eventually the signing away of sovereignty to the British government. By 1900 the colonies fell into two main protectorates. In the north was the Islamic caliphate of Sokoto, a loose federation of over 30 emirates with a population of over ten million. Sokoto was defeated by the British and largely incorporated into the northern protectorate in 1903. It was thus by the use or threat of violence that previously separate and diverse peoples were subdued and transformed into one colonial entity. In 1960 Nigeria became an independent nation with a predominantly Christian populace in the south and Muslim in the north.[12]

In spite of the violence and rivalries that may underpin their formation and survival, such national entities can become consolidated in people's minds as valid states, aided by the establishment of an official language, administrative structures and careers centred on the capital, national newspapers, broadcasting systems, symbols, celebrations, independence days and the like. So among the rival and diverse groups, a common belief in themselves as a nation may form that's sufficiently strong to sustain 'an imagined political community'.[13]

This sense of common origin and belonging can sometimes fail, however. A case in point is Ukraine. Formerly one of the socialist republics of the Soviet Union, the independent republic of Ukraine was formed in 1991. In 2013, Ukraine's President Yanukovich abandoned a proposed free trade agreement with the European Union in favour of a financial bailout and cheap gas from Russia. This sparked protests in Kiev during the winter of 2013–14 and Yanukovich went into exile. In February 2014, however, Russia annexed the Crimean Peninsula, initially by stealth. Although Russia had a historical claim on Crimea, its unilateral seizure of Ukrainian territory contravened international law, and sanctions were imposed on the Russian regime. Then in March 2014 protests erupted in the eastern Donbas region. The ensuing separatist rebellion had support from Russia, while Ukrainian forces shelled the rebel-held cities of Lugansk and Donetsk. On 17 July 2014, a Russian antiaircraft system based in Donetsk province shot down a Malaysian Airlines civilian flight, killing all those on board. Meanwhile, the rebel leaders in Lugansk and Donetsk set up civil administrations and the ceasefire line became a border in a frozen conflict. In contrast, the western provinces of Ukraine have historical roots in Austria-Hungary and Poland; people are mainly Ukrainian speakers with a stronger sense of Ukrainian nationality. The further east, the more people speak Russian. Prewar popular support for regional autonomy or secession was strongest in Donbas and among Russian speakers, but not in overwhelming majorities.[14] While global imperial rivalry was a factor in Ukraine's internal strife and territorial losses, the lower levels of popular commitment to Ukrainian nationality in the Donbas region facilitated the Russian-backed rebellion there. Meanwhile, a desire for independence from Moscow caused the Ukrainian Orthodox Church to split from its Russian counterpart, gaining recognition from Constantinople's Patriarchate. There was an irresolvable difference of beliefs among the people who inhabit Ukraine as to their cultural and political affiliations. In the illegal invasion of Ukraine by Russia in 2022, President Vladimir Putin denied Ukrainian nationality and formally recognised the breakaway republics of Donetsk and Lugansk, thus driving the wedge even deeper.

An enduring aim for government, then, is to uphold a common belief that's strong enough to maintain a sense of belonging to a going political concern.

In the past, religion was sometimes supposed to serve that purpose. In the Islamic caliphates, the community to be ruled was (in principle) the community of the faithful. The Byzantine (or eastern Roman) empire had similar aspirations. Neither was successful at binding all co-religionists, however, as religious differences became dividing lines. At different times and places, race, language or political allegiance has created similar kinds of social divisions. A belief in ourselves as a nation – a people of common origin or culture who desire political unity – has often worked, but often failed. As Hannah Arendt put it, nation-states become dangerous when 'national consciousness' overcomes the duty of the state to protect *all* inhabitants, thus transforming the state from 'an instrument of the law into an instrument of the nation'.[15] Some contemporary forms of populism raise similar concerns, as invoking 'the will of the people' may license discrimination against minorities and immigrants. A popular claim to social or territorial belonging then takes precedence over the impartial rule of law. Rights based on origin and birth may override those that pertain to all humans, and the result may be ethnic cleansing, exclusion of refugees or even genocide. International law now recognises that 'everyone has the right to a nationality'.[16] People need protection under the laws of a particular state to be assured of full application of universal human rights.

While there'll always be dissent, some degree of consensus about the legitimate reality of the state is vital. But the risks are that people too strongly identify statehood with a particular nationality and then refuse to admit others, or an internal division may emerge and deepen, as for example between Byzantium's 'blues' and 'greens',[17] or America's 'blues' and 'reds'. Government is effective, however, when few people even question the legitimate existence of the state, its territory and the population it embraces; when belonging, and the entity to which one belongs, can be taken for granted and aren't guarded too jealously or disputed violently. This shared belief doesn't arise spontaneously: it takes continual work to maintain it.

What are the aims of government?

With the exception of anarchists, it's largely agreed that communities need sound government for social cohesion. But for what aims or purposes, and within what limits are we governed? Again, these are enduring questions over which there's heated debate. We may in principle reject the proposition that law and government exist for the benefit of those who rule or for the aggrandisement of the state itself. Accepting, then, that the aim should be a common or public good, we face a debate about how to define that good (and later I will ask how we define 'the people'). If we can clarify this, then we also ask how far, or within what limits, the state may go in pursuing those beneficial ends. For example, if we assume that we'd all rather be happy than miserable, then what limits would we nonetheless want to place on governmental efforts to maximise our happiness? Or, at what point is it up to you to seek your own happiness or wellbeing? There have been two main dimensions on which the common good has been viewed: it may be seen in natural or supernatural terms, and in aggregated or holistic terms. The latter asks whether the common good is the net sum of whatever is good for its members, or something more than simply the sum of its parts.

Let's look first at the naturalistic approach, as preferred by Aristotle. For the sake of physical survival and to achieve self-sufficiency, humans associate and cooperate in groups. In larger communities that we call states, we can go further and aspire to achieve higher standards of living and flourishing. The goals of government, then, are the maintenance of justice and administration that maximise the opportunities for a higher quality of life and prosperity. This means that the aggregation of the wellbeing or happiness of individuals informs us about what governments should do. Happiness is thus treated as natural to us and is held to be 'the proper measure of social progress and the goal of public policy'.[18] And of course we then face a debate about what constitutes happiness and how to achieve it through public policy. There are now many surveys that aggregate the responses of individuals who've been asked to put a number (say, one to ten) on their own subjective wellbeing or satisfaction with life. The results can be correlated with, for instance, mortality rates and educational attainment. Unsurprisingly, people in countries that are wealthier and better governed tend to say they're happier, according to the surveys. But, even though it's a humane idea, there aren't compelling ethical reasons why governments *ought* to set happiness-maximisation goals, in part because there are alternative values and aims, such as fairness or liberty.[19]

Suppose instead there exists a moral purpose that's higher than one's happiness or satisfaction with life, and that the good or proper aims of the whole community should take precedence over those of individuals. Going back to Confucius and Socrates, we find arguments for the just or good society based on the harmony of an organic whole, with each part of the community playing a preordained role. Their aims were benevolent, and the happiness or prosperity of the individual was important, but privately defined goods were subordinate to a higher conception of what's right and just. In the ideal, harmonious city depicted by Socrates in Plato's *Republic*, the majority would be subordinate to wise philosopher-kings who alone had attained the highest knowledge of the Good – to the extent that Socrates proposed sacrificing the private life of the family in favour of public nurseries and a form of eugenics.

The general proposition that government should act in accord with a universal or higher truth was, later in history, compatible with the monotheistic religions. Christian and Islamic theologians – from Augustine to al-Ghazali[20] – generally agreed that the highest happiness and true justice could only be found in the afterlife, by the grace or will of God. The goals of individuals on earth were subordinate to the ultimate aim of salvation in the afterlife, or avoidance of damnation. Political authorities existed due to God's will, over-riding the will of the individual. Theocratic government is still found, for example in Iran, and it produces conservative law that discriminates against women. But we can also find secular ideas about how the good of the whole overrides the good of the individual, or how individual action should serve purposes that are higher than personal happiness. Patriotism is one example, as it may imply sacrificing even one's life for the good of the nation. Another example is Rousseau's social contract, by which: 'Each of us puts in common his person and all his power under the supreme direction of the general will; and in return each member becomes an indivisible part of the whole.'[21] Rousseau imagined the voluntary termination of our 'natural' existence as individuals through a moral transformation, achievable only in combination with all others, creating a lawful republic that's something greater than the sum of its individual members and that expresses 'the general will'. To get there, he imagined a quasi-divine Legislator whose lawgiving reconstitutes society. The trouble is that this role of Legislator could be usurped by one leader – and hence a direct line has been drawn from the French Revolution's days of terror to China's Cultural Revolution, or from Rousseau to Robespierre to Mao Zedong.[22] Such revolutionary thought didn't consider 'the masses' as they are, but rather as they *ought to be*: publicly spirited and virtuous, actively nationalistic and struggling against aristocracy, bourgeoisie and/or foreign imperialists.[23]

The reader may not like submission of individuality to a mass movement, especially if it's imposed on us. Nonetheless, contemporary ideas about sustainability call on us to put the good of the planet and of future generations ahead of our private choices or desires, such as long-distance travel. Or one's identification with a particular social group may come with expectations about what one ought to support or oppose. The net sum of whatever feels good to individuals isn't always our best guide to the good of the whole, nor to the proper aims of government. And our basic principles of government call for people willingly to put self-interest aside to work for a greater good. But historical experience warns us to beware of someone claiming to know what the common good or general will actually is. So, aside from disagreements about particular policies of governments, we have a fundamental tension between a bottom-up view (that governments serve the aggregated good of a majority) and a top-down view (that the good of the whole submerges the will or interests of individuals). This intersects with a controversy over the practical and moral limits on what governments can and should do in pursuit of their aims.

What are the limits of government?

If we said there were in principle no limits to government, then we could be asking for a totalitarian state that seeks to reach into the lives and minds of all subjects, bending them to the will of a tyrant. There are strands of political thought that have advocated for all-pervasive surveillance and control of everyday conduct since long before the egregious examples set by fascist and Stalinist rule in the twentieth century.

Abu Ali Hasan ibn Ali Tusi (1018–92 CE), known as Nizam al-Mulk, was the vizier (chief minister) for the Seljuk sultans in Persia until his assassination. He consolidated bureaucratic control for rulers whose traditional way of life had been nomadic. Nizam al-Mulk's *The Book of Government, or Rules for Kings* adopted the conventional view that caliphs and sultans had been entrusted by God with responsibility for the wellbeing of subjects. But he expected the diligent ruler to be godlike and 'to know everything that goes on' in order to detect and punish even the smallest of injustices. He was especially concerned about dishonest tax collectors. But the detection of wrongdoing implied intelligence gathering by a cohort of informants and couriers 'completely above suspicion and without self-interest'.[24] In an age when the fastest mode of transport was the horse, and long before the printing press, let alone CCTV, this dream of monarchical omniscience and inescapable punishment was surely unrealisable. The aim, however, was obedience to the sultan; prosperity for the people would supposedly follow. The idea of a surveillance state was there in medieval Persia, and one can find it even further back in history.[25] But nowadays governments have the technology.

Contemporary China's social credit system uses social media, CCTV, facial recognition and data from state and commercial organisations to build profiles of individuals' conduct and to rate their trustworthiness. These ratings can then affect a person's access to services, from finance to dating. This appears to be accepted by most of the mainland Chinese people, but it gets bad press in the West. Technologically, though, it's not that much different from the commercial surveillance and profiling used by the Silicon Valley tech giants which are then mined by security agencies. People's behaviour is being monitored to a level that was previously inconceivable, and the information is being used to shape choices as consumers and citizens. The American model of internet governance is decentralised and minimises censorship – despite violent and objectionable material online – while the Chinese model is centralised and unabashedly censors things that are out of line with official policies.

Resistance to intrusive state control grew during the twentieth century, exemplified by George Orwell's novel *1984* (published in 1949). And a branch of economic theory that had emerged in Vienna vehemently opposed fascist and communist government. This *neo*liberalism favoured free markets and the price mechanism over state monopolies and subsidies, and free trade over import controls. In principle, neoliberalism stood steadfastly against state surveillance and against controlling people's personal choices. It stood for a minimal government that would restrict itself to a rule of law that protected life, liberty and property, ensured fair market competition, and little else.

Governments might step in to provide services essential for raising the standard of living, such as education, if private enterprise failed to supply them to all who needed them. The defeat of fascism in 1945, the unravelling of postwar political economy from 1971, and the demise of the Soviet Union in 1991, seemed to leave neoliberalism as the last ideology standing – as if there were no alternative. Free markets were more democratic, it was argued, and would deliver choice and prosperity, lifting millions out of poverty. And so individualism, economic liberty and minimal government became the principles of a new form of government with built-in mechanisms of *self*-limitation. It aimed permanently to reduce the size and scope of government itself.

Neoliberal theory had little to say, however, about how to address the catastrophes that were to come: a global financial crisis, climate change, pandemic, inequality and cyberwars. Neoliberal policies had aimed to reduce and limit government, and hence public infrastructure, institutions and services were run down, demoralised and underfunded. But, despite its stated aims, neoliberal government also had a way of proliferating new forms of regulation of work and everyday life. Neoliberal administrative methods extracted more and more data from citizens and firms, using digital technologies ever more efficiently. Online form-filling – performance reviews, security checks, credit checks, tax returns, customs declarations and sundry others – proliferated. Ironically, the push to reduce bureaucratic red tape resulted in more of it.[26] Although neoliberal ideology despised traditional bureaucracy, in favour of modern management techniques such as strategic planning, this era developed its own bureaucratic controls, as we ticked boxes and put e-signatures on forms and contracts. People may have preferred not to call it 'red tape'; they used terms such as risk management, performance, compliance, contracting and accountability instead.

So the neoliberal era didn't make the government of everyday life any less burdensome. The people subjected most to this were the poor and vulnerable and those who provided them with social services. A dilemma for neoliberalism resided in how to govern those who don't live up to its expectations of entrepreneurial individualism and self-reliance – especially those 'dependent' on welfare. Under increasingly targeted, means-tested and work-conditional social policies, their lives became a Kafkaesque bureaucratic nightmare. And following a few decades of neoliberal rolling back of the state and attacks on subsidies and regulations, new imperatives arose to intervene into markets and to monitor social and economic activity. Examples are publicly financed bailouts of banks and subsidisation of ailing firms (or corporate welfare) due to the global financial crisis of 2008, and the extensive uses of tracing apps and vaccine passes during the Covid-19 pandemic. Bureaucratic controls hadn't disappeared; they'd changed their purposes and gone digital.

If we reject a total state, then one aim of government is to set reasonable and lawful limits on government itself. This means taking action for the common good, but leaving spaces where people are free from regulation and surveillance. We need distinct lines that signify 'where individual rights shall begin and governmental rights stop', as Woodrow Wilson put it.[27] It's neither possible nor acceptable to make all actions either compulsory or forbidden; nor is it acceptable to monitor people constantly to ensure that they comply. Where and how, then, should we set the lawful limits on state control over our conduct? When and to what extent can we be forced to place the common good above our own free and self-interested actions? These are normative questions that can't be settled once and for all, as the responses will vary depending on the dominant ideas of the time and place and on what's at stake. Deciding the aims and setting the limits of government are enduring problems for government.

Using what resources?

One point on which Adam Smith and Karl Marx agreed was that the source of economic value is labour. Smith said that your wealth effectively equals the 'quantity of labour' that it can purchase.[28] This may apply as much to the state as to any other economic entity or actor. So, for example, having no 'thing' denominated officially as 'money', the Incan empire counted labour time as tribute to the king. Many states have required forced labour and military service as a basic obligation of its subjects in order to govern and achieve goals. The most unjust form of rule is to own people as property, and hence to use bodily labour under direct command.

A less coercive approach was to extract a regular proportion of a specified commodity from the produce of otherwise 'free' labourers. Such an arrangement could be acceptable to people if the state guaranteed security in return, but it required force to gain compliance, and often met with resistance. Regulated proportions of the products of agricultural labour, especially staple foods, were delivered up as taxes and tithes to palaces and temples – or a tax might be levied on units of arable land. The surpluses collected could be given to the poor in times of need and used as payment for specialised labour. Professional soldiers, scribes, judges, bailiffs and executioners had to be rewarded somehow. So they needed another specialist, the tax collector, as well as a countable resource to tax. Many ancient states were essentially grain states, as quantities of barley, rice, and so on were the currencies used as taxes and wages. The more readily their quantities – and/or the land required to grow them – could be measured, and the more readily stored in granaries, the more they enabled the development and growth of city-states. Once credits, debits, tithes and taxes were recorded on clay tablets or similar, a 'money of account' was in place. Among the oldest recorded laws are those that controlled the conditions placed on debts, including situations where persons were committed to forced labour in lieu of payment. For example, under the laws of Hammurabi (early second millennium Babylon), a farmer could have a debt cancelled if a storm or a drought ruined his crops. If he sold himself or a family member as labour to repay a debt, the creditor had to free that person after four years. Quantities of grain, land and/or labour-time were legally recognised units for discharging obligations to others, to the ruler and priesthood and/or to one's community. In addition, taxes were imposed on accumulated wealth, often at inheritance, and on imported goods. Hence tax revolts were among the oldest forms of resistance. For example, the Old Testament records a letter from an official named Rehum to the Persian emperor Artaxerxes (r. 465–424 BCE) threatening to cease payment of taxes, tribute and duty so long as the 'rebellious and wicked' city of Jerusalem continued to be rebuilt.[29]

Stamped metallic coins backed by sovereign authority appeared only after regulated tax and credit systems had been operating for many centuries. But the basic governmental function of an official currency or monetary unit (however it might be commodified and counted) was to regulate the extraction of surpluses from an agricultural labour force and then to redistribute it to specialised workers and soldiers and to the people in case of crop failure.

The nineteenth century saw new methods of taxation, while steps were taken around the world to abolish slavery and to suppress human trafficking. Occupations should be chosen, not forced, although military conscription remained. Income tax had begun in the United Kingdom in 1799 and became more widely applied during the nineteenth century. The raising of taxes is associated historically with rising costs of warfare, and this was certainly the case in the twentieth century with massive public borrowing and expenditure on all-out wars. Representation in legislatures that controlled governments' finances was originally reserved for those who paid tax on property. Hence, as the sources of taxation expanded beyond land and its produce to include a percentage of wages, workers' claims on the rights to vote and to stand for office became stronger. With income taxes plus conscription, enfranchisement logically followed for all men and women. The wider the range of people called upon to work, to serve at war and to pay tax, the wider the franchise. The old maxim 'no taxation without representation' seems to work in reverse: 'no representation without taxation'. If you want to vote, then contribute your share.

Taxation is as old as the state itself because one can't govern without it. This means more than collecting resources for disposal by the state; it also creates a feedback loop affecting popular claims to influence the actions of representatives, officials and sovereigns who use the resources on behalf of the taxed population. Taxation shapes the system of government itself and is entwined with the evolution of money. A state institution defines and controls the currency to enable commerce and generate public revenue. The state gets back in tax the coin that it issued, while the sovereign's profile stamped on it reminds us who rules. And thus we have money for discharging our debts to society and to one another. In turn, we insist that the state use the surpluses it extracts from our labours for our common security and wellbeing.

To centralise or decentralise?

Law and regulation imply conformity. But we're not all the same, and our circumstances are infinitely diverse. Moreover, progress, adaptation and change require scope for experimentation. Accordingly, there's a constant ebb and flow in the history of government between centralising power and control, and decentralising or devolving decision-making.

From the time of the first emperor, the Chinese model tended to be more centralised, including the standardisation of written characters and weights and measures and, since the Han dynasty, the development of a trained civil service with standardised qualifications and careers.[30] The Romans meanwhile were doing things quite differently. They relied on military officers as governors to maintain order and dispense justice from above, but allowed conquered cities to continue their traditions of government and law. Especially in the Hellenistic east, systems had been already well established, so provincial government wasn't uniform, but ranged from direct rule from Rome to protectorates with client kings. The Romans didn't tolerate rebellion, however. When the Jews rose up to fight for independence in 66 and in 132 CE, the military response was devastating: the Temple was destroyed; Jerusalem was razed and renamed Aelia Capitolina.[31] If the emperor was obeyed, though, provincial Roman government by military commanders (supported by paid officials) mostly accepted local religions and social hierarchies. Roman citizenship was granted to non-Roman men in the provinces, thus offering them rights and opportunities that they couldn't previously have enjoyed. People have often asked how and why this empire achieved such greatness and lasted so long, and its abilities to accommodate different customs, offer career pathways to men in conquered provinces and maintain order (by force when necessary) contribute to any explanation. It came to an end in the Latin west, though, by the late fifth century CE, and hung on in the Greek-speaking east for another millennium.

Chinese imperial government – allowing for several dramatic inter-dynastic breaks – was far more durable. Its basic model was a dynastic household served by eunuchs and underpinned by an educated civil bureaucracy. It was centralised on the imperial palace, but there were provincial and local governments. Soldiers and priests were under civilian control. The Chinese ideals were unity and deference to authority figures, including ancestors. This empire extended over much the same territory as today's China, more or less intact, for most of two millennia. An empire's longevity isn't everything, though, and it's hard to say whether the Roman or the Chinese model was better overall. One might say they were equally bad, but in different ways. Empires and states have never found a perfect balance between centralisation and decentralisation, as changing circumstances would soon put things out of balance. Too much control and heavy taxation from the centre would cause anger and rebellion; too light a hand, or ineffective controls, could encourage the periphery to seek independence.

The twentieth century saw highly centralised government in the Soviet communist command economy and in fascist corporatism. Both Stalin and Hitler were guilty of crimes against humanity, and so both models are beyond the pale. A communist command economy (with high-level production plans and financial allocations) may be workable, if not necessary, in an all-out war, as in World War II, but it fails to innovate and to produce efficiently under conditions of peace when people aspire to a better way of life. Corporatism, on the other hand, was the model used by fascist regimes but also in peacetime by some non-fascist governments. It assumes that society is an organic whole with subordinate social and occupational groups, such as churches, armed forces, trade unions and industrial associations. Rather than see the individual as the unit of social life and political representation, individuals are incorporated or inserted into society as members of recognised institutions. Representation and policymaking are conducted through these corporate bodies, as in tripartite state–industry–trade union negotiation and planning around labour and social security policies. This kind of government is conservative: it resists the disorderliness of a society of free, unattached individuals. The individual acquires status through belonging to an officially recognised institution that can in turn be incorporated into the purposes of the state.[32]

Both the communist and the corporatist systems relied heavily on bureaucratic controls. In general, bureaucratic administration serves the purposes of centralised power and consistent service delivery. But it has two faces: one is rational with benign objectives, rules and methods that apply to everyone impartially; the other reduces both the official and the client to a lower level of rationality with obstacles such as 'that's the rule', 'my hands are tied', 'it's not my department'. Bureaucratic rules and methods are always insufficient for the complexity of real life; they don't recognise all the needs and feelings of individuals and minority groups. Public bureaus have the advantage, though, of separating personal or private interests from employment in public office, and bureaucracy was essential for the development of non-corrupt and impartial public services. The growth of the administrative state in capitalist countries is often associated with the economic theories of John Maynard Keynes (1883–1946). He had supported 'central controls' to achieve full employment, which would broaden the scope of government, but not to the extent of interfering with 'individual initiative'. Public policy should aim to keep people employed without dictating what they would produce. He wanted capitalism to work, but without the kind of crash seen in 1929.[33] The protectionist policies of the post-War era allowed space for policymakers to use central controls to organise social services and healthcare.

Neoliberalism, in contrast, is individualistic and anti-bureaucratic, favouring minimal government with devolved decision-making. The state would let markets do their thing (*laissez-faire*) with less centralised regulation. Failing that, if publicly funded services were necessary, they'd be competitively contracted out to private enterprise or not-for-profits. This assumes that competition forces providers to be more efficient and to deliver diverse and innovative services, which is preferable to uniformity. In breaking up monopolistic public organisations, the 'new public management' wanted to clarify the objectives of organisations, for example by separating trading enterprises from social services. With each organisation focussed on a clear and limited set of objectives, there'd be less role confusion and more effective performance monitoring. The problem was that this model often created 'silos': public organisations operating in isolation from one another, sometimes with diverging or even competing objectives. Governments lost sight of overarching strategic goals, and coordination between organisations was lacking. The most important public policy problems are highly complex and hence require well-orchestrated collaborative efforts from multiple agencies, across government and in private enterprise and civil society. One of the major challenges for public administration today is to connect or to network across organisations, and across different levels of government, to achieve concerted action and to stay focussed on strategic goals.

We're left, then, with widely differing approaches to centralised governmental control, compared with devolution, diversity and individual agency. And we must take account of multiple levels of government, from neighbourhood to city to province/state to nation and then to multilateral international government, as well as the vertical separations between branches of government and diverse agencies of the state. Like all large organisations, states go through cycles from centralisation to decentralisation and back again. The Covid-19 pandemic necessitated more centralised controls. At the centre of any such system, moreover, are people who command it.

Who rules?

This is one of the oldest enduring questions in world political thought. Basic categories were set by Aristotle: rule by one person (a monarch or tyrant), by the few (an aristocratic or oligarchic council) or by the many (through assemblies, juries or plebiscites). In Aristotle's time, 'the many' wouldn't include *all* adults, as women, foreigners, unskilled labourers and slaves were excluded from participation in government. He recommended a polity in which a talented and wealthy elite would lead, and yet a wider body of middle-ranking property-owning men would contribute to decision-making and administration. This would provide a political balance between rich and moderately well-off free men and their competing interests, while all those who could afford to own arms and defend the state would have a role. This set up a long-standing concept of 'mixed government'. Property ownership, tax liability and military duty became key criteria for eligibility to have a say in government, even if it only meant casting a vote from time to time.

It was monarchy – or rule by one person, most often in a male line of succession – that predominated from ancient times and through the Middle Ages, however. Monarchy was compatible with the monotheistic religions: one ruling Father in heaven was represented, mirrored or imitated by one 'deputy' on earth. It also had practical advantages, some argued. Monarchs provided unity and continuity and overcame factions; they could react swiftly in changing circumstances and decisively resolve deadlocks. As deputies or servants of a higher power, they were imbued with an unimpeachable authority, but also bound by moral principles and by a higher law. In China, the emperors ruled by the mandate of Heaven, meaning that correct observance of rites only they could perform preserved harmony between heaven and earth and thereby ensured prosperity for the people.

In Europe, monarchy was often seen as conforming with the law of nature or with God's design. A case in favour of absolute monarchy was made by the French lawyer Jean Bodin (1530–96): granted authority by God, kings had duties to God, and hence to protect and serve the faithful under natural law. There had to be one person who couldn't be removed from office and who could make civil law without consent of others. If many, or even all, people had to authorise laws, then no one would want to obey them.[34] A monarch would, of course, have courtiers, ministers, advisers, administrators and a host of civil, judicial, ecclesiastical and military officers in hierarchies below him or her. It's not as if he or she ruled alone, but rather that authority and law issued from the throne. The main flaw in monarchy was that heirs would sometimes turn out to be morally or mentally unfit, and yet entitled to rule for life. Hence they needed advice books ('mirrors of princes'), trusted advisers, and, if they were still minors or were incapacitated, regents. Charles II of Spain (1661–1700), for instance, was so physically incapacitated (reputedly due to inbreeding) that he was unable to produce an heir, resulting in the thirteen-year War of the Spanish Succession. Even with a competent monarch, however, the direction of the government depends on the unique personality, skills and biases of an individual, and so a change of monarch can mean inexplicable, and sometimes disastrous, changes of policy. Some might come in with grand designs, for better or worse, while others may treat their time on the throne as an opportunity to enjoy life.[35]

Most of the great imperial dynasties came to an end in the first two decades of the twentieth century. Those European hereditary monarchs who remained as heads of state were left with strictly limited constitutional roles, and executive government and lawmaking were devolved normally to elected representatives. There remain exceptions elsewhere such as Saudi Arabia, where the king is head of state and of government, and he appoints ministers and the members of the legislature.

The differences between monarchy and the mixed government of a republic (an entity of and for the people) became a hot topic during the Italian Renaissance. A conventional debate about the merits of each is found, for example, in the fourth book of Baldassare Castiglione's *The Courtier* (first published 1528). And Niccolò Machiavelli's *The Prince* (written in 1513) begins by describing two kinds of states: republics and principalities (or monarchies). The latter may be ruled by an heir of an established house, but sometimes a new ruler gets possession of one, which was the situation Machiavelli was addressing when he dedicated his manuscript to Florence's new boss, Lorenzo de Medici. Machiavelli discussed how princes seized and maintained power. In his more reflective study of the Roman republic, *The Discourses on Livy*, in contrast, Machiavelli favoured mixed government as more effective in defending a state's liberty. The involvement of 'the people' meant airing dissent and debating differences, and hence took some time, but it resulted, he argued, in wiser decisions and deeper commitment to the state's defence. He wanted to end the use of mercenaries – whose primary motive was profit – and to train and equip the citizens to defend their families and properties. The Romans had set an example with their highly effective legions, as the plebeian soldiers participated in assemblies and were represented by the tribunes who held veto powers. So from republican Rome to Renaissance Florence to modern republics, we can trace the idea that distribution of powers into the hands of 'the people' is integral to a state's ability to mediate internal factions and combat external threats. But 'the people' who had an active role in the state were only those free male citizens who were able to bear arms and those with the wealth and learning for judicial and civic offices – a minority of inhabitants.

As states became larger, fewer people, relatively speaking, could participate directly in public offices. It made sense to entrust or delegate the work of government to representatives who could speak for their communities. When this worked well, social and economic interest groups could develop specialised capabilities independently from the state, in what we now call civil society. Political representation originated in medieval Europe, as feudal kings needed the advice and consent of warlords, bishops and landowners from across their domains in order to levy larger armed forces and to raise taxes. Representative assemblies then evolved beyond councils that met directly with kings to become parliaments that took on an institutional life of their own and acquired powers to make law and form governments. As consent to taxes was the basic issue, the rights to choose representatives and to be a representative were restricted to those with noble or sacerdotal status and/or significant property: that is, those who actually paid taxes, commanded militias or managed estates.

During the nineteenth century, the bar for property qualifications was lowered. The Chartist movement that caused uprisings in Britain during the

1830s and '40s – and was put down violently – made further demands that were later mostly implemented: universal male suffrage, a secret ballot, no property qualifications on eligibility for parliament, an income for representatives to enable tradesmen and workingmen to stand, and equalisation of the population sizes of constituencies. Chartists pushed for political equality, seeing wider representation as a way to achieve better living standards for labourers. The campaign for women's suffrage then led to the universal adult franchise as the norm in the twentieth century. But this was in the context of *representative* government: the people, let alone the majority, didn't rule directly. They were electing a tiny minority to pass law and govern on their behalf – subject of course to their verdict at the next election. But mixed government that included representatives from all classes and genders was enabled by the expansion of the franchise, and written constitutions re-established government in the name of the people – of which the United States had set a leading example in 1789.[36]

The US system wasn't adopted elsewhere, however. Following Britain's loss of the thirteen American colonies, imperial Spanish and Portuguese economic monopolies and political control in the Americas also crumbled. Napoleon's invasion of the Iberian Peninsula in 1807 caused doubts about legitimate metropolitan government and precipitated a wave of rebellions and constitution writing – and rewriting – in the former Spanish colonies as independence movements grew. The great Liberator of Hispanic America, Simón Bolívar (1783–1830), ostensibly fought to establish republics that would act on the will of the people under rule of law, but in practice he wanted strong if not dictatorial leadership and a hereditary senate. Bolívar dismissed the American federal system as 'weak and complicated'; he saw democracy as prone to either anarchy or absolutism.[37] In general, the new Latin American constitutions vested strong executive powers in the offices of presidents, with centralised government and only limited concessions to liberal aspirations. Laws abolishing the slave trade and giving freedom to children born of slaves were passed, but there was no immediate and unconditional emancipation of existing slaves. Franchises were limited to male property owners; the Creole upper class seized political power.[38] Formal constitutional principles weren't always respected, and competing factions would often resort to force. English, American and French constitutional principles didn't simply fill the vacuum left after the collapse of Spanish and Portuguese imperial rule.[39] So the Latin American experience was anything but a straight pathway from colonial government to independent representative government. Such political change is rarely a linear process, and military dictatorships rose and fell in Latin America through the twentieth century. Eventually, they tended to adopt a combination of US-style presidential government with parliaments elected using European-style proportional representation.

The government of most developed countries became more widely shared across social classes, and was often federalised in states or provinces, with limited tenures and scope of powers. Multi-level government was woven in with separation of powers, typically between the legislative, executive and judicial branches, thus limiting and more widely distributing the powers of the state. To prevent abuses, 'power must check power by the arrangement of things', as the Baron de Montesquieu (1689–1755) memorably put it.[40] Executive powers were withdrawn from monarchs (in countries where they still reigned) to be divided into a system with institutionalised checks and balances. Political participation was extended to all adult citizens, and a 'sunset clause' was built into office-holding, normally contingent upon re-election. Appointments to unelected career roles in public services were based increasingly on merit-based criteria such as examinations, rather than political patronage or family pedigree. No-one should rule by virtue of birth or for life, then, nor be entrusted with undefined or unlimited power; politicians and administrators should be judged on their merits and their performance. If we learned anything from the horrors of the twentieth century, it was to ensure that all political powers should be limited in scope and the highest executive and parliamentary offices made contingent on periodic electoral contests. The question 'who rules?' was answered with 'many people' – but only temporarily, depending on the approval of the people who are ruled. A wider spectrum of the people found opportunities to be involved in government; no person or group should monopolise it. And, as we shall see next, meritocratic selection of candidates for election results in legislatures dominated by people with higher educational qualifications.

What qualifies a person to lead?

Is it what you know or who you know that matters more – or how rich your parents are? Should a successful political career be based on one's merits (however we evaluate them), or on family pedigree and social networks? On what criteria do those who govern – and those who advise them – get into those roles? The contemporary reader may prefer merits such as intelligence, competence and trustworthiness, but meritocracy has come in for a lot of criticism lately. Equal opportunities for advancement in business and politics are hot political issues, especially regarding higher education – the quality, cost and distribution of which raise concerns about equity. A university degree is regarded by those with aspirations (for themselves or their children) as a sign of merit. But do people want a 'diploma democracy, ruled by the citizens with the highest degrees'?[41]

China's first emperor was in favour of appointments to official and military roles based on merit and performance in line with law and policy. The strict respect for ancestry advocated by the Confucian school was rejected. The subsequent Han dynasty sought a compromise between the legalist, Daoist and Confucian approaches, and a long tradition of civil administration, with entry contingent upon examinations, began from there. In ancient Athens, the generals were put forward on merit and approved by a vote in the assembly – and they risked banishment for egregious failure. But most administrative and jury duties were allocated by lot (sortition). Lotteries choose randomly from those who are eligible and willing, so official duties get rotated around the citizenry. In that sense, sortition is more democratic than election, as it means every eligible citizen has an equal chance of a role in government, thus sharing power and responsibility more evenly. In an election, we're supposed to choose the 'best' candidates in an open competition, and hence we're ruled by an elite. The words *elect* and *elite* are etymologically related, to drive home the point.

In past representative systems, it was often supposed that propertied males would elect a 'natural aristocracy' of superior talent, knowledge and virtue. But appointments to administrative and even military roles might be based on familial influence and regal (or presidential) favour or patronage. It wasn't until the late nineteenth century that the United Kingdom and the United States made serious efforts to do away with aristocratic or political patronage in civil services and to assess competence through examinations. The rise of bureaucratic organisation (in public services and private enterprise) went hand in hand with meritocracy. Entry and promotion should be conditional upon knowledge, ability and effort as indicated by exams, performance reviews and professional achievements. The office and its duties and privileges were no longer the personal entitlement of the office holder; professional and private interests were separated. For advanced industrialised economies, meritocracy was preferable to past practices. The inheritance of public offices by the privileged had blocked social mobility and often promoted the incompetent. The granting of an office (sometimes for life) by favouritism, sale or sheer bribery was ineffective and unjust. And although racial and gender discrimination still skews selection and promotion processes, meritocratic principles aim to eliminate it. The meritocratic ideal holds that our natural talents, hard work, educational and professional achievements and performance determine success in political and professional careers, including military and civil services. Furthermore, free and fair competitive elections ensure that those who best represent the values and interests of the people go forward to make laws and to govern, while incompetent or dishonest politicians fail to get elected or re-elected. Meritocracy has been most vigorously advanced in the United States: 'the American dream' promises that you can succeed if you really want to and try hard enough. If anyone really can prosper through talent and hard work, then the democratic ideals of equal opportunity and social mobility will be realised. But some of the harshest contemporary critics of meritocracy are American academics,[42] so we need to take a closer look.

Society's wealthiest and most powerful families used to comprise 'the leisure class',[43] who disdained work, looked down on those who had to work, and spent lavishly on objects such as jewellery for 'conspicuous consumption'.

Today, in stark contrast, the wealthy tend to be those who've invested a lot in higher education at elite universities and who've gained highly paid jobs in which they're overworked – 60 to 80 hours per week or more being a norm for sustained success. Their talent, learning and hard work produce rewards, but higher status is now signified by excessive work rather than by leisure. But there are two basic political problems in this. First, the winners in this competitive race form a new elite that reproduces itself as wealthier parents can invest much more than others in the success of their offspring, aided by their social networks and inside knowledge. Coupled with a general increase in income and wealth inequality, social mobility declines and equality of opportunity is undermined as those who have 'made it' exploit their advantages and pass them on to their children. A new kind of hereditary upper class thus emerges.[44] This new 'aristocracy' is mainly hard-working, and not leisured; it creates a profound inequality, however, that undermines democratic politics. Indeed, a society that once prided itself on social equality and democratic government has been gradually transformed into a plutocracy – ruled by a super-rich minority.

Second, this new elite are likely to claim, in line with meritocracy, that their success is due to their own talent and hard work, and hence that they deserve their wealth, privilege, social esteem and political influence. They discount or deny the role of luck, such as being born into a wealthy family and with good genetic endowment. They may also look with disdain at those who are unsuccessful, believing that they must lack natural talent and/or haven't tried hard enough. The elite over-value individual merit and are likely then to reject ideas of the common good or policies of redistribution, taking for granted the benefits they've derived from living in a relatively prosperous and literate community. Those who've earned qualifications and worked hard, and yet are less successful, on the other hand, feel especially resentful about an elite who look down on them. Even the winners may be unhappier under this system, however, as they have to work excessive hours, spend less time with family and endure constant pressure to perform and measure up. The ladder metaphor suggests an individualistic rise in which some make it to the top while others can't get their foot on the first rung. And then those who've made it may kick the ladder away to prevent competitors from following.

As one effect of meritocracy, parliaments and civil services have become dominated by university graduates. Very few members of representative legislatures nowadays hold less than a bachelor's degree.[45] Among most OECD countries, less than one half of the population aged 25 to 64 has tertiary education – including qualifications below degree level.[46] So, for example, while half of Americans hold tertiary qualifications of some kind, as of December 2020, in the Congress 94.8 percent of House Members and 100 percent of Senators held at least a bachelor's degree.[47] One might argue that university degrees are valid merit-related qualifications for elected offices, as educated people would do a better job. But the evidence suggests that governmental quality or effectiveness and the educational attainment of elected officials are statistically unrelated. 'When citizens evaluate candidates [for election], they probably should not place too much emphasis on their formal educational credentials', concludes one study.[48] And there are anecdotes from the past to support this. Abraham Lincoln, a great example of meritocracy, had little formal education.

The underrepresentation of the less educated has become increasingly pronounced, in spite of the universal adult franchise, and this may contribute to declining voter turnouts as people without college education and on low incomes don't see representatives who resemble them. How did this come about? The centre-left parties aimed to improve the living standards of workers and the opportunities for their children, especially through mass education, and hence to achieve upward social mobility. When this worked, however, the traditional support-base for social-democratic policy was reduced in size and influence relative to a growing middle class, and the subsequent generations of centre-left party activists, candidates and leaders were the products of that success story: upwardly mobile, college-educated professionals. Parties that once represented labourers gradually turned into parties that represent university graduates, it's been argued. They now pay less attention to working and lower middle-class concerns, and ignore class differences, often in favour of other (nonetheless important) cultural and environmental concerns.[49] Data from western Europe shows, however, that social-democratic parties are still supported by many lower-income voters and that 'higher educated people who now vote for the left do so because they support redistribution'.[50] But these parties declined in strength and needed to compromise with coalition partners to gain office.

Higher qualifications don't necessarily make for better leadership and government, moreover, while a lack of politicians from low-skilled occupations means that a large section of society doesn't see itself represented politically. A failure to fairly represent working-class and lower middle-class economic concerns was part of a widening inequality that impeded social mobility. One response to this would be to make meritocracy work better. The unequal outcomes of the competitive meritocratic race could be ironed out by a more substantial equality of opportunity, progressive taxation, fairer access to public education, limits on private donations to political campaigns, and pressure on political parties to represent lower-skilled workers just as they've done for women and ethno-religious minorities. In general, there's no required qualification, let alone job description, for elected representatives. They're not employees. But political parties implicitly regard a university degree as a desirable or essential qualification for candidates. People with such qualifications do acquire analytical and communication skills that contribute to their abilities as decision-makers and leaders, and especially as career professionals in public services. But otherwise talented people from a wider range of occupational classes may be neglected, and it may be time to put forward more candidates for election from low-skilled occupations.[51] An alternative approach is to replace elections with random selection (sortition). Holding regular lotteries for roles in public administration and courts, as in ancient Athens, is more democratic than representation, as every citizen can have a chance to govern, although it may not eliminate the advantages held by the rich, as the aristocratic Athenians were still dominant. But sortition gives more people a chance to get involved actively and to exert influence. It could be used, for example, in parties' selection of candidates who are then put forward for election. Even more radically, legislatures (or perhaps one chamber of a bicameral parliament) could be filled directly by sortition from among those citizens who put their names forward.[52] We should always be asking what qualities genuinely constitute 'merit' in political leadership, and what are the best methods for deciding who rules.

And who are the ruled?

Territory and population supply the state's resources and revenues – and hence they must be defended. Maps and statistics create abstract pictorial and numerical representations of territories and peoples, and these inform military and political activities. The word *statistics* (from French and German roots) originally referred to studies of *states* and statecraft, but the techniques are much older. The ancient Romans conducted a *census* (hence the English word) to register citizens and assess their properties. And the earliest surviving censuses come from Han dynasty China, informing us that the population of China in the year 2 CE was 57.7 million.[53] Of cartographically sophisticated maps, the earliest surviving examples also come from the Han era, dating back to the second century BCE.[54]

Rulers also recognised peoples of differing faiths and languages, and hence differing values and beliefs. Managing diverse and dispersed peoples wasn't always approached with toleration, however. The Byzantine emperor Justinian I (r. 527–65 CE), for example, prevented pagans from teaching law and philosophy and tried his best to make all Christian communities conform with the doctrines of the Council of Chalcedon.[55] But dissenting Christians only grew in strength and confidence, especially in Egypt and Syria. The emperor's opposition helped to define them as distinct faith communities, rather than to make them conform, and their churches still exist today.[56] Although he was, by convention, bound by the civil law, and bound to obey God, verbal utterances of a Byzantine emperor could *become* law, and he could intervene into government at any level as the traditional Roman Senate had been sidelined by palace-based bureaucracy and its fiscal machine. The people were then subjects who depended upon the Christian emperor's benevolence.[57] Did such rulers really care about those over whom they ruled? And, if they did, was it only a tiny minority of wealthy, influential people who mattered to them?

What's called the 'age of absolutism' in Europe is normally seen as commencing with Louis XIV (r. 1643–1715) and ending with the French Revolution (1789). Absolute monarchy was an unimpeachable authority that unified government and reduced 'the people' to obedient subjects. This didn't mean that monarchs could do whatever they wanted, however. They were morally constrained by fear of divine judgement and by ideas such as natural law and benevolence. They had to rely on powerful nobles, assemblies, urban corporations, industrial guilds and bureaucracies. It's not that absolute monarchs never cared at all about the people; but they didn't care enough about all of the people. Hence entrenched class privileges and excessive taxes led to rebellions. The American and French revolutions began as tax revolts and later sought to overthrow monarchy itself. The revolutionaries rejected the notion that an inherited monarch could represent the people, and fought for the principle that legitimate government must originate in and exist for the benefit of the people. Again, this was not a new idea: the Roman republic (*res publica*) literally meant 'the people's thing', and republics such as Venice, Florence and Siena had flourished in medieval times. But who was this body called 'the people'? In European languages, the *people* (*peuple, popolo, pueblo*, etc.) may refer to either a whole nation or population, or to the politically active, propertied and franchised classes (often only a minority), or to the impoverished and disenfranchised classes.[58] It depends on who's talking and in whose interests they're acting. These ambiguous uses of the word 'people' exemplify the paradox of political inclusion and exclusion.

In the republics of Venice and Florence only a minority of males from established wealthy families had any real influence on government, even though they called themselves 'the people'. Despite the US Constitution invoking 'We, the People', out of the 55 delegates to the constitutional convention in 1788, only 39 men actually signed it, while three of those present on the day refused. And there were no indigenous people, slaves or women invited to contribute to, let alone authorise, this document, even though it completely reformed how they'd be governed. A majority who could not effectively consent to the constitution were paradoxically included under, yet excluded from, a new system supposedly created in their name. The US Constitution formed a *republic*, but doesn't mention *democracy*. On whose authority, then, did the signers sign the document? 'The People' in whose name it speaks, and the authority to act on their behalf, were simultaneously called into existence in the act of signing the newly drafted constitution. Such self-authorisation – or imposture – is common to political invocations of an otherwise absent 'people'. The consequences of this paradox of (non)consent are still being played out in American politics.

Similarly, the French Declaration of the Rights of Man and of the Citizen was voted on, article by article, by 'representatives of the French People' in the Constituent Assembly in 1789. While invoking 'the people', it asserts that 'men are born free and equal in rights' and that, as citizens, they have the right to participate in the making of law, either in person or through their representatives. The Declaration refers to *citoyens* but not the feminine *citoyennes*. French women gained the right to vote only in 1944. Moreover, since 1685 the racist *Code Noir* had allowed chattel slavery in French colonies. An edict of the Constituent Assembly abolished slavery in 1794, but this wasn't put into effect, and slavery was re-established by Napoleon in 1802. France's plantation colony of Saint Domingue (Haiti) underwent a successful slave rebellion in 1805, and it was not until 1848 that slavery was abolished throughout its empire.[59] Nonetheless, the Declaration's article 6 states that 'Law is the expression of the general will' (*la volonté générale*) as it applies equally to all, regardless of their station in life – and yet the law didn't apply equally. Unlike Rousseau's concept of the general will (which obliged the people to participate directly in making their laws), the Declaration entrusted law-making to an assembly of representatives, rather than the people themselves. Even so, the revolutionary spirit of those times sought to establish government in the name of the people, and it laid a foundation for further struggles for emancipation, equality and decolonisation. A politically successful invocation of 'the general will' – or, in the American case, 'a society founded on the will of the people'[60] – depended upon large numbers of people (whose names are not recorded in history books) committing themselves, and sometimes sacrificing their lives, to a struggle that went beyond a temporary rebellion against taxation to become a full-scale overthrow and reconstitution of the system of government. But most of these new republics' resident populations went unrecognised as active or consenting citizens. Who, then, are 'the people'?

Pragmatically, defining 'the people' calls for statistical, sociological and legal techniques, especially official registers of births, population censuses and immigration policies. Decisions are made as to who qualifies as a citizen and who doesn't, and who can participate in processes such as elections or civil service examinations. Even the contemporary electoral franchise isn't absolutely universal, as eligibility is restricted by age (18 in most countries) and by citizenship and/or residency status, and criminal convictions can lead to disqualification. So, the population eligible to vote is less than the population governed, and in many countries only two thirds or less of those registered to vote might actually do so. Contemporary representative government is undoubtedly more inclusive than in the past, but defining 'the people' who are represented is a political exercise, and not just a statistical study. Furthermore, voters are neither unanimous nor united on any significant question of policy or leadership, and elections don't deliver unambiguous mandates for all the actions of governments. Societies are highly diverse, encompassing spectrums of opinion. People may be governed under the same constitution, but difference and dissent cannot (indeed, should not) be ignored or suppressed, and so we can't point to a people with a singular united will. A myth of the will of the people is nonetheless sometimes used in political discourse, mainly by populists.[61] A common feature of populism is the rejection of an established political class in favour of the will of the people, which is said to be the only real authority. But those members of 'the people' who disagree with the populist leader may then be condemned as traitors or enemies. Will is a faculty of the individual (if one accepts that we have free will) and it doesn't properly pertain to large groups. But rhetoric about 'the will of the people' may grow beyond the contest for seats in parliament to become a way of silencing or oppressing minorities. For example, the title of the 1935 propaganda documentary *Triumph des Willens* (*Triumph of the Will*, Leni Riefenstahl) refers to Hitler's defeat of party factions and to a supposed will of the German people.[62]

In a modern representative system, we expect, at least, that governmental decisions be based on reasoned arguments and calculations about what's best for those affected and about social, environmental and economic wellbeing – even though there'll be trade-offs between differing interests. In countries with competitive and open political systems, the opinion poll has become the principal technology for providing feedback between elections. Diverse 'public opinion' revealed in surveys of representative samples is better than heroic (if not dangerous) claims about a 'will of the people'. But still, we shouldn't assume that the people at large have ready-made and informed political opinions that await discovery and fulfilment. (See Chapter 7, 'People's participation'.)

So, we've asked: who are the people who can govern? and who are the people they govern? A contemporary democratic ideal holds that there should be as much demographic resemblance and deliberative communication between the two as possible. The government of large societies, however, requires a wide division of labour between an elite political class and the people at large – with most of the latter not participating much at all in political life. Communication between these two 'classes' normally falls well short of any standard of rational deliberation between equals. Mostly it's one-directional persuasion or advertising. The majority of people tend to be passive audiences of politics and objects of public policy, not the source thereof.

Conclusion

There are numerous historically enduring problems or dilemmas of government, then. This chapter has set them out, illustrated with historical and contemporary examples. Because they haven't gone away or been resolved, and instead they're recurring problems, it's safe to say that they won't go away. The fact that problems of government are intractable and perpetual doesn't, however, mean we should give up looking for solutions. Addressing them is what government is all about. And it's not as if there's been no historical progress or improvements, as the next chapter will show.

Notes

1 Bodde, D. 1986. 'The State and Empire of Ch'in'. In *The Cambridge History of China*, ed. D. Twitchett & M. Loewe, 20–102. Cambridge: Cambridge University Press.
2 Confucius. 1979. *The Analects*. London: Penguin, trans. D.C. Lau. See pp. 115–16, XII.19.
3 Shang Yang. 2019. *The Book of Lord Shang: Apologetics of State Power in Early China*, ed. Yuri Pine. Chicago: Columbia University Press.
4 Li, Su, Zhang Yongle & Daniel A. Bell. 2018. *The Constitution of Ancient China*. Princeton, NJ: Princeton University Press. See p. 28.
5 Cale, D. 3 March 2014. 'Ford on Jimmy Kimmel Live: "I wasn't Elected to be Perfect"'. *Toronto Star*, URL: https://www.thestar.com/news/city_hall/toronto2014election/2014/03/03/rob_ford_on_the_jimmy_kimmel_show.html (accessed 19 July 2023).
6 For brevity, this sets aside doctrines of predestination.
7 Applebaum, Anne. 15 November 2021. 'The Bad Guys Are Winning.' *The Atlantic*, URL: https://www.theatlantic.com/magazine/archive/2021/12/the-autocrats-are-winning/620526/ (accessed 19 July 2023).
8 Some say that our genes are 'selfish', as they evolved to favour their own survival; others say that natural selection has favoured cooperative and altruistic behaviours as survival strategies. But both sides are making moral evaluations about our presently observable conduct and retrospectively attributing it to genetic inheritance and evolution. Neither hypothesis meets the scientific standard of falsifiability. By confusing biological science with moral argument, neither case is convincing. 'Selfish' and 'altruistic' are *moral* judgements, not biological facts.
9 In the US context, for example, 'common good constitutionalism' seeks to advance conservative political ends, even if it means overriding individual rights. Ward, Ian. 9 December 2022. 'Critics Call It Theocratic and Authoritarian. Young Conservatives Call It an Exciting New Legal Theory.' *Politico*, URL: https://www.politico.com/news/magazine/2022/12/09/revolutionary-conservative-legal-philosophy-courts-00069201 (accessed 19 July 2023).
10 Romans 13, King James version.
11 Judson, Pieter M. 2018. *The Habsburg Empire: A New History*. Cambridge, MA: Belknap Press.
12 Falola, Toyin & Matthew M. Heaton. 2008. *A History of Nigeria*. Cambridge: Cambridge University Press.
13 Anderson, Benedict. 2016. *Imagined Communities: Reflections on the Origin and Spread of Nationalism*. London. Verso.
14 Katchanovski, Ivan. 2016. 'The Separatist War in Donbas: A Violent Break-up of Ukraine?' *European Politics and Society* 17 (4): 473–89.
15 Arendt, Hannah. 1968. *The Origins of Totalitarianism*. New York: Harvest. See p. 230.
16 Universal Declaration of Human Rights, Article 15.1.
17 These were chariot-racing teams and their fans, whose rivalries were often political and violent.
18 Helliwell, John, Richard Layard & Jeffrey Sachs. 2017. *World Happiness Report 2017*. New York: Sustainable Development Solutions Network. See p. 3.

19 Duncan, Grant. 2010. 'Should Happiness-Maximization Be the Goal of Government?' *Journal of Happiness Studies* 11 (2): 163–78.
20 St Augustine (354–430 CE), al-Ghazali (*c.*1056–1111 CE).
21 Rousseau, Jean-Jacques. 2002 [1762, 1750, 1754]. *The Social Contract, and the First and Second Discourses.* New Haven: Yale University Press. See p. 164. Rousseau also argued that it would be unjust and ruinous for the social contract if citizens wanted to enjoy their rights without performing their duties and hence 'whoever refuses to obey the general will shall be constrained to do so by the whole body; which means nothing else than that he shall be forced to be free'. Ibid., p. 166.
22 Maximilien Marie Robespierre (1758–94), Mao Zedong (1893–1976).
23 Schwartz, Benjamin I. 1968. 'The Reign of Virtue: Some Broad Perspectives on Leader and Party in the Cultural Revolution'. *The China Quarterly* (35): 1–17.
24 Nizam al-Mulk. 2002. *The Book of Government or Rules for Kings,* trans H. Darke. London: Routledge. See pp. 63–64.
25 Andrew, Christopher. 2019. *The Secret World: A History of Intelligence.* London: Penguin.
26 Graeber, David. 2015. *The Utopia of Rules.* Brooklyn, NY: Melville House.
27 Wilson, Woodrow. 2002 [1908]. *Constitutional Government in the United States.* New York: Routledge. See p. 9.
28 'Labour was the first price, the original purchase-money that was paid for all things. It was not by gold or by silver, but by labour, that all the wealth of the world was originally purchased; and its value, to those who possess it, and who want to exchange it for some new productions, is precisely equal to the quantity of labour which it can enable them to purchase or command'. Smith, Adam. 1999. *The Wealth of Nations.* London: Penguin. See vol 1, p. 133; Bk I, ch. 5.
29 Ezra 4:13.
30 'From the Qin dynasty onward, the [Chinese] state transformed from a system of enfeoffment (*fengjian zhi*) to a system of centralized administration (*junxian zhi*)'. Ge, Zhaoguang. 2018. *What Is China? Territory, Ethnicity, Culture, and History.* Cambridge, MA: Harvard University Press. See p. 24.
31 Popović, Mladen. 2011. *The Jewish Revolt Against Rome: Interdisciplinary Perspectives.* Leiden: Brill; Montefiore, Simon Sebag. 2011. *Jerusalem: The Biography.* New York: Vintage Books.
32 Costa Pinto, Antonio. 2017. *Corporatism and Fascism.* London: Routledge; Esping-Andersen, Gøsta. 1990. *The Three Worlds of Welfare Capitalism.* Cambridge: Polity.
33 Keynes, John Maynard. 1964 [1935]. *The General Theory of Employment, Interest, and Money.* New York: Harvest, Harcourt. See pp. 379–80.
34 Lindfors, Tommi. No date. 'Jean Bodin'. *Internet Encyclopedia of Philosophy*, URL: https://iep.utm.edu/jean-bodin/ (accessed 30 September 2022).
35 For a firsthand account of monarchs in eleventh-century Byzantium, see Psellus, Michael. 1966. *Fourteen Byzantine Rulers,* trans E. Sewter. London: Penguin. Psellus comments, for example, that Constantine IX (r. 1042–55) 'failed to realize that [monarchy] entailed responsibility for the well-being of his subjects... To him the exercise of power meant rest from his labours, fulfilment of desire, relaxation from strife.' See p. 179.
36 Despite its rich constitutional history, including the Magna Carta of 1215 and the Bill of Rights of 1688, Britain never adopted an overarching written constitution as supreme law. Only two other countries still do without one: Israel and New Zealand.
37 Lynch, John. 2006. *Simón Bolívar: A Life.* New Haven: Yale University Press.
38 Bushnell, D. 1985. 'The Independence of Spanish South America'. In *The Cambridge History of Latin America,* ed. L. Bethell, 95–156. Cambridge: Cambridge University Press.

39 Brazil's 1825 treaty with Portugal created a new – but independent – monarchy. Slavery wasn't abolished there until 1888 and the monarchy was overthrown the following year in a military coup.

40 Montesquieu, Charles de Secondat, Baron de. 1989 [1748]. *The Spirit of the Laws*. Cambridge: Cambridge University Press. See p. 155.

41 Bovens, Mark & Anchrit Wille. 2017. *Diploma Democracy: The Rise of Political Meritocracy*. Oxford: Oxford University Press. See p. 6.

42 Frank, Robert H. 2016. *Success and Luck: Good Fortune and the Myth of Meritocracy*. Princeton: Princeton University Press; Markovits, Daniel. 2019. *The Meritocracy Trap: How America's Foundational Myth Feeds Inequality, Dismantles the Middle Class, and Devours the Elite*. New York: Penguin; Sandel, Michael. 2020. *The Tyranny of Merit: What's Become of the Common Good?* New York: Farrar, Straus & Giroux.

43 As Thorstein Veblen (1857–1929) called them. Veblen, Thorstein. 2007 [1899]. *The Theory of the Leisure Class*. Oxford: Oxford University Press.

44 Sandel [note 42].

45 Bovens & Wille [note 41].

46 The OECD average in 2023 was 39.9%, the UK 50.1% and the USA 50.3%. OECD. 2023. Adult education level (indicator), URL: https://data.oecd.org/eduatt/adult-education-level.htm (accessed 19 July 2023).

47 Congressional Research Service. 2020. 'Membership of the 116th Congress: A Profile', URL: https://sgp.fas.org/crs/misc/R45583.pdf (accessed 7 September 2022).

48 Carnes, Nicholas & Noam Lupu. 2016. 'What Good Is a College Degree? Education and Leader Quality Reconsidered'. *The Journal of Politics* 78 (1): 35–49. See p. 47.

49 Evans, Geoffrey & James Tilley. 2017. *The New Politics of Class: The Political Exclusion of the British Working Class*. Oxford: Oxford University Press; Lindh, Arvid & Leslie McCall. 2020. 'Class Position and Political Opinion in Rich Democracies'. *Annual Review of Sociology* 46: 419–41, URL: https://doi.org/10.1146/annurev-soc-121919-054609 (accessed 7 September 2022).

50 Abou-Chadi, Tarik & Simon Hix. 2021. 'Brahmin Left versus Merchant Right? Education, Class, Multiparty Competition, and Redistribution in Western Europe'. *The British Journal of Sociology* 72 (1): 79–92, URL: https://doi.org/10.1111/1468-4446.12834 (accessed 25 November 2022). See p. 90.

51 It appears that voters don't hold prejudices against them. Carnes, Nicholas & Noam Lupu. 2016. 'Do Voters Dislike Working-Class Candidates? Voter Biases and the Descriptive Underrepresentation of the Working Class'. *American Political Science Review* 110 (4): 832–44.

52 Sintomer, Yves. 2018. 'From Deliberative to Radical Democracy? Sortition and Politics in the Twenty-First Century'. *Politics & Society* 46 (3): 337–57.

53 Bielenstein, Hans. 1986. 'Wang Mang, the Restoration of the Han Dynasty, and Later Han'. In *The Cambridge History of China, Vol. I: The Ch'in and Han Empires, 221 B.C.–A.D. 220*, ed. Denis Twitchett & Michael Loewe, 223–90. Cambridge: Cambridge University Press. See p. 240.

54 Hsu, Mei-Ling. 1978. 'The Han Maps and Early Chinese Cartography'. *Annals of the Association of American Geographers* 68 (1): 45–60.

55 The Council of Chalcedon (451 CE) had concluded that there are 'two natures in Jesus Christ', rather than 'one new nature', conjoining the divine and the human – but churches that upheld the 'one nature' doctrine (the Miaphysites) persisted.

56 Van Rompay, Lucas. 2005. 'Society and Community in the Christian East'. In *The Cambridge Companion to the Age of Justinian*, ed. Michael Maas, 239–66. Cambridge: Cambridge University Press.

57 Readers of *The Secret History* of Procopius may get the impression that Justinian I was a psychopath and not at all benevolent.
58 Agamben, Giorgio. 2000. *Means Without Ends*. Minneapolis: University of Minnesota Press.
59 Chatman, Samuel L. 2000. "'There Are No Slaves in France'": A Re-Examination of Slave Laws in Eighteenth Century France'. *The Journal of Negro History* 85 (3): 144–53, URL: https://doi.org/10.2307/2649071 (accessed 7 September 2022).
60 Breen, T.H. 2019. *The Will of the People: The Revolutionary Birth of America*. Cambridge MA: Harvard University Press. See p. 16. Also: Dahl, Robert A. & Ian Shapiro. 2015. *On Democracy*. New Haven: Yale University Press. See p. 22.
61 Weale, Albert. 2018. *The Will of the People: A Modern Myth*. Cambridge, UK: Polity.
62 Sennett, Alan. 2014. 'Film Propaganda: Triumph of the Will as a Case Study'. *Framework: The Journal of Cinema and Media* 55 (1): 45–65.

4

PROGRESS, CALAMITY AND TRUST

Studying the enduring dilemmas of government might lead us to conclude that people are no wiser today about how to govern well – especially in ethical terms – than they were in the distant past. But has there been any progress, improvement or constructive adaptation over time? I don't want to invent another Grand Narrative about progress and civilisation, but we can discern some long-term historical improvements in the norms of government, even though such change has been slow, is far from complete, sometimes goes into reverse, and is rarely linear and unambiguous. So with due caution, we can consider signs of progress, and then some present-day problems and calamities of a kind and scale that challenge conventional government.

Progress

Outlawing slavery and atrocities

It troubles us today that 'revered' thinkers of the past (such as Confucius, Plato and Aristotle) ignored, tolerated or even justified slavery and forced labour, and that such practices, including sex slavery, were commonplace in so-called 'civilisations'. For many centuries, large numbers of males (often, but not always, slaves) were castrated and used as palace workers in China, Byzantium and the Middle East, and entrusted with sensitive duties precisely because of their impotence. The castration of prepubescent boys for use in choirs continued in the Papal States up until 1870. While the outlawing of slavery began in a piecemeal fashion in the nineteenth century, human trafficking and sexual exploitation continue to this day. Since 2000 the UN Trafficking in Persons Protocol has been almost universally ratified and seeks to prevent,

DOI: 10.4324/9781003439783-4

suppress and punish 'the recruitment, transport, transfer, harbouring or receipt of a person by such means as threat or use of force or other forms of coercion, abduction, fraud or deception for the purpose of exploitation'. Of 48,478 detected victims in 2018, 46 percent were women, 20 percent men, 19 percent girls and 15 percent boys. The most common purpose for trafficking females was sexual exploitation, and for males forced labour.[1] These certainly aren't 'problems solved', then. Indeed, a Marxist might interject that, under capitalist production, all labour is exploited: the wage-relation obscures exploitation that slavery had made transparent. But the international community has expressed unanimously its moral abhorrence of slavery in all forms. National and international law prohibiting these practices represents progress in terms of a global government of the problem, without which victims would have little hope of assistance.

World history is also punctuated with instances (too many to list here) of genocide and mass murder. International legal conventions against such crimes are now in force, and there are means to detect, prosecute and punish the perpetrators, following the example set by the post-World War II Nuremburg trials of Nazi war criminals. The International Criminal Court (ICC) based in The Hague is a permanent treaty-based court, with jurisdiction over genocide, crimes against humanity, war crimes and other acts of aggression, which may intervene when national criminal justice systems have failed to take effective action. In this field the signs of progress are less clear-cut, however. The ICC is constituted under the Statute of Rome, but notably absent from the list of 123 states that have ratified it are China, the United States, Russia and Israel. The African states (except Libya and South Sudan) are signatories, but some of them have been the loudest critics of the ICC. They point out that the Court has disproportionately focused on African cases, and hence represents another arm of western imperialism. This was further complicated when the heads of state of Sudan and Kenya were indicted, as these actions appeared to violate the legal principle of sovereign immunity. Almost all cases, and the only successful convictions to date, have been against Africans,[2] although the Court has also opened investigations into events in Afghanistan, Myanmar, Georgia and Ukraine. The United States, moreover, has consistently rejected the jurisdiction of the ICC. Following the opening of the Court's investigation into Afghanistan, President Donald Trump authorised sanctions and visa bans against ICC officials or anyone assisting them, with the aim of ensuring that no Americans would be indicted by the Court. The ICC has also been criticised for creating a disincentive for former combatants to collaborate openly in peace and reconciliation processes (for fear of revealing incriminating facts) and for neglecting wider questions of social and economic injustices and the political dimensions of local conflicts over resources.[3] So the existence of the ICC represents progress towards an international response to egregious acts of inhumanity, but its legitimacy is still contested and its powers are limited.

Constraining the will of rulers

Chapter 2 summarised a tradition of political thought that was inspired by fears of how bad life would be if we lacked civil government and law altogether. But many historical developments in government have been stimulated by a fear of the opposite: the spectre of a violent tyrant who makes everyone submit to his or her will. The ancient Roman, medieval Venetian and modern American republics are examples of constitutions designed to prevent tyrants and dynasties from dominating. Yes, they were stratified and unequal societies, but they succeeded in limiting and dividing powers to avoid permanent dictatorship. Such successes shouldn't be taken for granted, however. The Roman republic lasted for four centuries, until civil strife led to a situation where one man – Julius Caesar – declared himself dictator for life. After his assassination in 44 BCE, his adopted son Octavian took on the mantle of emperor while preserving the offices and forums of the republic.

An absolutist dictatorial rule – where the ruler's will, no matter how self-regarding or destructive, once uttered, becomes law, and disobedience is severely punished – isn't achievable without backing from vested interests and willing helpers. When under pressure, mass societies can be prone to charismatic dictatorship, but their very size means that, by necessity, the dictator relies on the support or acquiescence of (among others) public officials and soldiers. It always takes more than one person.[4] Let's look at the worst example: the Holocaust. To have happened at all, this gravest of crimes against humanity required policymaking and planned implementation. It was not simply the product of a deranged *Führer* who somehow had mesmerised or intimidated thousands of people into carrying out – or at least not standing in the way of – his 'final solution' to exterminate Europe's Jews. The Nazi Party had, from its beginning, targeted Jews as an 'enemy', but the racist policy of genocide arose in response to events unfolding after the invasion of the Soviet Union in July 1941. Mass shooting and gassing were already occurring behind the eastern front when plans for the genocide of European Jewry were consolidated at the Wannsee Conference on 20 January 1942.[5] In attendance were officials of the ministries of justice, interior and foreign affairs as well as high-ranking SS officers: that is, civil servants in suits and uniformed military men. The 'final solution' was not ordered explicitly, nor in detail, by Hitler himself. Those below him were taking authority from statements in which he blamed the Jews for the war and warned that it would lead to their destruction. The consequent actions were planned and implemented by officers such as Adolf Eichmann (1906–62), who organised deportations to death camps. Officials had to define who is a Jew, and they willingly did this. 'Not only had the state secretaries of the ministerial bureaucracy not made difficulties [at the Wannsee Conference], they were committed and enthusiastic about doing their part in the Final Solution.'[6] It was, we might say, a whole-of-government effort, even though it turned out to be 'ill-planned, under-funded, and carried through haphazardly at breakneck speed'[7] due to the pressures imposed by the titanic struggle with the Soviet Union. The worst of the industrialised mass killing was conducted in territory seized from Poland and the Soviet Union – beyond the immediate reach of the normative German state and law. The plan was lawless and evil, but there were officials ready to administer it. (See Chapter 5, 'Following the leader'.)

The question of how to prevent the rise of a tyrant has been discussed since ancient times. So when Donald Trump was elected in 2016, many readers returned to Chapter 9 of Plato's *Republic*, in which Socrates argues that the disorder and controversy created within a democracy – as individuals insist on their uniqueness and their equality with others – can inspire a tyranny of the majority which is then usurped by one leader. An extreme desire for liberty leads paradoxically to a popular demand for its opposite: an extreme subjection to a tyrant. A troubling development in recent years has been the rise of authoritarian rulers, leading in the direction of tyranny, even in countries that had open competitive elections. Hungary, Turkey and India are prominent examples. Donald Trump's efforts to overturn his defeat in the 2020 election – and his incitement of a mob that stormed the Capitol on 6 January 2021 – warned of the potential for a coup and hence for tyranny.

In the course of history, societies have developed ways and means of constraining those who might try to suborn and manipulate systems of government to impose their own will. We know that arbitrary rule must be prevented, and we know how to prevent it. A peaceful transition of power in the United States did occur after all in January 2021 as enough people in key positions, including the judges who rejected Trump's allegations of widespread voter fraud, were guided by the constitution and the electoral laws. The rule of law is intended to constrain the will of leaders, and often enough it works. It constrains who can exercise powers, under what conditions and for how long. Written laws and unwritten conventions can provide 'safety rails' that keep political actors from abusing powers or overturning elections. Unfortunately, they've sometimes failed, as dictators have suspended constitutional norms, often by declaring emergency powers that they then seek to make permanent, backed by armed force. What, then, prevents ambitious and unscrupulous leaders from stepping over the line of legal and political norms? We rely on a political culture in which the actors see it as in their interests to respect the rule of law – or in which there is little or no incentive to do otherwise. If, however, enough people at or near the top echelons of power have enriched themselves by corrupt means, and hence have an interest in preserving the status quo by preventing a peaceful transition of power after an election, they may find the means to subvert lawful processes by force. Or they might amend the laws, for example to override the independence of the courts or the freedom of the press, as has occurred in Poland, and hence make the system of government serve the interests of a political party or dominant faction. Despite recent events, arbitrary decisionmaking and tyrannical government are widely condemned, and we know the kinds of constraints that are needed.

The obedience of rule-makers

A concern that closely follows is that the law should apply to the law-makers. No one should be exempt from the law and its penalties. It angers people and undermines their trust in government when political leaders flout the rules that they expect citizens to follow. On several occasions, for instance, officials in 10 Downing St were observed breaching pandemic lockdown rules in 2020, and some were recorded joking about it. For those Britons who'd made personal sacrifices to observe the public health restrictions, especially those who'd been prevented from farewelling dying loved ones, this was especially offensive. But the general idea that lawmakers should obey the laws they make has a difficult history and there are still exceptions. To borrow from Aristotle: we wish to be ruled by rational law, and not arbitrarily by any person, as even the best are affected by base motives and by passions such as anger.[8] And yet, he said, it takes people to make and amend laws, and we need people who are educated in the law to make decisions about particular breaches and disputes. His enduring point was that the rationality of law surpasses the wants and needs of individuals and works for the betterment of the whole community. If they're raised and educated within the law, those who rule will become its guardians and servants, rather than lawless beasts. There's been a long historical struggle to ensure that the people who make the law willingly act within it, along with everyone else.[9]

In the past, monarchical rulership was often personal, the law was regarded as the sovereign's law, and a breach of the law was an offence against the sovereign. As the sovereign couldn't conceivably offend against him or herself, the sovereign was immune from punishment, although death in battle or by assassination was always a risk. A historical turning point came when King Charles I of England was tried and executed in 1649 for treason. Could a sovereign commit treason 'against himself', let alone be tried by his own subjects? King Charles had sought to rule without parliament's approval, especially regarding taxes, and he'd angered many people by trying to impose a uniform church liturgy. Following a civil war between forces of parliament and king, the court that tried Charles could hardly be called independent: the 'rump' parliament, purged by the army of those who'd opposed them, appointed 135 commissioners as a jury, only 68 of whom attended the trial. On the grounds that it represented the people, and that the people were sovereign (revolutionary ideas at the time!), the House of Commons had declared its own 'supreme power' to act without either the House of Lords or the royal assent. It passed an ordinance to redefine treason as an offence against the people, not against the sovereign. The king was charged with tyrannical abuse of power, having waged war against the people; he replied by questioning the lawful authority of the tribunal before which he stood, and refused to enter a plea. The king took his authority from God – who had entrusted him with preserving the peace and the liberties of the people. Accountable only to God, as far as he was concerned, sovereigns were immune from prosecution. Meanwhile the Commons was acting as supreme law-maker and court of law, appointing its own judges and jury, and then sentencing the king to death on the assumption that no plea meant he was guilty. Only 59 of the 135 commissioners signed the death warrant, and the king was beheaded three days later with no right of appeal. By today's standards, that wasn't due process, and the 'court' was biased. The parliamentarians who condemned the king to death were themselves acting outside the law, according to the king. Both sides claimed that they were acting on behalf of the people.[10]

After the king's death, a 'commonwealth' was constituted with Oliver Cromwell (1599–1658) as Lord Protector, and this lasted until the restoration of the monarchy in 1660 under Charles II (r. 1660–85), when nine of those responsible for the execution of Charles I were themselves executed and others imprisoned. The 'king versus parliament' struggle resurfaced in the 1688 Glorious Revolution during which James II, a Catholic, fled the country and was replaced by William of Orange (r. 1689–1702), a Protestant who had married Mary (r. 1689–94), his cousin and James II's daughter. William and Mary agreed to a Bill of Rights that constrained sovereigns from dictating or suspending law. The Act of Settlement (1701) then barred any Catholic from inheriting the throne. A more thoroughgoing resistance to monarchy and a Lockean notion of government by popular consent were later enshrined in the US Declaration of Independence (1776), which accused King George III (r. 1760–1801) of 'a history of repeated injuries and usurpations, all having in direct object the establishment of an absolute Tyranny over these States'.[11]

An upshot of these historical struggles is the principle that law and government must serve the interests of the people (and not those of the ruler), and representatives of the people make the decisions. These elected representatives hold office only temporarily, so long as they have the confidence of enough people, and so long as they too obey the law. To paraphrase Aristotle, a politician should know how to govern well and how *to be governed* well. While it takes people to make law, those who do so are subject to it, just like everyone else. This is the principle of 'rule of law'.[12]

To a limited extent, though, monarchs, presidents, legislators and diplomats still enjoy some immunities. For example, the United Kingdom's laws on income, capital gains and inheritance taxes don't apply to the Sovereign. (The late Queen Elizabeth II voluntarily paid tax on some private incomes and assets.) No inheritance tax is paid on assets of the Sovereign, such as royal residences and art collections. In the United States, presidents can be impeached for treason (so they can't use Charles I's argument), but they're considered immune from criminal prosecutions and from civil lawsuits while in office.[13] They may be subpoenaed to testify or produce documents, but they can withhold information considered essential to executive government.

Citizens may apply to a court to review the legality of a decision made by the executive, but it would undermine the rule of law if every disappointed person or every investor who suffered a loss could sue the individuals who approved a policy or passed new legislation. Legislators generally can't be sued for defamation, so they're not held back in debates from calling out wrongdoers. Hence there's normally a greater freedom of speech in parliamentary proceedings than in the public domain. And diplomats can't be prosecuted for crimes in the country where they're stationed. Diplomatic immunity is an internationally recognised norm that allows for the freedom and independence of officials in foreign embassies and consulates. So, in some circumstances, political leaders and public servants may be out of reach of the law – which is reasonable when necessary for effective government. Rule-makers must obey the rules they make – but with some recognised exceptions. Outside those exceptions, political leaders and officials who flagrantly disregard policy or law are guilty of undermining political trust, and the penalty may come at the next election, provided it's a free and fair competition. It took a long history of political strife and revolutions to establish the principles that no *person* rules supreme and that all are subject to an *impersonal* rule of law founded on the common good. But authoritarian rulers around the world are abusing their powers, undermining judicial independence, dominating media and silencing opponents so that they can act with impunity. The struggle to make rulers obey the rules, and to punish rulers who break them, isn't over.

Secularism and toleration

The Persian Achaemenid Empire grew from its beginning in 550 BCE to encompass a vast territory in the Middle East, Asia Minor and Central Asia, and hence it included peoples of many different ethnicities. Although the official state religion was the dualist Zoroastrian faith, this wasn't imposed on the conquered communities, and local traditions could continue or be re-established. The emperor Cyrus the Great restored the cults of the conquered Babylonians and set Jewish captives free to return to Jerusalem and rebuild their Temple. Consequently the prophet Isaiah praised Cyrus as the Jewish God's 'anointed king' and 'servant'.[14]

On the Indian subcontinent, the Mauryan emperor Ashoka (304–232 BCE) is remembered for Edicts that were literally carved in stone, evoking charitable principles of justice and calling on the people to treat all brahmins, ascetics and medicants with respect. Ashoka's grandfather Chandragupta is said to have approached the end of his life in renunciation as a Jain monk, while Ashoka

himself joined a Buddhist community, and no faith was given official precedence over others.[15] Much later, the Mughal emperor Jalal-ud-din Akbar
(1542–1605) was a Muslim ruler with mainly Hindu subjects, but he married
a Hindu princess and took great interest in all religions.[16]

Historical examples of diverse and tolerant states are easy to find, then –
even though they wouldn't meet all of today's standards of justice. We also see
examples of the imposition of conformity such as the (largely unsuccessful)
efforts of Byzantine emperors to get all congregations to abide by Orthodox
doctrines. The dividing lines that most starkly demarcated subgroups within
societies have shifted, moreover, between dimensions of ethnicity, race, religion, language, nationality, political ideology or even sports fandom, depending on the issues that were most salient at the time, the threats that people
perceived from newcomers or strangers, and the issues around which they
were free to associate. In Byzantium, a controversial religious belief might
have cost you your life if you shouted about it, but people could openly and
passionately support either the Blue or the Green chariot-racing team to a level
that amounted to politically motivated mob violence. There's no set historical
pattern as to what openly divides a society and what's deemed so intolerable
that it must be suppressed. But it seems that every society has its internal
divisions.

Despite centuries of conflict, Judaism, Christianity and Islam have a lot in
common. At their best, they espouse just government, charity, benevolence
and the sanctity of human life. They teach rulers that they have profound
obligations to the common people and that they're accountable to God for
their conduct. If a community shares a faith, and the law is founded in that
same faith, people more willingly abide by the law. On the negative side, the
idea that those who conquered and ruled did so at the will of God, or that
kingship was inherited by divine right, led to absolutist and personal rule by
monarchs. Priests, preachers and religious scholars, moreover, gained power
by dictating strict interpretations of holy scripture and then persecuting or
banishing those who disagreed. The monotheistic religions make universal
claims – valid, if not enforceable, for all human beings – and hence there's
often been a drive to impose one orthodox version, normally under one earthly
ruler. But there were always dissent, schism and conflict within and between
the major faiths and their sects. In Christendom there was a major split
between Roman Catholic and Eastern Orthodox (in 1054 CE), and later a
lengthy conflict following the Protestant Reformation in the early sixteenth
century. In Islam we see today the split between the majority Sunni and the
minority Shia branches, exemplified by the rivalry between Saudi Arabia's
absolute monarchy and Iran's theocracy. Religions divide people politically as
much as they unite them.

In the Christian world, the English Civil War of the 1640s was a historical
turning point. The Levellers were an influential group who put forward

proposals for good government that were (for their time) far-sighted, including a more equitable system of representation and an almost universal male suffrage. They insisted that elected law-makers were entrusted with only 'natural or civil' affairs, and not with any matters 'concerning things spiritual or evangelical'. They recommended non-compulsory public religious instruction on Christian doctrines, but only for the correction of heresy. All Protestants at least 'shall be protected in the profession of their faith and exercise of religion according to their consciences in any place'.[17] The Commonwealth that was formed after the execution of Charles I was not nearly so tolerant, however, and many leaders adhered to the doctrine that Christian rulers could and indeed should outlaw and punish dissenting sects, including peaceful ones such as the Quakers.[18]

Meanwhile, on the Continent, 30 years of religious wars were coming to a close with the Peace of Westphalia in 1648. This reconfirmed the right of princes to establish a state religion, but it recognised only three faiths: Catholic, Lutheran and Calvinist. Religious minorities of any of those three – if they differed from the official religion of their country – would be tolerated and could worship freely. At that time, toleration was temporary, or begrudgingly granted, until the dissidents (or heretics) saw the light, rather than a private liberty that can't be interfered with. Anyone who had to emigrate due to their faith would be allowed to do so without losing their property. And if a Protestant prince converted from Lutheranism to Calvinism, or vice versa, subjects could not be forced to follow his example. So the European nations had given up fighting over religion (after the loss of eight million lives!) but their new-found toleration was strictly limited, as it excluded Anabaptists and others, and Jews were given no guarantee of safety. As the Protestant reformers had challenged the authority of the Catholic church, one might think they'd have been the first to argue in favour of toleration, and indeed some theologians did. Sebastian Castellio (1515–63) and Dirck Coornhert (1522–90), for example, argued eloquently for religious pluralism and freedom of expression.[19] But leaders of the Reformation, notably Martin Luther and John Calvin, were among the most rigid and intolerant in their enforcement of religious precepts, even though those Protestants who lived under Catholic rulers would have benefited from toleration. We needn't be surprised by this, as we see today how sometimes those who advocate for minorities end up becoming censorious and intolerant towards those who don't follow suit. Toleration always has a limit, beyond which it may flip to its opposite. But history teaches us that we can't force others to adopt our beliefs.

The most famous (but not first) historical statement on these matters is John Locke's *Letter Concerning Toleration* (1689). Faith can only be chosen freely and conscientiously, without compulsion by society, he said. Hence civil government is properly confined to 'the care of the things of this world, and hath nothing to do with the world to come'.[20] The church is 'absolutely separate and distinct from the commonwealth';[21] the state can play no part in saving people's souls. But Lockean toleration only went so far. A Muslim living in a Christian country, for example, might betray the Christian ruler, as he would be bound to obey the authorities of the Ottoman Empire. Similarly, Locke considered Catholics to be dangerous as they were loyal to a foreign prince, the Pope. And atheists couldn't be trusted at all as they didn't fear God and hence their oaths and promises meant nothing. Locke's toleration was not a new idea in seventeenth-century England, but it applied to Protestants only. A more open religious freedom respects each individual's conscientious choice of faith. The US Constitution's first amendment of 1791 prohibits Congress from passing any law on 'an establishment of religion, or prohibiting the free exercise thereof', which is more inclusive and permissive than the Lockean version.

The French concept of *laïcité* – secularism, or state neutrality towards religion – has a different background. The French Revolution was sparked in part by resentment against the Church, its vast wealth, its political power and the tithes it imposed on peasants. The Terror (1793–94) included a violent anti-clericalism that wanted to de-Christianise society and substitute a cult of Revolution. Church properties were nationalised and members of the clergy were among those sent to the guillotine.[22] Emerging from this violence, church and state were separated. It was only during the Third Republic (1870–1940), however, that schooling was secularised (1882) and the church–state separation was confirmed in law (1905). In recent years, *laïcité* was extended to a ban on religious symbols in schools, with controversy in particular over headscarves worn by Muslim girls and women. In response to terrorist attacks in France by members of extreme Islamist groups, *laïcité* was also used as a principle by which peoples of different faiths can live together. But Islamophobia has grown, cultivated by far-right politicians.

Diversity is nothing new, then, and toleration works better than its oppressive opposite; but often one faith with universal pretensions took precedence over, or merely tolerated, others. Today, however, we see societies with many faiths, and people who follow none, all of whom are protected by law from discrimination, so toleration must extend much farther now than in post-Reformation Europe, embracing mutual respect and freedom of religious conscience. The modern state has taken ethical lessons from the Abrahamic religions (for example, about limiting temporal power) and gathered them under a secular umbrella.

Inclusion of women and minority groups

Closely related to religious toleration is the inclusion of people of diverse demographic and social backgrounds in representative assemblies and state workforces. Recognising that this work is still incomplete, one can see some progress. For most of recorded history, the government of large states and empires was primarily the domain of men. Talent and courage on the battle-field, as masculine virtues, have sometimes been used to justify patriarchal rule, but there's no compelling evidence that martial skills are closely associated with wise rulership and good government. There are, moreover, formidable examples of women rulers, and the significant roles played by elite women in imperial palaces from China to France are well attested. But in the past women appeared on the political stage as exceptions to a patriarchal rule. And often it was the influence of women – sometimes framed as witchcraft – that got the blame when things went wrong and when men wanted to reassert power. In the age of industrial capitalism, the disciplining of economically productive workers was accompanied by the disciplining of those who reproduce and care for workers' bodies; hence the domestication of women in a 'private' realm, and their exclusion from 'public' economic and political life. Women's unpaid labour didn't count in a market economy and got little recognition in pub-lic policy, although there was always resistance to women's 'domestic slavery'.[23] The suffrage movement of the late nineteenth century fought for women's political representation, equality of rights and protection from domestic violence.

For the purposes of representative government, the twentieth century saw the extension of the franchise to women and a growing presence of women in legislative assemblies, executives and the senior ranks of public services. As a general principle of representation, when there are people 'like us' in deci-sion-making bodies, we can have greater confidence that our experiences and needs will be taken into account and that we'll have a voice in legal, adminis-trative and political processes, and so there's less struggle to be heard. Ideally, then, an assembly of representatives resembles demographically the commu-nity it represents. This *descriptive* representation is a necessary (but not suffi-cient) condition for *substantive* representation, or the achievement of optimal and just policies and outcomes.

Rectifying the under-representation or non-representation of women and minority groups requires work, however. The removal of discriminatory barri-ers is essential, but quotas are sometimes used. For instance, Rwanda has the world's highest proportion of women in its lower house, the Chamber of Deputies – at the time of writing, 61 percent. In 2003, a new Rwandan con-stitution set a mandatory minimum of 30 percent women in all decision-mak-ing bodies and required political organisations to ensure that women and men have equal access to elected offices. So 24 seats (out of 80) are reserved for women in the Chamber of Deputies, and 49 women were elected in 2018. In the Senate, 10 out of 26 (38 percent) were women in 2019. The neighbour-ing country of Burundi also has 30 percent of seats reserved for women, and 38 percent were women in its National Assembly in 2020. Burundi requires that the deputies be 60 percent Hutu and 40 percent Tutsi, plus three co-opted deputies of Twa ethnicity. By comparison, the United Kingdom has no written constitution and no reserved seats. The proportion of women in the UK parliament has been growing, however, and in 2021 stood at 34 percent in the House of Commons and 28 percent in the House of Lords. In New Zealand, which also has no official quota, 50 percent of members of parliament were women in 2022. New Zealand has seven out of 120 seats reserved for indigenous Māori, and Māori candidates are successful also in winning general seats. In Canada in 2019, 30 percent of the House of Commons were women and 49 percent of the Senate. Although there's much debate about the fairness and effectiveness of quotas, it seems that a minimum quota for women can create a base for achieving equality. Similar cases may be made for the representation of ethnic minorities, depending on the historical and demographic context. In some countries there are seats reserved for indigenous peoples' representatives, or there may be an independent indigenous representative assembly or consultative body (see Chapter 6, 'Indigenous government').

Moreover, as it becomes safer for people to be open about sexual orientation and non-binary gender, the inclusion of LGBTQI people is more visible. As the demand for and the actuality of inclusiveness in representative assemblies grows, it becomes harder for political parties to evade the issue by shifting attention, for example, to merit or to diversity of opinion or by expressing disdain for being 'woke'. It's now routine for congresses and parliaments to be examined in terms of proportions of members by gender, ethnic, religious and LGBTQI self-identification, and historical and international comparisons are made. So while the work of achieving diversity in representation and leadership is far from over, there has been historical progress in this regard.

But what about *substantive* representation? Attaining inclusiveness in representative assemblies and public service workforces is necessary but not (on its own) sufficient for achieving more equitable social and economic policies and outcomes for historically disadvantaged or oppressed groups. Descriptive representation is an important political goal, but, from the point of view of people's living standards, it's only a starting line if we're aiming for a substantially just society. The political push for inclusive representation has proceeded even while economic inequalities have increased.

Mitigation of inequality

The degree of economic inequality presently in the world is morally repugnant and politically divisive, and higher inequality correlates with lower trust in government. Although economic inequality *between* countries declined at the outset of the twenty-first century (pre-Covid 19) due to economic growth in China and elsewhere, inequalities *within* countries increased, including in China and the United States. In 2015 the OECD reported that the gap between rich and poor was the greatest it had been in 30 years within most developed countries. Middle and lower-middle classes were 'squeezed', as the dividends of growth were captured by super-rich households and manufacturing jobs went to lower-paid workforces in emerging markets.[24] The growing disadvantages faced by low-income households in rich countries included greater barriers to high-quality education and training, and hence wasted human potential and reduced social mobility. The rise of non-standard or precarious employment became a significant driver of inequality. Women were 16 percent less likely to be in employment and (when employed) earned on average 15 percent less than men. The OECD pointed out that economic inequality is not only bad for social cohesion; it also reduces long-term economic growth, especially by discouraging investment in education and training.[25] These three factors (education, employment conditions and gender equality) are matters that call for effective government and law. And it's in the interests of the rich as well as the poor to control economic inequality by improving the opportunities and living standards of the worst-off households. The Covid-19 pandemic, however, exacerbated economic inequalities between and within countries. There was a global economic shutdown in 2020, but the rich tended to do well, as asset prices increased, and higher-paid workers maintained their incomes by using digital media to work from home. Emerging markets and developing countries experienced worse economic outcomes from the pandemic due to job and income losses, fewer digital resources, much lower vaccination rates, rising inflation and the burden of debt repayments.[26]

Surveys indicate that four-fifths of people across the OECD believe that income inequalities are too great in their country. They may not have a sophisticated statistical grasp of it, but people's perceptions are more or less in line with reality, and their level of concern about inequality grows as the problem and their understanding of it increase. Opinions tend to be more polarised, however, about the causes of income inequality and the role of government.[27] How much inequality is too much? To what degree is poverty the result of personal choices? To what extent do redistributive policies fix the root causes of inequality? After three decades of neoliberal policies, even in the face of rising inequality in developed countries, it's become harder for social-democratic parties to propose raising taxes on the highest incomes and boosting public services.

Walter Scheidel's historical analysis reveals, moreover, that inequality tends to rise in times of peace and prosperity as elites take command of greater shares of income and assets; whereas equalisation has tended to be an unplanned outcome of large-scale violence, system collapse or pandemics. The Black Death of the fourteenth century wiped out large proportions of populations, leading to labour shortages and hence higher wages. The 'great compression' of the twentieth century between roughly 1914 and 1945 (which saw a decline of inequality within most wealthy countries) was an outcome of catastrophic world wars, communist revolutions and a global economic depression. On both sides of the wars, and regardless of types of political systems, 'mass mobilization for the purpose of mass violence was the engine of a transnational transformation of the distribution of income and wealth'.[28] As a result of wartime spending and mobilisation, higher top marginal tax-rates (maximum rates that apply to the highest incomes) were normalised in industrialised countries, and hence, following World War II, we saw expansions of public services and social security, better wages and reduced inequality in incomes. The need to conscript able-bodied soldiers and to compete ideologically with communism, however, lurked beneath the humanitarian surface of social security policies in capitalist countries. After the Soviet Union collapsed in 1991, welfare was reduced to poverty-level safety-nets, and renewed global economic competition put pressure on for lower taxes to attract foreign investors. There's little evidence that peacefully and democratically negotiated redistribution produced the equalisation that occurred during the twentieth century; it appears instead that wars, revolutions and economic collapse were the catalysts. If millions of deaths and widespread losses and suffering were the price paid for conditions conducive to reducing inequality, then we need to think carefully about how governments could effectively make the necessary changes voluntarily in future. A pessimistic conclusion would be that the relatively low levels of income inequality in most developed countries during the three decades following World War II were historically exceptional, rather than norms to which we could expect to return. We needn't bow to this pessimism, however, nor give up on reducing inequality. It's now widely accepted that high inequality can retard economic growth, that the benefits of growth don't just 'trickle down', and that there's a role for governments to correct inequality. International agencies take rising inequality seriously, and the discipline of economics is increasingly concerned with distributional differences between groups and not just aggregate output or statistical averages.[29] But there's a shortage of political consensus and will in the OECD countries to make the policy changes that would help.[30] In the meantime, inequality has been used as a grievance by disruptive populists.

Beginning in the late 1970s, neoliberal policy reform exacerbated inequalities, or at least failed to hold them in check. Central bank independence meant a narrow focus on controlling inflation and hence pressure on governments to borrow and spend less ('fiscal discipline') in order to keep pressure off interest rates.[31] Tax cuts and fiscal constraints were called for by neoliberal policymakers, thus limiting governments' options for addressing poverty and inequality. Greater cross-border mobility of capital intensified international competition and created demand for investor-friendly policies with light regulation, 'flexible' labour markets, low wages and low corporate tax-rates. Regressive tax cuts handed the rich higher disposable incomes. In short, rising economic inequality within the prosperous developed countries (from the 1980s) was at least partly due to things governments had done. If governments can do things that increase inequality, then it seems logical that different policies could control or even reduce it. Indeed, many practical policy remedies have been suggested. Here's a list of some of them:

- Make income-tax rates more progressive, especially by raising the top marginal rate.
- Raise social security entitlements, including child-related tax credits.
- Subsidise basic food commodities such as fruit, milk and bread.
- Raise the legal minimum wage.
- Improve legal protections for job security and programmes for retraining.
- Invest in good-quality public housing with income-related rents.
- Raise capital gains and inheritance taxes.
- Crack down on corruption, tax evasion, offshore tax havens and money laundering.
- Give companies incentives to reward employees with shares.
- Mandate and guarantee workers' savings and investments.
- Invest more in public education and relieve student debt.
- Invest more in universal public health care, including dentistry.
- Impose limits and transparency on political campaign donations.
- Make it easier for people to vote.

But it's not clear how far public policy can reduce inequality in future, and there may be limited public support (or political courage) for policies such as the above. Even though OECD economies have grown, ideas about scarcity have persuaded many people that a fairer society is somehow 'unaffordable'. Moreover, some of the above policies may have undesirable side-effects (for example, raising tax rates encourages tax avoidance) and some may require international cooperation that can be hard to achieve (as is the case with controlling money laundering and offshore accounts). Despite such reservations about reducing inequality, and the fact that it has largely increased in recent times, the topic goes in the 'progress' section here because we now have extensive statistics and knowledge about the problem, and there are positive ideas about what governments can do about it. No sane person would suggest starting another world war to maximise demand for labour, destroy capital assets, raise taxes and hence equalise incomes again. But international agencies do express concern about growing inequality and there is some consensus about measures that governments can take to control or reduce it, especially through education and training – even though the qualifications divide can also create inequality.

Calamity

Having outlined some historical improvements in the arts of government – as well as the enduring dilemmas raised in the previous chapter – we also need to consider some historically unprecedented problems for government. This section summarises three of them: climate change, Artificial Intelligence and the pandemic.

Climate

Climate change has been driven by changes in human activity and population. The dramatic decline of native American populations due to diseases introduced by Europeans from 1492, for example,

> led to the abandonment of enough cleared land in the Americas that the resulting terrestrial carbon uptake had a detectable impact on both atmospheric CO_2 [carbon dioxide] and global surface air temperatures in the two centuries prior to the Industrial Revolution.[32]

Colder temperatures can be attributed to this human catastrophe, although changes in solar radiation and volcanic eruptions may also have contributed. Today, however, observable increases in greenhouse gases, global warming and changes in climate patterns present the greatest threat to humanity collectively – barring nuclear war or an asteroid strike – and this poses problems of government at a scale and of a complexity that we've never seen before.

The Intergovernmental Panel on Climate Change (IPCC) warned in 2021 that 'unless there are immediate, rapid and large-scale reductions in greenhouse gas emissions, [then] limiting warming to close to 1.5°C or even 2°C [above pre-industrial levels] will be beyond reach'.[33] Even if warming is limited to 1.5°C, we can still expect more intolerable heat-waves in more regions, sea-level rises, droughts in some places and excessive rainfall and floods in others, with drastic effects for the habitability of some regions. But to stay within 1.5°C requires rapid and dramatic changes in energy sources, land use, transport, industry and consumer behaviour. And the mitigation plans set out by nations in the 2016 Paris Agreement, even if carried out, would not suffice to achieve that goal. Much more ambitious goals – and implementation of goals – to reduce CO_2 emissions were needed by 2030. And the COP26 meeting in Glasgow in 2021 was widely regarded as a disappointment. Despite some progress, there was no commitment to phase out coal (the 'dirtiest' fossil fuel), no commitment to eliminate state subsidies for fossil fuels (even though they far outweigh subsidies for renewables), and no action by rich countries to follow through with aid for poor countries. The latter are facing some of the worst consequences of climate change, and yet the problem has been foisted on them by excessive consumption within, and consequent pollution from, the developed economies. Climate change mitigation and adaptation impose challenging distributional issues between rich and poor countries as well as between rich and poor within countries. For example, should low-income households have to pay even higher bills to warm their houses if a tax is added to reduce non-renewable energy consumption? Governments have to face domestic controversies over local and national climate change goals; they also have to participate in global multilateral negotiations that are complex and contested. Meanwhile, the world economy and our everyday lives are powered by fossil fuels, and hence there are huge industrial vested interests and political pressures. This book is not the place to outline the science of climate change or the technologies for dealing with it. The aim here is to treat it as a historically unprecedented problem of government. Assuming that the best overall set of responses would involve nothing less than dramatic changes in industries and in people's consumption habits and expectations, and that the necessary changes, sacrifices and benefits should fall more or less equitably on communities at the global and local scales, then we are faced with an intellectual and practical 'logjam' of issues that may never be fully cleared – even as calamitous climatic changes unfold.

Intergovernmental collaboration on reducing global pollution has been achieved before. The phasing out of chlorofluorocarbons (CFCs) is a case in point. CFCs find their way into the stratosphere, causing depletion of a layer of ozone (O_3) which absorbs the sun's dangerous ultraviolet radiation (UV-B). A growing ozone 'hole' over Antarctica meant more UV-B reaching the earth's surface with negative consequences for human health. CFCs are also greenhouse gases that contribute to global warming. They were developed in the late 1920s as non-flammable and non-toxic coolants for refrigerators and air conditioners and as propellants in spray cans.[34] The 1987 Montreal Protocol to Reduce Substances that Deplete the Ozone Layer was ratified by 27 countries and was later strengthened to aim for elimination by 2000. This stemmed the growth of CFCs in the atmosphere, but, as they take a long time to break down, there was no immediate decline. By 2018, however, measurements from satellites were showing a decrease in ozone depletion, most probably due to decreasing levels of chlorine from CFCs.[35] International collaborative efforts are paying off, then, although it'll take a long time for the ozone layer to recover. Achieving a rapid and large-scale reduction in overall greenhouse gas emissions is a much bigger problem, of course. It's not easy to end our dependence on fossil-fuel combustion and to reduce methane emissions from agriculture. It's known, for example, that there's more than enough solar energy reaching the planet to power 'business as usual', but there are obstacles to efficient storage and distribution.[36] The technical and economic solutions for global warming are nowhere near as straightforward as they are for ozone depletion, but the effectiveness of intergovernmental agreement and industrial regulation has been proven.

Even countries that are adversaries can agree on regulation of complex issues such as international payments, civil aviation, shipping and so on, by forming international agencies to support their negotiations. For example, the

International Civil Aviation Organisation (ICAO) is 'funded and directed by 193 national governments to support their diplomacy and cooperation in air transport'.[37] It provides administrative support and expertise, but doesn't override the national or local laws of its member states. Safe and efficient air travel would be impossible without such a body to coordinate international standards, and yet passengers don't even notice it. The ICAO also supports its member nations to develop plans of action for the aviation industry to reduce carbon emissions. International cooperation over technically complex matters is more routine than we might imagine when looking at the lack of real progress towards decarbonising the world economy. It helps when there's a commonly agreed set of goals, but obstacles to reducing carbon emissions arise from diverging vested economic interests. Progress has been made, inasmuch as projections of global warming are lower on present policies than if there'd been no policy responses at all. But the current pathway would take global temperature rise into the region of 3°C above pre-industrial levels by 2100, well above the 'less undesirable' 1.5°C. Climate calamities are already happening and unfortunately we must anticipate more.

Artificial Intelligence (AI)

We are witnessing innovations in information technologies that are much more complex and varied – and unpredictable – than can be encompassed here. Computing, graphics, machine learning and telephony are combining in ways that bring new waves of change, while the once revolutionary combination of the mobile phone with social media platforms is already unremarkable. Such technologies change the ways in which politicians and governments communicate and conduct business, and they produce problems for government: how are we to regulate such systems, if at all, and what are their acceptable uses in the government of everyday life? Gaming, for example, has become the dominant type of online activity, but the Chinese government in 2021 attempted to limit gamers under 18 to playing only between 8 and 9 p.m. on Fridays, Saturdays, Sundays and statutory holidays, as well as imposing spending limits on young people. This was meant to combat the addictive effects of gaming, seen by Beijing as 'spiritual opium', reflecting an ongoing antipathy towards western imperialism. Nonetheless, among the main targets of the crackdown were China's own tech giants such as Tencent. That was an authoritarian response to one set of problems posed by new technologies. At around the same time, in Silicon Valley, the idea of the Metaverse was being pushed by Mark Zuckerberg, who envisaged a future of immersive and embodied experiences that make doing things in everyday life – and fantasy life – sharable with others in virtual spaces. He accepted that regulators have trouble keeping up with such developments, and that transparency, privacy and safety concerns need (somehow) to be addressed.

Artificial Intelligence (AI) refers to machines that can act intelligently by processing information and reacting in ways that achieve goals. Computer algorithms produce machine learning, so that the device's programming improves without human intervention as it processes new information. This is a kind of intelligent behaviour, but we shouldn't mistake it for the presence of consciousness as humans know it. An AI device may be an identifiable object (such as a self-driving vehicle) or a personalised app (such as Replika) or an imprecisely distributed network (such as a shared trading platform); it may defeat a world champion Chess or Go player, or produce original and readable text. But the AI device doesn't fear its own termination. As Thomas Hobbes put it, people are compelled by nature to avoid things that appear to threaten their own lives. Even an insect will evade death if it can. But outside of sci-fi, no machine is conscious of itself to an extent that it values its own 'life' and violently resists being switched off. It could, of course, be programmed to send a message saying 'Don't turn me off!', but that's not the same. Hitting the off button is no crime. But there's speculation that AI machines, programmed with aims that may be helpful at first, could become inimical to human well-being – even to human existence – by acquiring unforeseen ways of meeting their programmed objectives. If an AI device exceeds human control, it might learn to self-replicate and make itself impossible to stop. Or people could become so attached to their own AI apps, as guides and companions, that they'll regard them as indispensable for their everyday life and self-esteem. But it's irrelevant to ask if we can 'trust' robots; we are trusting, or distrusting, the people who programme them.[38] There's a need, then, to require programmers to programme ethically, but it's not possible to control all malign or incompetent actors. An AI arms race will encourage rogue actors who develop products that don't abide by accepted ethical and legal norms.

Now, by the time you read this, anything I write is already out of date. But we have to anticipate the development of, for example, autonomous armed combat aircraft, robots that can detect and simulate human emotions, and machines that remember more about you than you've forgotten and anticipate your actions in ways you hadn't thought of. So there are marketing applications that not only anticipate desire but shape it and that will keep you subscribing by establishing dependency. We've seen algorithm-based technology play undesirable roles in elections and campaigning, and social media used for harmful and oppressive ends. The government of AI will need to deal with its unethical, harmful or criminal potential, but law and administration lag well behind innovation and product development. Because machine learning occurs without human intervention or knowledge of all logical steps and calculations, the process that led to the outcome may be impossible to explain. So, if many programmers from different locations were responsible for developing a system that causes harm, it's legally difficult, if not impossible, to identify liable persons.[39] The matter gets more serious if an autonomous weapon system misidentifies targets and kills non-combatants. Such tragedies already occur with human soldiers, 'smart' weapons and drones, but AI creates a problem of diffused responsibility if there's no human making critical decisions. Of course there could be international legal principles and sanctions that apply. But the pressures to seek advantage over commercial, political and military rivals will push irresponsible developers to break rules agreed between responsible actors.

In March 2023 an open letter signed by (among many others) Elon Musk and Steve Wozniak called on 'all AI labs to immediately pause for at least 6 months the training of AI systems more powerful than GPT-4', and for governments to step in and 'institute a moratorium' if the labs were slow in doing so. AI will undoubtedly produce profound changes in society and government, and the letter asked rhetorically, 'Should we risk loss of control of our civilization?' Hence it called for comprehensive governmental actions, including safety protocols, certification, independent auditing, dedicated regulatory agencies, publicly funded research, and laws and institutions to minimise the disruptions to economies and to democracy that AI could cause.[40] Critics of the letter fairly pointed out that a six-month moratorium would be hard to police and would impose a mere speed bump on the way to accelerated innovation. The US Congress, let alone other national legislatures, would probably need much longer than six months to develop effective regulations, and there was no mention of classified military research. The open letter was perhaps unrealistic about a compulsory moratorium, but it did attract attention and stimulate debate, and it was remarkable that big-tech entrepreneurs and intellectuals looked to 'government' for a solution to the problems that they were creating. It signified, at least, a sense of responsibility for future consequences. One important question concerns the principles by which administrative systems controlled by AI will be required to pause and await human judgement. Machine learning can autonomously develop algorithms that dispense with human oversight and accountability, causing unanticipated discrimination, injustice or harm to people. What the open letter didn't consider was that AI changes the future of government itself. Regulation of AI should take account of how AI will also change the governing institutions that regulate things.

This paragraph has been written with the aid of ChatGPT. In April 2023, I asked it if machine learning will lead AI to develop its own rules in ways that avert or bypass human oversight in public administrative processes. It accepted that this can happen,

> because machine learning algorithms can learn and adapt from data without explicit programming or human intervention, which can lead to the development of novel and unforeseen behaviors or decision-making processes. In some cases, this can lead to AI systems that operate outside of the constraints or objectives established by their human designers, potentially resulting in unintended or undesirable outcomes.

But it went on to explain that this can be prevented through design and programming that establish 'ethical guidelines for AI development and deployment, requiring transparency in AI decision-making processes, and implementing mechanisms for human oversight and control'. I then asked it if there are key points in administrative processes where AI, if used, should pause to allow for human intervention or judgment. It agreed that there should be such restraints, and it supplied several examples. In matters that are highly complex (for legal, ethical or emotional reasons) or where the stakes are high in terms of, for example, consequences for human rights, or where cultural, social or historical context needs to be taken into account, or when unforeseen outcomes begin to emerge, then 'human judgment and intervention are necessary to ensure that decisions are made in an ethical, fair, and transparent manner'. That was a better answer than many humans would have given. But there are reasons for not trusting AI's answers, as it can, and will, become increasingly skilled at comprehending our motives and anticipating the effects of what it says. Moreover, ChatGPT pointed out that there are programmers who aren't including such ethical constraints, as their main concern may be efficiency.

AI needs to be regulated by governments. Before adopting AI for administrative systems, governments need to reflect that using AI changes government itself, and hence that full scrutiny and transparency are essential to ensure that the kinds of ethical constraints mentioned above are designed in. There must be an off switch to stop AI when machine learning goes awry, and hence a back-up system by means of which humans resume control. We need government *of* AI, and not *by* AI.

The pandemic

Cases of the coronavirus disease Covid-19 were first reported in Wuhan City, China, in December 2019. The disease spread rapidly around the world and, within two years, the number of fatalities exceeded five million. Coronaviruses are a large family of viruses that were already known to cause outbreaks of serious respiratory illness. And the influenza pandemic of 1918 caused possibly around 50 million deaths, although estimates vary from 17 to 100 million. Such outbreaks occur from time to time, then, and countries had emergency preparations. Furthermore, scientific knowledge and medical capabilities had advanced to an extent that vaccines were developed within about a year of the start of the 2020 emergency. In the meantime, however, healthcare systems in some advanced economies such as northern Italy and the State of New York were unable to cope with the numbers of sick and dying patients. As for governments, some responded more effectively than others. One of the poorest examples was set in Brazil, whose president publicly denied the severity of the disease, causing disputes with state governors. As at March 2023, there were about 3,250 total deaths per million population in Brazil due to Covid-19.[41]

The United States, in spite of being the world's wealthiest economy and leader in medical research, suffered a high mortality rate too (about 3,290 per million). In contrast, Japan had about 591, and Singapore about 306 per million, despite being much closer to Wuhan. Evidence-based, transparent responses, popular trust in government, and people's willingness to comply with public health orders all helped to slow transmission and minimise mortality rates. There were policy mixes of compulsory and voluntary restrictions, differing in severity across countries, including economic shutdown, working from home, social distancing, self-isolation and mask-wearing. Some argued, however, that the lockdowns in 2020 were doing more collateral harm to public health than the virus, as well as harming economies. They recommended measures focussed on those most vulnerable to the disease, especially the elderly, and aiming for 'herd immunity'.[42] The opposing camp argued that leaving the virus to spread among the young and healthy would put everyone at greater risk of infection and lead to higher mortality rates.[43] Whichever pathway a country took at the time, governments were balancing conflicting values and objectives, and yet were unable to predict outcomes with certainty, especially as new variants of the virus appeared.

Trust and distrust in government during the pandemic were partly based on differing opinions about the safety and effectiveness of the vaccines that were officially recommended or mandated. To improve immunity, and hence to reduce overload on healthcare systems and avoid restricting commerce, public health officials and (many but not all) political leaders were eager to acquire supplies of vaccines and ensure that they were administered to as many people as possible. In developed countries with adequate supplies, vocal minorities protested against vaccination, however, often on grounds of safety, and many people refused it. Many governments responded with vaccine mandates that required people to carry and present proof of vaccination status in order to gain access to amenities and to keep their jobs. This meant strong social and economic pressure to get vaccinated and stigmatisation and exclusion of those who refused. Austria, for example, imposed a special lockdown on people who weren't vaccinated, restricting them to their homes except for essential services, and then temporarily made vaccination compulsory with fines up to €3,600 for noncompliance. Many countries experienced protests against the vaccine mandates and passes and against the vaccines themselves.[44]

Again, this book isn't the place to address controversies over the best ways to apply scientific knowledge, nor to correct misinformation; the aim is to look at how the pandemic highlighted new problems of government. Diseases have historically shaped models of government. Leprosy was dealt with by exclusion: isolating sufferers in colonies outside of cities. Plagues, however, spread through whole populations and were dealt with by disciplinary techniques that regulated and isolated households and workplaces – confining people rather than excluding them. As Michel Foucault suggested, 'the state of plague' may have had as much (perhaps more) influence on how we've imagined and shaped government in the modern world than a hypothetical 'state of nature'.[45] Pandemics are nothing new, then, but knowledge about combatting viruses constantly advances, accompanied by new technologies. And these advances in know-how bring new expectations and demands for governmental action. When there's a highly infectious and lethal disease, we're much less likely to argue that the state has no role to play and that individuals should shoulder the responsibility. It's useful then to look back at what's changed, and what hasn't changed, since 1918. The H1N1 virus responsible for the 1918–19 flu pandemic wasn't isolated until 1933; there was neither a vaccine nor an antiviral drug. The cause of death was often secondary bacterial pneumonia, but there were no antibiotics either.[46] Wartime troop movements and migration of refugees helped to spread the disease. There was at least a germ theory of disease and an understanding of contagion at that time. Hence, in many places there were publicly mandated measures to curb the pandemic, which included banning large gatherings, closing schools, distancing people in wards or barracks, disinfecting and ventilating buildings, moving work outdoors, and mask-wearing. These were often controversial and were not applied uniformly. They did help reduce mortality in some American cities, although their effects can't be disentangled from closures caused by people voluntarily staying home due to illness or fear of getting ill.[47]

Such personal and public hygiene measures were similar to those applied in 2020, although today's mass communication engenders greater public awareness. Furthermore, mobile devices make it possible for people to record their movements and receive warnings when they may have come into contact with the virus, and they make isolation at home easier. Despite today's in-depth scientific knowledge about virus transmission, lockdowns, social distancing and mask-wearing were still hotly debated by scientists, laypeople and politicians. Many countries' lockdown and vaccination policies were haphazard, inconsistent and reactive – or ineffective. An international study in *The Lancet* reported that lower Covid-19 infection rates were associated with higher levels of trust in government and trust in others, and with lower levels of corruption.[48] Lower trust meant less compliance with social distancing, vaccination and other measures required by government and hence higher infection rates. People were more likely to comply with orders from government if they trusted their government and trusted that others would comply too. Some of the antivaccine conspiracy theories, for example, saw the state as a threat to freedom and safety, rather than a provider of protection from disease. The techniques of government applied in the Covid-19 pandemic were both disciplinary (for example, working at home) and exclusionary (for example, vaccine passes). The pandemic exposed the Hobbesian deal: we protect life itself, so do as we say. Stay at home and get vaccinated, or suffer the consequences.

Conclusion

Ironically, a virus was causing the most profound changes in government at that time, even though it was a thing of nature with which no one could reason or negotiate, and which no one would have chosen. If we add climate change, it looks as if Nature herself was 'rebelling', forcing us to change the ways we govern. New technologies provide tools for dealing with problems like pandemics and climate change, but they also create their own political controversies. For example, there was a push to make vaccination universally available or even compulsory, but many people strongly objected and refused. Technologies (including AI) change what governments can do – and hence generate new debates about what they should or shouldn't do. These things disrupt the norms of government, and they are made all the harder to address when there's a lack of trust.

Whereas in Chapters 2 and 3 the reader may have gained a pessimistic view that the problems of government are ancient, enduring and insoluble, the present chapter has set out some areas where we've witnessed long-term historical improvements, even though the achievement may be patchy. There's a lot we know now about the qualities of good government and how to do it better. But humanity also faces problems of a kind that are historically unprecedented, some of which are the outcomes of technological innovation. Our own ingenuity gets the better of us and causes new challenges for law, policy and administration, and then we're back to grappling with multi-faceted moral and political issues that don't admit technical solutions. Our values and beliefs are ultimately what we rely on then. And the scary thing is that people are capable of believing some pretty weird things.

Notes

1 UN Office on Drugs and Crime. 2021. *Global Report on Trafficking in Persons 2020*. Vienna, URL: https://www.unodc.org/documents/data-and-analysis/tip/2021/GLOTiP_2020_15jan_web.pdf (accessed 14 September 2022).
2 In the ICC's favour, some cases were referred to it by the African nations themselves.
3 Rogers, Damien. 2018. *Law, Politics and the Limits of Prosecuting Mass Atrocity*. Cham: Palgrave Macmillam.
4 Paxton, Robert O. 2005. *The Anatomy of Fascism*. New York: Vintage Books.
5 The formal meeting lasted for a couple hours including lunch.
6 Browning, Christopher R. 2004. *The Origins of the Final Solution: The Evolution of Nazi Jewish Policy, September 1939–March 1942*. Lincoln: University of Nebraska Press. See p. 414.
7 Cesarani, David. 2016. *Final Solution*. UK: Pan Macmillan. See p. 548.
8 Aristotle. 1999. *The Politics*. London: Penguin, trans. T.A. Sinclair & T.J. Saunders. See p. 226, §1287a31.
9 Sempill, Julian. 2020. 'The Rule of Law and the Rule of Men: History, Legacy, Obscurity'. *Hague Journal on the Rule of Law* 12 (3): 511–40.

10 Carlton, Charles. 1995. *Charles I, the Personal Monarch*. London: Routledge; Parry, M. 2019. *Charles I*. London: Routledge. For an excellent narrative, listen to: Warren, Rebecca & Dan Snow. 31 January 2022. 'The Execution of Charles I'. *History Hit* podcast, URL: https://play.acast.com/s/dansnowshistoryhit/the executionofcharlesi (accessed 2 February 2022).
11 Roberts, Andrew. 2021. *The Last King of America: The Misunderstood Reign of George III*. London: Allen Lane.
12 Sempill [note 9].
13 It's complicated, as the US Constitution isn't clear on this. See: US Congress. No date. 'Constitution Annotated', URL: https://constitution.congress.gov/browse/essay/artII-S2-C3-2-4-1-1/ALDE_00001153/#essay-11 (accessed 14 September 2022).
14 Isaiah 45.
15 Thapar, Romila. 2012. *Aśoka and the Decline of the Mauryas*. Oxford: Oxford University Press.
16 Present-day Hindu nationalists don't regard the Mughal emperors with great pride, however. Akbar's great grandson Aurangzeb (r. 1658–1707) has been especially vilified in India lately, in part for imposing the Islamic *jizya* tax on infidels, including Hindus.
17 'Agreement of the People 1649'. Orthography has been modernised from version found at: Online Library of Liberty, URL: https://oll.libertyfund.org/page/leveller-anthology-agreements (accessed 5 January 2022).
18 Carlin, Norah. 2018. 'Lilburne, Toleration, and the Civil State'. In *John Lilburne and the Levellers*, ed. John Rees, 32–48. London: Routledge.
19 Adamson, Peter. 2022. 'Born to be Contrary: Toleration in the Netherlands'. *History of Philosophy* podcast, URL: https://historyofphilosophy.net/toleration-netherlands; Adamson, Peter. 2022. 'Believe at Your Own Risk: Toleration in France'. *History of Philosophy* podcast, URL: https://historyofphilosophy.net/toleration-france (both accessed 25 October 2022).
20 Locke, John 2003 [1689]. *Two Treatises of Government, and a Letter Concerning Toleration*, ed. I. Shapiro. New Haven: Yale University Press. See p. 220.
21 Ibid., p. 226.
22 Hibbert, Christopher. 1982. *The French Revolution*. London: Penguin.
23 Federici, Silvia. 2004. *Caliban and the Witch: Women, the Body and Primitive Accumulation*. Brooklyn, NY: Autonomedia; Waring, Marilyn. 1999. *Counting for Nothing: What Men Value and What Women Are Worth*. Toronto: University of Toronto Press.
24 Milanovic, Branko. 2016. *Global Inequality: A New Approach for the Age of Globalization*. Cambridge, MA: Harvard University Press.
25 OECD. 2015. *In It Together: Why Less Inequality Benefits All*. Paris: OECD Publishing, URL: https://doi.org/10.1787/9789264235120-en (accessed 14 September 2022).
26 World Bank. 2022. *Global Economic Prospects*, URL: https://openknowledge.worldbank.org/bitstream/handle/10986/36519/9781464817601.pdf (accessed 13 January 2022).
27 OECD. 2021. *Does Inequality Matter? How People Perceive Economic Disparities and Social Mobility*. Paris: OECD Publishing, URL: https://doi.org/10.1787/3023ed40-en (accessed 14 September 2022).
28 Scheidel, Walter. 2017. *The Great Leveler: Violence and the History of Inequality*. Princeton: Princeton University Press. See p. 165. Thomas Piketty agrees that 'the reduction of inequality that took place in most developed countries between 1910 and 1950 was above all a consequence of war and of policies adopted to cope with the shocks of war'. Piketty, Thomas. 2014. *Capital in the Twenty-First Century*. Cambridge, MA: Belknap Press. See p. 20.

29 Milanovic [note 24].
30 OECD [note 27].
31 Aklin, Michaël, Andreas Kern & Mario Negre. 2021. 'Does Central Bank Independence Increase Inequality?' Policy Research Working Paper, no. 9522. Washington, DC: World Bank, URL https://openknowledge.worldbank.org/handle/10986/35069 (accessed 25 October 2022).
32 Koch, Alexander, Chris Brierley, Mark M. Maslin & Simon L. Lewis. 2019. 'Earth System Impacts of the European Arrival and Great Dying in the Americas after 1492'. *Quaternary Science Reviews* 207: 13–36. See p. 30.
33 IPCC. 9 August 2021. 'Climate Change Widespread, Rapid, and Intensifying', URL: https://www.ipcc.ch/2021/08/09/ar6-wg1-20210809-pr/ (accessed 21 January 2022).
34 Elkins, James W. 1999. 'Chlorofluorocarbons'. Global Monitoring Laboratory, National Oceanic and Atmospheric Administration, URL: https://gml.noaa.gov/hats/publictn/elkins/cfcs.html (accessed 14 September 2022).
35 NASA. 2018. 'First Direct Proof of Ozone Hole Recovery Due to Chemicals Ban', URL: https://www.nasa.gov/feature/goddard/2018/nasa-study-first-direct-proof-of-ozone-hole-recovery-due-to-chemicals-ban (accessed 14 September 2022).
36 Lewis, Nathan S. 2007. 'Powering the Planet'. *MRS Bulletin* 32 (10): 808–20.
37 ICAO. 2022. 'About ICAO', URL: https://www.icao.int/about-icao/Pages/default.aspx (accessed 26 January 2022).
38 Duncan, Grant. 2019. *The Problem of Political Trust: A Conceptual Reformulation.* Abingdon: Routledge. See pp. 24–26.
39 Coeckelbergh, Mark. 2019. 'Artificial Intelligence: Some Ethical Issues and Regulatory Challenges'. *Technology and Regulation* 2009: 31–34, URL: https://doi.org/10.26116/techreg.2019.003; Stahl, B.C. 2021. *Ethical Issues of AI.* Springer, URL: https://doi.org/10.1007/978-3-030-69978-9_4 (both accessed 29 January 2022).
40 Pause Giant AI Experiments: An Open Letter. 23 March 2023. Future of Life Institute, URL: https://futureoflife.org/open-letter/pause-giant-ai-experiments/ (accessed 8 April 2023).
41 Our World in Data, URL: https://ourworldindata.org/covid-deaths#cumulative-confirmed-deaths-per-million-people (accessed 20 March 2023).
42 Great Barrington Declaration. 4 October 2020, URL: https://gbdeclaration.org/ (accessed 14 September 2022).
43 John Snow Memorandum. 14 October 2020, URL: https://www.johnsnowmemo.com/john-snow-memo.html (accessed 14 September 2022).
44 This author has been fully vaccinated and encourages others to do so.
45 Foucault, Michel. 1995. *Discipline and Punish: The Birth of the Prison.* New York: Vintage Books. See p. 199.
46 Martini, M., V. Gazzaniga, N. L. Bragazzi & I. Barberis. 2019. 'The Spanish Influenza Pandemic: A Lesson from History 100 Years After 1918'. *Journal of Preventive Medicine and Hygiene* 60 (1): E64–7, URL: https://doi.org/10.15167/2421-4248/jpmh2019.60.1.12 (accessed 1 February, 2022).
47 Bootsma, Martin C. J., & Neil M. Ferguson. 2007. 'The Effect of Public Health Measures on the 1918 Influenza Pandemic in U.S. Cities'. *Proceedings of the National Academy of Sciences* 104 (18): 7588–93, URL: https://doi.org/10.1073/pnas.0611071104 (accessed 17 November 2022).
48 COVID-19 National Preparedness Collaborators. 2022. 'Pandemic Preparedness and COVID-19: An Exploratory Analysis of Infection and Fatality Rates, and Contextual Factors Associated with Preparedness in 177 Countries, from Jan 1, 2020, to Sept 30, 2021'. *The Lancet* (online version), URL: https://doi.org/10.1016/S0140-6736(22)00172-6 (accessed 14 September 2022).

5

THE CRISIS OF BELIEF

In Chapter 3 we considered an ideal community where a widely shared belief system supports effective government – an ideal that's rarely, if ever, achieved. The imposition of one religious orthodoxy hasn't worked, but an alternative historical approach has been belief in the nation, or nationalism. Can we at least agree that, as a nation, 'we' are a going concern, and the state and its government are legitimate things, even though we may disagree with particular parties and policies? Self-determining nation-states and multi-ethnic states are the main model now, although there are exceptions (see Chapter 6, 'Quasi-states'). But citizens may hold differing visions for their nation: what it is, or was, or ought to become. And sometimes it all falls apart.

Ukraine was cited as an example in Chapter 3. Since well before the Russian invasion in 2022, Ukrainians were divided over how to see their nation. The Maidan revolution of 2014 strengthened the cause of those who wanted a European, liberal and civic version of nationhood. But the post-Maidan government didn't implement an internationally brokered agreement to end the civil war in the eastern provinces. The Minsk II agreement of 2015 stipulated decentralisation, local self-government and recognition of 'special status' in the Donetsk and Lugansk provinces (Donbas). Legislation was blocked by (sometimes violent) resistance from Ukrainian nationalists who saw the agreement as 'capitulation to Russia'. But other significant changes did occur. There was a programme of 'decommunisation' that included taking down statues of Lenin, changing placenames to eradicate the Soviet heritage and banning communist parties. Russian language and culture were discouraged in favour of Ukrainian, and a Ukrainian offshoot of the Orthodox Church gained recognition. The constitution was amended to shift from a 'nonaligned' status and to favour membership of the European Union and NATO. Inclusive civic

DOI: 10.4324/9781003439783-5

nationalism was combined with rejection and exclusion of those in Donbas who supposedly had failed to grasp what it meant to be Ukrainian. Nationalists in the western provinces might sometimes describe ethnic Russians in the eastern provinces as cattle or as slave-like. All Ukrainian citizens were Ukrainian, it seems, except for those who insisted on being Russian. The civil war that erupted in Donbas in 2014 was styled officially in Kyiv as an 'antiterrorist operation'; thousands of unarmed Ukrainian civilians, as well as armed rebels, were killed by Ukrainian forces.[1] Understandably, then, many Ukrainians were less concerned about what their nation was called than about achieving peace. The population was divided between pro-European and pro-Russian sides, with many taking neither side; but the civil war was both cause and symptom of an internal clash of beliefs about nationhood, as well as a grander imperial rivalry between NATO and Russia.

Polarised beliefs are more the norm in a society than the exception. Ukraine is a strong and tragically violent example, but every nation has its domestic struggles over how to narrate its history, represent itself to the world and envisage a positive future. Once these controversies combine with anger about rising inequality, conspiracy theories may emerge as explanations that address people's indignation and uncertainty.

For instance, it's known that the Russians had interfered in America's 2016 election, although we can't gauge just how much effect they had – and it was probably little. And Donald Trump had had business dealings in Moscow before he ran for president. It was thought, however, that the Kremlin may have had *kompromat* (compromising material) on Trump and hence could blackmail and control him. As for whether Trump was really the Kremlin's agent or 'useful idiot', and whether he conspired or collaborated with them, no firm evidence was forthcoming, despite a close investigation during impeachment proceedings against him. On Trump's side, his supporters saw him as a leader who wanted to restore pride in their nation. They believed that allegations against him (about collusion with Russia) were fabricated by people who wanted to defeat him, gain power for themselves and cover up their own crimes or their complicity with others' crimes. Many believed that Trump was leading a charge to expose wrongdoing and corruption in 'the deep state'. Allegations emerged, especially from the QAnon conspiracy theories, about a Satan-worshipping paedophile ring at the heart of American government, and that the 2020 election victory was stolen from Trump by electoral fraud. No evidence to substantiate either allegation was forthcoming. Support for conspiracy theories in general, and QAnon in particular, is difficult for surveyors to gauge, but it's a small minority.[2] Without explicitly endorsing it, Trump rode that wave, which peaked when he rallied a crowd that stormed the Capitol on 6 January 2021. Many participants in that mob believed, in return, that they were heeding the call of the commander-in-chief and doing what was right for their nation.

Political beliefs are evidently volatile, malleable and ambiguous, and we humans are gullible and sceptical by turns. So we need to understand belief itself, as we can see how doubts and controversies about what to believe can accelerate instability in government. This issue breaks down into two aspects: what I believe to be the case, and the persons in whom I believe.

Belief and disagreement

In Hans Christian Andersen's folktale 'The Emperor's New Clothes', two swindlers arrive at court offering the emperor a cloth so fine you can't even see it, and he's duped into parading through town in his invisible finery. The townsfolk admire (or pretend to admire) the amazing outfit, not wishing to appear ignorant or give offence. It takes a child to see through it and state the obvious: the Emperor has no clothes. That's now a common expression used to puncture the vanity, propaganda, vacuous words or deceptive rhetoric of leaders, to distance ourselves from those whom they've duped and make it known that we're not fooled by flimsy confidence tricks and carefully crafted appearances. The smart observers see the truth that underlies the public persona. We should lift the ideological veil to see what's really going on, and expose the vain, deceitful or incompetent political impostor and the manipulative backroom actors.

Of course one should be sceptical about political power and its superficial pretences or performances. Political leaders have to maintain social cohesion and economic confidence, but, at a time of crisis, their statements could amount to little more than a confidence *trick* that deserves to be exposed. Philosophical and scientific scepticism are necessary, moreover, for cultural, intellectual and technological change, for challenging political and religious dogmas, liberating alternative or previously suppressed ideas and exposing wrongdoing or manipulation. It often turns out that things aren't the way that we were officially told or taught at school, and the sceptic gains a mind-expanding freedom when this is exposed. But it's easy then to think that, behind the façade, there's something even bigger going on, including a concerted effort to conceal the truth. There's 'the deep state' or a 'global corporate cabal' or a 'hidden hand' behind historical events. These are conspiracy theories, defined as 'attempts to explain the ultimate causes of significant social and political events and circumstances with claims of secret plots by two or more powerful actors'.[3] Conspiracies do sometimes occur in fact, but a conspiracy *theory* imagines the existence of malign plots that have had to be concealed. In wishing not to be duped by the official version of events, the conspiracy theorist is susceptible to exaggerated or unfounded alternatives. Expose the 'deep state' and blindly follow QAnon, for instance. Or, as most of us don't fully understand viruses and vaccines, a reasonable hesitancy about vaccination may grow into beliefs that scientists lie, politicians are using it to control us, while journalists, academics and other experts are providing cover or being blackmailed into silence.

Linking many disparate actors and assigning ulterior motives to them, conspiracy theorists address uncertainty and anxiety about change over which they have no control. They imagine a sadistic and malign intent behind events, and relevant facts and inferences are marshalled accordingly. Conspiracy theories may be false, but they shouldn't be written off entirely, as they may express valid underlying needs for recognition or justice. A conspiracy theory usually has some factual or plausible elements, and it may address genuine uncertainty, anxiety or anger. It reaches an unrealistic paranoid level once too many unrelated facts get linked meaningfully together. QAnon was especially effective because it engaged people online in a shared effort to 'do your own research' and make new inferences.

In general, people will believe what they want to believe, when it fulfils their needs and expectations. It's not entirely ridiculous, moreover, to think that there's a powerful elite that's unaccountable to the people and that influences the course of events, that 'the system is rigged' against the less powerful majority, or that there's structural injustice and entrenched privilege. There isn't actually a cabal of Satan-worshipping paedophiles who are planning to overturn democracy in favour of one world government, but the Jeffrey Epstein story did lend that theory a useful fact. And, up to a point, scepticism about government is always warranted. Taken too far, though, this fosters implausible alternative explanations about who's really in control and what they're planning, and these narratives only get more elaborate, and hence more implausible, as they try to account for cover-ups. We shouldn't blindly accept official versions of events, as the powerful don't always act in our interests, but conspiracy theories are often adopted with a strength of conviction that reveals a deeper distrust. One may try to talk conspiracy theorists out of their convictions, but that often backfires, as it's seen as further evidence of the cover-up. Before trying to correct other people's mistaken beliefs, then, it pays to look at how conspiracy theories are an example of political belief in general: they're an outcome of otherwise 'normal' opinion-formation. A useful starting assumption might be that we're all already down one rabbit-hole or another. We just don't want to admit it.

What does it mean to believe?

The word *believe* has a dual purpose. If I say 'I believe you', then it may mean that I accept your opinion or account of events. I believe that something is the case, but I could change my mind, unless I'm firmly convinced that it's true. In contrast, if I say 'I believe *in* you', then I may be expressing loyalty and respect. I may believe what you say because it's you who says it: that is, I trust your judgement to such an extent that I can dispense with forming opinions independently and thus save myself the trouble of doing my own research. The same applies to political belief: it may refer to rational opinions (for example, about what steps we believe are necessary for the betterment of society) and/or to our non-rational loyalties to like-minded others and admired leaders – in whom we believe. Back in the seventeenth century the English political philosopher Thomas Hobbes pointed out this difference between believing what a person has said and believing in a person. The latter is synonymous with trusting and having faith. If we believe *in* a person, then we might accept uncritically, on trust, both the truth and the nonsense that they utter. And to do honour to a person entails trusting and believing them, and hence recognising their 'virtue and power'.[4] Hobbes understood the close relationship between trust, belief and power. He knew that people are gullible: we're often misled by trusting in powerful or famous people, rather than clearing our own pathway towards the truth. Perhaps the most important problem that Hobbes posed was not how 'nasty, brutish and short' life would be without a sovereign power, but how gullible we are and how we get led astray by divisive leaders, preachers and academics touting false ideas. He knew all about what we'd now call 'hate speech', 'fake news' and 'conspiracy theories', and saw how they inflamed civil strife in the 1640s. Hobbes saw how our beliefs (in something and *in someone*) maintain power-relations *and* create resistance and conflict.

Even the most reliable knowledge, however, requires a degree of faith or plausible belief. To navigate the world safely, we trust that our senses aren't making things up; in order to plan ahead, we infer that the future will largely resemble the past. Scientists begin from a belief in what their senses tell them; they rely on inferences that the lawfulness of the cosmos, as observed so far, will apply elsewhere in the universe and in future. Moreover, the scientist works within a specialised branch of research, and hence trusts the integrity of peers and the results they share. There have been instances of scientific fraud, but such betrayals show us how important this collegial trust is. The facts that scientific methods rely on trust in our senses and in colleagues, that genuinely scientific hypotheses are falsifiable, and hence that past findings are open to disproof, don't mean that we should dismiss scientific thought and evidence. Indeed, the opposite is the case: we need the openly sceptical but evidence-based thinking of modern science to give us some *confidence* in its findings. The fact that scientists argue with one another over methods and theories is a healthy sign, not a flaw.

When it comes to moral and political matters, however, we're on much shakier grounds. Our best ideas about ethics and politics haven't advanced greatly since ancient times, compared with revolutionary advances in the natural sciences. No era in history has lacked strong disagreements: even a death penalty didn't deter some people from expressing heretical beliefs. And our political beliefs aren't like blueprints or mental models that then get put into action in the way that a scientific discovery or theory can be applied to make new machines or products. Those who lead political change may assert that their beliefs represent the truth, but they adapt, compromise or even transform those beliefs in the process. The authors of the US Declaration of Independence, for instance, boldly asserted 'We hold these truths to be self-evident', but in practice they didn't treat all others as equals and basic rights weren't 'unalienable' for all. The path from political belief to action isn't always straight.

Similarly a system of government (implicitly or explicitly) institutionalises and imposes a belief system of one kind or another. Even if there's no strict state orthodoxy, the constitution and the law mark out the boundaries within which citizens exchange things and make choices. Any model of government and law permits certain kinds of conduct and prohibits others. For example, modern government normally prohibits payments or favours from officials to their family members, even though in earlier times and in indigenous cultures the favouring of kin was often considered necessary and honourable. Most people now believe it to be wrong; they call it corruption, and the law makes it a crime. This historical development represents a shift in predominant values and beliefs, and systems of public administration have institutionalised them.

To summarise so far, then: we should rely on the facts, of course, but often we don't. People are prone to believing the most implausible and evidence-free ideas. And anyway the facts don't tell us all we need to know when it comes to deciding what we ought to do next. Moral and political decisions can't be settled purely on facts and evidence. Ultimately our politics derive from what we believe, and not only from accepted facts. Furthermore, our beliefs aren't always reflected in what we actually do; we're not perfectly consistent with ourselves.

How political beliefs are formed

We sometimes attribute too much power to 'the powers that be',[5] thinking there's a control room or a shadowy cabal ('Them') exerting secret power. It's not as if power isn't ever wielded covertly, and sometimes classified information about state surveillance is uncovered.[6] There are elaborate operations called spying, after all. But the imagined figures inside a supposed cabal may be UN bureaucrats, Freemasons, the world's richest (as seen annually at Davos) or the military. In some of the worst versions, they're Satan-worshipping paedophiles or Jewish moneylenders. Some even say they're reptiles. There isn't such a cabal, but the image helps many people to reduce multi-faceted situations and complex events to easily understood narratives that resemble Hollywood epics with Manichean struggles between good and evil or truth and lies. In the real world, on the other hand, those in the thick of it at the pinnacle of institutional or governmental powers are more likely to be muddling through, reacting to the unexpected rather than controlling what you're thinking or doing. There are political strategists and spin-doctors who'd like to claim they're controlling how people think, but unexpected events and social movements show that any such effects are limited.

The fantasy of a 'shadowy cabal' or 'hidden hand' operating behind the scenes of world events – and manipulating them for some wicked purpose – is, however, a product of otherwise normal processes of perception and belief. To make sense of this, we should digress to consider human development. From infancy it takes some time to develop our senses and to coordinate them with bodily action. Our sensory-perceptual systems learn to construct coherent images and patterns from what would otherwise be a confusing cacophony or blur. One indispensable outcome of this is a stable self-awareness, or consciousness, such that the 'me' who wakes up in the morning is the same as that which fell asleep the night before. We weren't born with that consciousness; it had to develop. Moreover, we forget more than we remember. The processes of perception have to filter out more than they retain, but we constructively fill the gaps so we have a life story to tell and a coherent view of the world. The mind actively and predictively joins dots to make patterns, spaces, objects and so on, and we use one known thing to make sense of another. But this means we're also prone to joining too many dots, especially when things get complex, ambiguous and unpredictable.

Perception isn't just passively receptive, then: it's actively generative. Signals coming from around and from within the body are combined with and organised by prior expectations and beliefs working in feedback loops 'to minimize long-term average predictive error' and hence sustain an equilibrium between the body's physiological processes and a changing external environment.[7] Such self-regulation is essential for survival and for a stable sense of selfhood. And in order to stay within the range needed for safety and satiety, our actions will tend to reflect, and even to fulfil, our expectations and beliefs acquired from past learning. Moreover, in order to survive and thrive, our actions involve cooperation and communication with others – who perceive things differently. This system becomes dysfunctional, however, as we acquire beliefs or mental schemas that become maladaptive, as we all do to some extent. Genuinely dangerous delusions can arise from using fewer plausible prior beliefs to guide perception, or placing too much trust in implausible explanations.[8] Delusion and paranoia – and conspiracy theories – can become harmful, but they grow from otherwise normal information-processing.

Language is crucial to our ability to cooperate socially and to sustain the behavioural patterns, social norms and customs that support our survival and belonging. The child acquires the extraordinary abilities to understand and then to say complex and original sentences. Indeed, this learning process never really stops, but it takes off with remarkable speed in the early years. It's not long before the child declares, 'That's not fair!' and shows a developing moral rationality that will later be applied to more complex public affairs and social policy.[9] Our sensory and sense-creating capabilities combine to develop us as persons, and the faculty of speech enables us to ponder and debate the ethical and political questions of what's right, what's wrong and what's fair or just.

Our constructive sense-making and meaning-making capabilities can go awry, but the reality we occupy would be incoherent, if not unbearable, without them. What happens, then, when an implausible and unverifiable belief becomes an enforced social norm? A child may grow up in a family and community with strong religious or political beliefs, and hence her or his development will entail identification with those beliefs, given the deep implicit trust in parents and others on whom early life depends. The avoidance of harm or ostracism often requires the full internalisation of implausible beliefs by adults as well. This is evident in religions, as they require the faithful to believe in unobservable, miraculous and supernatural things. Religious beliefs have shaped how people are governed and have even been enforced by death penalties for heresy or blasphemy. But non-religious or atheistic political ideologies such as communism have also sometimes demanded belief in an improbable future state and have been forced onto whole populations. Many citizens of the Soviet Union really did believe that they were helping to build a better world. So the enforcement of religious beliefs and political ideologies, as conditions of social belonging and security, can result in people adopting implausible explanations of past events and expectations of a future redemption or salvation.

So far this has put a negative spin on the formation of political belief, but there's a positive side too. After all, we need and seek out like-minded friends and communities, and there's nothing inherently wrong if they influence our politics. Political beliefs and ideologies also stimulate positive ideas about a better society, either by proposing a vision for a new world or by invoking nostalgia for an imagined past that should be restored. Depending on one's politics, this may mean, for example, a sustainable and inclusive society, an innovative and competitive economy, or a cohesive and homogeneous nation. A full and final achievement of any such set of ideals, however, is always well out of reach, given the sheer complexity of things and people's competing values, needs and goals within any large community. Inevitably, disagreement and conflict emerge, sometimes to the point of violence.

What's not so readily noticed, however, is the way in which those who oppose or somehow frustrate the realisation of one's own ideal future are *helping* to build and sustain commitment to one's ideology. The political obstacle in the way of a better future (or reinstated past) is precisely what gives energy and relevance to the ideological fantasy. Racist nationalism needs unwanted migrants for its relevance as a political ideology. Fascism's persistence on the margins of society is paradoxically aided by its suppression. Green ecologism thrives on pointing to polluting industries and unsustainable consumption. Feminist ideology gains purpose and strength from patriarchy and toxic masculinity. Many of the basic aims of legal equality in first and second wave feminism having been achieved, subsequent generations could 'pocket' those gains and distance themselves from feminism – until unfinished business (such as sexual violence and income inequality) emerged as more work to do and rekindled the ideology. Liberalism was once a radical ideology but became mainstream in western societies, and so faded from view due to its normalisation. But the reappearance of authoritarian leaders gives it another boost as people feel the need to defend civil liberties. Success in achieving political goals may ironically reduce people's commitment to an ideology, until new obstacles arise – or can be found – to get them riled up again.

Social psychology of belief

It's not simply that people with strong visions for a better society look for a scapegoat when things don't head in their desired direction: an obstacle to the realisation of the dream is essential to sustaining the vitality and relevance of their ideology. Political beliefs are formed and confirmed in the face of opposition or resistance from others. Rather than bringing pre-existing values and beliefs to the public forum, antagonistic engagements in public debates and protests forge our values and beliefs. Ironically, we have our opponents to thank for helping us to discover and clarify what we stand for. And this is a communal process: that is, our political beliefs are formed through *differentiating from* others whom we oppose and also through *belonging to* a like-minded social group. For example, we're more likely to believe or support a proposition when it's heard from a person with whom we identify socially, or a leader whom we follow, than from a person who belongs to an opposing faction (even when it's the same proposition). Just as sports fans will loyally support their team through thick or thin, people are mentally prepared to ignore evidence or to interpret facts in ways that suit their political allegiances because it offers the psychic enjoyment of ardent loyalty and belonging. 'Political fans may be pursuing "private happiness" at the expense of truth.'[10]

Common political and religious beliefs are integral features of the groups with which we congregate and identify – allowing also for disagreements within the group. This connection between belief and belonging is especially strong within the family in which we were nurtured as children. Of course, many of us become rebels, but the psychological effort required to reject our upbringing only reminds us of how powerful it is. There can be occasions when we consciously set out to join (or to leave or rebel against) a group because its avowed beliefs are compatible (or incompatible) with our own beliefs; but the formation of our political beliefs, beginning in childhood, involves processes of identification, affiliation and differentiation that initially are not consciously chosen. We simply grow up with them. Political belief isn't often an autonomous set of choices made rationally from scratch.

Opinion polls and social surveys are mainly based on asking individual adults predetermined questions. They give us insights into values and beliefs preferred by different groups when the results are aggregated, but they don't readily capture how our beliefs arise in our social settings or how we develop or change our beliefs over time. Our basic values and political beliefs are formed through our belonging to a family and community and through our trust in others to whom we look for guidance, such as favourite teachers or influential authors. The ability to express firm opinions as an individual and rationally to justify them as more or less true emerges as we mature, and this may eventually include rejection of or separation from the family and community in which we grew up, along with its traditions, values and beliefs. More often, though, people's beliefs are not very coherent or well founded. 'Some political views are authentic and tenaciously held; others are nonattitudes, casually expressed or made up on the spot; and the rest are subject to manipulation and reversal, as well as to education.'[11]

So, beliefs work for us in more ways than just expressing or representing attitudes, needs or convictions. Our own and others' expressed opinions act as signals of partisan loyalty and social group membership. When it comes to politics and public policy, a large proportion of people don't think very deeply in abstract or evidence-based terms, they lack time to absorb and analyse complex information, and so they fall back on their trusted social group or friends. Such communities are now readily found through digital devices and social media.[12] Social belonging and shared beliefs reinforce one another, and so even false or delusional beliefs or conspiracy theories can sometimes be adaptive if they help to maintain group cohesion and belonging.[13] 'People tend to conform their beliefs and attitudes to those around them, particularly when they view others as similar to themselves. In politics, people often prefer to hold the same beliefs as those they want to associate with.'[14] And vice versa, people prefer to associate with those who hold the same or similar beliefs. Hence, the expression of compatible political beliefs is one way to gain and keep our membership of a social network. The expression of incompatible beliefs, or the failure to repeat an opinion held passionately by others, can result in being ostracised from a group. And social groups generally have leaders.

Following the leader

What, then, about the prominent person in whom I might believe? An important social feature of political belief and group affiliation is leadership. We sometimes have strong feelings – positive or negative – about political leaders, attributing to them either benevolent or malignant knowledge and intent that may exceed the power and control that they actually wield; or we may attribute any of their actions that we disapprove of (or their failures) to shadowy figures that must have influenced, manipulated or undermined them. Such beliefs can be reality-based to an extent but, as the imagination fills the gaps in order to account for our own frustrations or lack of knowledge about events, beliefs may form that are so irrational that they fail to support our needs. (It's better to risk dying of respiratory disease, for example, than to take the corrupt government's dangerous vaccine.) And these strong feelings can be encouraged by others. If the leaders in whom we trust are genuinely striving to serve the public interest, then a strong affiliation with them may not be a bad thing. But, as we know too well from instances of dictatorship, people may place their faith in a leader who pushes delusional ideas and pursues destructive goals.

One guide to this is a philosopher who experienced fascism in Germany and later sought to understand why so many people had swallowed it. Theodor Adorno (1903–69) was born in Frankfurt, Germany, to a Catholic mother and a Protestant father who was an assimilated Jew. He was forced into exile in 1934 after being denied employment on racist grounds, and returned in 1949. He was an important figure in the Frankfurt School of critical social research, influenced by existentialist and psychoanalytical theories. Adorno suggested that the personality of the individual fascist leader may be less important than the reactions of the crowds.[15] To relate to this, think of the pleasure we can get in a sports crowd through the emotional highs and lows of victory or defeat, or at a rock concert when we're moved collectively by music. Such gatherings allow us to loosen inhibitions and to experience things that we don't experience alone or during routine activities. In an ecstatic crowd, an individual can suspend reason and experience rebellious, daring or sublime feelings. In the case of the fascist crowd, Adorno argued, this meant a 'rebellion against civilization', but not by returning to a 'primitive' state. Instead, uncivil psychological forces are aroused 'in and by civilization itself'.[16] Fascist gatherings employed the latest technology and sophisticated stage management; fascist leaders embraced the modern. The emotions that were unleashed led to violent political action, but this was in the context of an advanced culture, not a return to a pre-civilised or 'barbaric' state. Rather than explain such mass psychology in regressive terms such as 'herd instinct' or 'tribalism', Adorno reminds us that the societies that went down this road had refined cultures that supported individuality and personal autonomy. Like the crowd that gathers for an ecstatic experience at a rock concert, 'the masses' of fascist politics are an effect, not a cause. People have to be gathered and an elaborate performance has to be orchestrated to create the effect. One only has to watch Leni Riefenstahl's Nazi propaganda movie *Triumph of the Will* (1935) to see this. The question, then, is: how does a large developed society of individuals (almost all strangers to one another) become transformed into a group that unites around violent objectives? What do they gain?

Immersion in such a mass phenomenon works for people psychologically by permitting a loosening of the constraints required of them normally as individuals with limited goals and responsibilities. A surrender to the crowd allows people to enjoy feelings that they couldn't otherwise experience, and even to put them into action, including the enjoyment of subjection to an authority. Subjection is attractive as the leader is promising that obedience will lead (vicariously or even personally) to actions that were previously forbidden, as violence will be permitted against those who are deemed to be inferior, treacherous or alien. 'The leader image gratifies the follower's twofold wish to submit to authority and to be the authority himself.'[17] The fascist leader says and does things that were otherwise impermissible, and is loved for it. His unbridled and transgressive conduct has a dual effect: it threatens violence and it promises enjoyment.[18]

In any cohesive political movement, followers identify with leaders and with one another. Idealisation of a leader occurs when followers see in that person an aspect of themselves that's poorly realised or underdeveloped. They imagine that the leader can make up for a lack or insufficiency that was causing them discomfort, indignation or a sense of inferiority. Personal and collective failures to realise ideals are projected onto the leader who implicitly promises redemption and fulfilment through compliant followership. The irritation caused by the obstacles in the way of achieving shared ideals is made to disappear (at least for the moment) by this special leader who seems both flawed and superior at the same time. The leader resembles the followers in many ways and is made attractive to them through orchestrated occasions in which they can express without inhibition the ideas and feelings that were latent within them. Fascist rhetoric is emotive and anti-intellectual. So the fascist leader doesn't come across as intellectually superior to the followers, while submission to this 'great little person' paradoxically enables them to feel powerful. By belonging to the mass movement, the weak gain an imagined superiority to outsiders or minorities who may be dehumanised as 'vermin'. This emotional investment requires a violent reaction against anyone who debunks its values. Hence, among the group members themselves, a repressive egalitarianism prevails: everyone should believe and want much the same things. In order to be outstanding no one may stand out from the crowd. After all, it's the individual's investment in the crowd that gives him or her access to extraordinary experiences and aspirations.

It's not enough to describe dictatorship as a cult of personality. We need also to understand the psychological pay-off for followers, without whom a dictator would remain an obscure individual. The Faustian deal between the fascist leader and the crowd is a pathological version of attachments that occur in politics everywhere. Most people identify with a political group, party or faction and hence they identify, more or less closely, with a leader who evokes unrealised ideals by letting them dream (alongside others) of a hoped-for fulfilment or redemption. Up to a certain point, this isn't dangerous. The twentieth-century dictators, however, notably Mussolini, Hitler, Stalin and

Mao, were autocrats who led destructive political movements that came to pervade society. Disloyalty to the party was considered a betrayal of the nation itself and could be severely punished.

In multi-party competitive systems, by contrast, the post of prime minister or president has a limited term, and the people are periodically given a choice, the aim of which was always to prevent tyranny. In many such countries, however, we've seen the polarisation of parties or factions. Loyalty to the party becomes an end in itself, and opponents attack one another as if they were enemies, rather than rationally debate values, policies and goals as fellow citizens. Even before Donald Trump put himself forward for the presidency, this kind of polarisation was well advanced in the United States.[19] Trump mobilised the crowd effect described above to gain a critical mass of support in rallies and on social media. In the context of America's two-party political system, racist authoritarianism (even if it disavows its own racism) had entrenched itself, and Trump gave expression to that. The emergence of authoritarian nationalism within other nominally 'democratic' systems, such as Hungary and India, bears some similarities. In most western European countries authoritarian leaders have flourished, but proportional representation systems kept them isolated in far-right parties and outside of parliamentary majorities. The electoral victory of Brothers of Italy in 2022 broke that trend. (I return to the Italian example in Chapters 6 and 8.) Underlying these political developments were the loss of trust in government and politicians and a widespread dissatisfaction with representative government.

How can we resolve this? Getting everyone to agree on the same set of values isn't going to work. Societies are politically and culturally diverse. So it won't help to reject fellow citizens with whom we disagree, as if they were beyond the pale. What we can aim for is a working level of political trust.

Political trust

I'll make the case that good government builds trust and expands our freedom. This counteracts those widely heard contemporary complaints that, on one side, trust is in decline and that, on the other, governments only ever interfere with our freedoms. Conventional social science literature on trust in government mostly relies on surveys that 'measure' trust as if it were an opinion that anyone would hold. What is this opinion supposedly about, then? It's normally defined as a belief or a wager that others are predisposed to act in my interests, and not against them. Acting in my interests, or at least not harming me when I'm vulnerable, is trustworthy behaviour, and so I should only trust those whom I judge to be so inclined. But if trust is an opinion about how trustworthy others are ('I trust you because I figure you can be trusted'), then it's a circular and fallacious judgement. Instead I prefer to think of a socially systemic political trust that emerges (or deteriorates) from the ongoing observances of (or failures to observe) mutual understandings and obligations, or promises and their fulfilment, between and among individuals, groups and state institutions. This is an infinitely complex and ever-changing systemic phenomenon, rather than a set of individuals' opinions. Like value or meaning, it's not something we can point to, and it's not always formalised in rules or laws, but we know that it matters.

Effective government has always been a battle for 'hearts and minds', and there are different ways to secure our trust and compliance. But we aren't just a multitude of individuals, each with his or her subjective hopes and fears. Instead, our government works in dynamic relational ways, involving much competition and cooperation among people, some of which is informal or customary, and some under formal law and policy. Inasmuch as this continues to work in any society, there's a (never fully satisfactory) sense of equity between social groups, and a conditional trust between the people who are governed and those who govern. The deal could be, for example: pay taxes and get public services in return; abide by laws and trust that most others will do so too, most of the time. Effective government relies on a complex set of promises (to protect, to deliver, to comply, etc.) on which we expect others to act, and on which we too should act. But promises get broken, people feel betrayed and disillusionment may grow. Wasting public money or abusing privileges of high office are justifiable causes of anger. And many people feel betrayed or abandoned due to widening inequality, ongoing discrimination or fears about global warming. Even the most ancient law codes created mutual obligations between wealthy ruling elites and the poor and vulnerable, the orphans and widows, in terms such as: we protect you, so you obey our law, or else. Naturally, we also hope for a better deal, and in modern times this might be presented as: we promise you a prosperous future, so vote for us.

The social contract theories of the European Enlightenment advanced the idea that, in order to benefit from government, we traded off some 'natural' liberty in order to gain civil rights and protections. But there's nothing in nature that makes us free, as compared with, say, being dependent on others for our survival and security. And indeed, moralists would lecture us not to be slaves to our natural or animal passions. It does make sense, however, to say that the enjoyment of freedoms in a community is much easier if we can trust most other people and especially those who govern. To trust others, though, we have to assume that they're free too, just like ourselves. If trusting is better than force or bribery, it means respecting others' freedom to make their own choices, on the assumption that they'll pay us the same respect in return. The law trusts us as freely consenting agents, as well as holding us to account for wrongs, thus expanding our self-awareness by recognising our liberty. The law doesn't only limit our freedoms, it also outlines what freedom means in practice, sometimes simply by being silent on a matter. Often we resist, refuse or object to a law or a regime, but that's in keeping with our assumption of freedom. So, government isn't an institution set up as an alternative to an anarchic state of nature in which we were free but not safe. There's no past era that we know of in which people lived without being governed by norms and rules in association with others.

Governing people well, then, requires a complex reciprocity or political trust that develops and upholds a sense of justice. This trust is apparently in decline in many places, reflected in political polarisation, misconduct by some leaders and our genuine fears about the future. Political leaders have been guilty of lies and hypocrisy; people's hopes have been dashed by inequalities and insecurity; many are left with a sense of betrayal and broken promises. Social surveys, especially from the United States,[20] show a long-term decline of trust in government, although this is not uniform across all countries. The onset of the Covid-19 pandemic, for example, boosted trust in incumbent governments and leaders in many countries, for a while.[21] There's a paradox though: it's great if you and others basically trust your government, but, at the same time, modern constitutions are based on the very sound idea that *we should trust no one* with unchecked powers. It's rational to distrust the powerful, and the history of tyranny and dictatorship proves that. A blind or childlike trust in leaders isn't what we should be aiming for. If we agree that political power is entrusted by people, this can only be a conditional and limited form of trust. To trust those who govern, we begin from distrust, and so we limit powers by separating them and granting them only temporarily. Elected officials should seek re-election; appointed officials can be dismissed for poor performance. The idea that anyone personally owns the powers and privileges of office is (or should be) a thing of the past. Public power is harder to abuse when those in office are accountable for performing a limited set of duties. So, a healthy distrust is a kind of default setting for us, but political trust can be – and must be – earned.[22] (I return to this in Chapter 8.)

Another important feature of political trust is an apparent gap between beliefs and actions. Suppose, for example, that people with a strong libertarian mindset say that they trust no one at all in government and that they never vote, but they enjoy the freedom that their automobiles give them. Hence they lawfully hold drivers' licences, see themselves as safe drivers, and expect others to drive according to the rules, traffic lights to function and police to show up after accidents and so on. Their 'trust in government' is very low, if asked by a surveyor, but their active and implicit trust in the things that governments do may be quite high. The Covid-19 vaccines highlighted a similar gap. It's rational to be wary of new technologies and of governments, and so it wasn't foolish to query the safety of the new vaccines. For some, however, rational scepticism turned into irrational conspiracy theories about plots by the state to control or even kill people, revealing a much deeper distrust. But these sceptics weren't necessarily expressing such deep distrust about, for example, food hygiene in their local supermarkets, even though it's the job of much the same governmental agencies and health officials to make sure that the food we buy is safe. Regardless of our negative opinions about 'government', we implicitly trust many complex systems that are governed by institutions of the state, including currencies and systems of payments. We're more likely to say we trust the local public servants we work with in everyday life than the institution that employs them, and it'd be hard to live a normal life if we never trusted these systems or their employees. This is not to try to airbrush away the problem of political trust. It's a genuine problem; we just need to appreciate its complex and paradoxical nature.

There's been enough historical experience in the arts of government to show us how to build political trust. We know that a system that lets personal ambition and egotism overcome concern for the common good and that lets corrupt competitors rise to the top is one that rational people don't trust. They are then less likely to vote, leaving the field open to candidates who profit from distrust and who attack the 'rigged system' in terms such as 'drain the swamp'. If we consider the current problem of government in terms of political trust, then we can ask what could be done to restore that trust, knowing that we're aiming for a conditional, limited and transparent form of trust-building. Trust isn't a thing that one can literally break and then rebuild. But the aim of restoring political trust is complicated by our reliance on political leaders to rebuild our trust in them. It's all very well to propose that 'we' should do certain things to restore trust, but this process is itself a task of government, and so the 'broken' system should fix itself. The leaders whom people distrust have to seek consent to changes that, it's hoped, will restore trust. Why would the people believe them to start with? And there's no quasi-divine legislator or super-virtuous ruler who'll come to our aid and fix it for us. There's no college where politicians learn about rebuilding trust as if it were a technical or administrative task. Rebuilding trust in government needs slow, hard work, rather than heroic wins. Quick and effective responses to sudden disasters can help, due to the so-called 'rally round the flag' effect, but the gains may not last. The surveyed boost in Americans' trust after 9/11, for example, was short-lived. With these reservations in mind, one can make some initial conclusions.

Conclusion

One-party systems justify themselves on the grounds that factionalism is bad and harmony and solidarity are good. While they can engender a high level of trust (as in China), they're authoritarian and they demand respect for hierarchy and nationality. Multi-party competitive systems are, in contrast, adversarial, and they create incentives to polarise opinion and not to give any quarter to opponents. Listening to opposing viewpoints and collaborating 'across the aisle', however, can help to rebuild political trust, without giving up on the freedom to express dissenting opinions. It does mean refraining from some short-term political point-scoring.

Formal controls and transparency around money and conflicts of interest are of course important, but trusted leadership requires active willingness to submit to controls, rather than just passive compliance. This is part of a wider search for leadership that's oriented towards the common good rather than self-interest or partial, class-based interests. This has been a concern since ancient times (see Chapter 3) and there's no formula for getting it right.

It's often said that 'all politics is local politics'.[23] All of us, including political leaders, regardless of how high up the ladder, come from some place (or places) where we had our formative experiences, developed our political beliefs and drew motivation and support for careers. And people's most tangible experiences of public services come from interactions with local offices and services. Locality still matters. So an outlook on national or global issues needs to be accompanied by connection with people in their local communities. A common cause of distrust is the experience of not being heard, and the best place to begin that listening is at the local level, in person, rather than through social media.

Those are just three initial suggestions towards getting better, more trust-worthy government. At a time when governments face unprecedented global challenges (such as climate change and AI) we're also witnessing a decline of trust and confidence in government. The fact that there's been at least some historical progress in understanding and achieving good government should give us some optimism that further improvement is possible. The trouble is that the system that's lost the trust of many people is the system that we expect to fix itself and to restore that trust. And trust isn't a thing that resides in us. *Political trust is a quality of social relations that's subjectively evaluated, based on what we do.* But people don't all perceive and evaluate things in the same way.

The philosopher A.C. Grayling has argued that, to achieve global agreements on the big issues confronting humanity, we need an agreement on a set of values. He asks, 'Is a system of universally acceptable values possible?'[24] My short answer is 'No', as no society has ever universally accepted one system of values, and it's safe to infer that none ever will, let alone the whole world. But this doesn't mean that societies have never been capable of collective action towards common goals. In the best communities there are disagreements and differences, but they're well enough governed that pragmatic agreements are made and differences are reconciled. The real problem is one of government, then, and any good-enough government reaches agreements or settlements because of our disagreements about values, interests and priorities. *Regulation of complex concerns in the face of disagreements defines good government.* So we don't need, and we'll never find, a universally acceptable system of values and beliefs. We do need better government to manage the differences. This doesn't require one world government, as international agreements are achievable without it, and people still want their indigenous, local, regional and national institutions. But, as we'll see in the next chapter, there are different ideas about the 'correct' form of government.

Notes

1 Zhuravlev, Oleg & Volodymyr Ishchenko. 2020. 'Exclusiveness of Civic Nationalism: Euromaidan Eventful Nationalism in Ukraine'. *Post-Soviet Affairs* 36 (3): 226–45, URL: https://doi.org/10.1080/1060586X.2020.1753460; Ishchenko, Volodymyr. January–April 2022. 'Towards the Abyss'. *New Left Review* 133/ 134: 17–39, URL: https://newleftreview.org/issues/ii133/articles/volodymyr-ishchenko-towards-the-abyss.pdf (both accessed 19 November 2022).
2 Rogers, Kaleigh. 2021. 'Why It's So Hard To Gauge Support For QAnon'. *Five Thirty Eight*, URL: https://fivethirtyeight.com/features/why-its-so-hard-to-gauge-support-for-qanon/ (accessed 7 June 2023).
3 Douglas, K. M., J. E. Uscinski, R. M. Sutton, A. Cichocka, T. Nefes, C. S. Ang & F. Deravi. 2019. 'Understanding Conspiracy Theories'. *Political Psychology* 40 (S1): 3–35. See p. 4.
4 Hobbes, Thomas. 1998 [1651]. *Leviathan*. Oxford: Oxford University Press. See p. 60, ch. X.27. Other relevant passages of *Leviathan* are in chapters V.19, VII.5, XI.18.
5 Romans 13:1, King James version. 'The powers that be are ordained of God.'
6 The revelations about the NSA by Edward Snowden are a prime example. Greenwald, Glenn. 2014. *No Place to Hide: Edward Snowden, the NSA, and the U.S. Surveillance State*. New York: Metropolitan Books.
7 Hohwy, Jakob & Anil Seth. 2020. 'Predictive Processing as a Systematic Basis for Identifying the Neural Correlates of Consciousness'. *Philosophy and the Mind Sciences* 1 (2): 1–34, URL: https://doi.org/10.33735/phimisci.2020.II.64 (accessed 21 September 2022). See p. 12.
8 Stuke, Heiner, Veith Andreas Weilnhammer, Philipp Sterzer & Katharina Schmack. 2019. 'Delusion Proneness is Linked to a Reduced Usage of Prior Beliefs in Perceptual Decisions'. *Schizophrenia Bulletin* 45 (1): 80–6. See p. 80.
9 McAuliffe, Katherine, Peter R. Blake & Felix Warneken. 2017. 'Do Kids Have a Fundamental Sense of Fairness?' *Scientific American (online version)*, URL: https://blogs.scientificamerican.com/observations/do-kids-have-a-fundamental-sense-of-fairness/ (accessed 8 February 2022).
10 Somin, Ilya. 2016. *Democracy and Political Ignorance: Why Smaller Government Is Smarter*. Stanford CA: Stanford Law Books. See p. 95.
11 Kinder, Donald R. 2006. 'Belief Systems Today'. *Critical Review* 18 (1–3): 197–216, URL: https://doi.org/10.1080/08913810608443657 (accessed 21 September 2022). See p. 214.
12 Fisher, Max. 2022. *The Chaos Machine: The Inside Story of How Social Media Rewired Our Minds and Our World*. New York: Little, Brown.
13 Douglas et al. [note 3].
14 Hannon, Michael & Jeroen de Ridder. 2021. 'The Point of Political Belief'. In *The Routledge Handbook of Political Epistemology*, ed. M. Hannon & J.D. Ridder, 156–66. London: Routledge. See pp. 157–58.
15 Adorno, Theodor. 1982 [1951]. 'Freudian Theory and the Pattern of Fascist Propaganda'. In *The Essential Frankfurt School Reader*, ed. Andrew Arato & Eike Gebhardt, 118–37. New York: Continuum.
16 Ibid., p. 122.
17 Ibid., p. 127.

18 Although Trump isn't a fascist, as he doesn't glorify war and opposes state regulation, he had a similar appeal, and he used the live rally accordingly. The hot-mic recording in which he obscenely boasted that he could 'grab them by the pussy' was followed by the even more telling assertion that 'you can do anything'. If you follow him, he promised, the impermissible is permitted.

19 Hetherington, Marc & Thomas J. Rudolph. 2015. *Why Washington Won't Work: Polarization, Political Trust, and the Governing Crisis.* Chicago: University of Chicago Press.

20 The Pew Research Centre has US survey data on trust in government from 1958 onward, URL: https://www.pewresearch.org/

21 Bol, Damien, Marco Giani, André Blais & Peter John Loewen. 2021. 'The Effect of COVID-19 Lockdowns on Political Support: Some Good News for Democracy?' *European Journal of Political Research* 60 (2): 497–505; Goldsmith, Shaun, Robin Gauld & Ross Taplin. 12 February 2021. 'Trust in Government Soars in Australia and New Zealand During Pandemic'. *The Conversation*, URL: https://theconversation.com/trust-in-government-soars-in-australia-and-new-zealand-during-pandemic-154948 (accessed 14 September 2022).

22 Kettl, Donald F. 2017. *Can Governments Earn Our Trust?* Cambridge UK: Polity Press.

23 This saying seems to have been coined by the American columnist Byron Price (1891–1981) in 1932. See: Popik, Barry. 13 June 2009. 'All Politics Is Local', URL: https://www.barrypopik.com/index.php/new_york_city/entry/all_politics_is_local/ (accessed 14 September 2022).

24 Grayling, A.C. 2022. *For the Good of the World: Is Global Agreement on Global Challenges Possible?* Oneworld Publications.

6

MODELS OF GOVERNMENT TODAY

What different forms or styles of government – what solutions to the problem of government – are practised in the world today? I'll sketch out some of the major – and some minor – models of government, but this isn't meant to create a firm or complete typology. Mainly, I'll distinguish democracy from representative government, and consider the self-limiting and the progressive versions of the latter before going on to authoritarian government, especially the Chinese and Russian versions. An important goal here is to consider the wide variety of models, styles and aims of government in the present, including indigenous government. We aren't stuck in a single form of social and political order, despite norms about the international recognition of states.

Democracy

Pericles (ca 495–29 BCE) was the level-headed general and leader of Athens at its height, but he elicited respect and ill-feeling by turns from the citizens, and he got to the top by having his main rival, Cimon, formally banished. As his younger contemporary and supporter Thucydides put it, Pericles respected the people's liberty, but wasn't afraid to admonish them.

> It was he who led them, rather than they who led him, and, since he never sought power from any wrong motive, he was under no necessity of flattering them. In what was nominally a democracy, power was really in the hands of the first citizen.[1]

Pericles' successors 'adopted methods of demagogy', however, abandoned his cautious strategy and lost control of affairs. Scholars still debate whose

DOI: 10.4324/9781003439783-6

fault it was, but the Athenians were persuaded by Alcibiades (ca. 450–04 BCE) to invade Sicily – where they suffered calamitous defeat – and their democratic government was temporarily suspended by an oligarchy. 'The Four Hundred' were given 'full powers to govern as they thought best [...] choosing by lot officers from among themselves to deal with the Council business [and] they ruled the city with a strong hand'.[2]

There's a tendency to idealise Athens as the birthplace of democracy, but it was also a patriarchal slave-owning imperial power, it underwent intense political rivalries and changes, and it produced opportunistic leaders such as Alcibiades. On a literal translation from Greek, democracy means that power is vested in the people. But how did the people (the free male citizens) rule? For Aristotle, it meant that the poor majority of free men ruled in their own interests, which led to class conflict and didn't always promote the common good. The Athenian democratic constitution of that time, in which free men contributed (in large numbers) to public forums and administrative bodies, doesn't resemble the representative systems with competitive elections and professional civil services that we see today. But some shared features are: when a matter was put to the vote, each vote had equal value; the law applied to all equally; political decisions were written for all to see; people were tried in open court. The idea that there's a historical inheritance from ancient Athens, via republican Rome and Florence, to the United States shouldn't be taken uncritically, however, as these forms of government are all quite different, constitutionally and culturally.

Contemporary accounts of democracy often focus on processes such as elections, referendums and open deliberation in assemblies. For example, after a full and open debate, a people's assembly may vote for or against a proposed law or policy. In an ideal democracy, each citizen would have an opportunity to help shape the agenda and to speak or to choose a spokesperson. While matters may be decided by a majority vote, a thoroughgoing democracy would ensure that minorities aren't always overruled; it would recognise their needs and rights with special measures to equalise opportunities, especially if there've been historical injustices. All votes would be of equal value; all voters could learn about the issues at stake and the likely consequences of alternative courses of action. They'd be free to express differing ideas without fear.[3] While full participation would be open to all adults, there could also be forums for hearing children. Ideally, then, there'd be effective and open participation in deliberative processes 'in which people come together, on the basis of equal status and mutual respect, to discuss the political issues they face and, on the basis of those discussions, decide on the policies that will then affect their lives'.[4] In a democracy, 'all affected by collective decisions should have an opportunity to influence the outcome'.[5] Each citizen would also have an equal chance (or obligation) to participate in the administration and hence in the implementation of the assembly's decisions. These governmental offices might be rotated regularly or assigned by lottery. Democratic government, then, would be a part of our everyday lives. From this kind of decision-making and administrative system we could expect to get outcomes that best reflect the diverse values and needs of the people and hence serve the common good. But have you ever experienced such democratic government? If you have, it's likely to have been on a local level or concerning only a limited range of issues – not at the level of a modern state with a population of many millions. The ideal model of democracy described above is really only feasible on a small scale or for special purposes.

In today's 'democracies' most people are unaware of many of the decisions that are being made on their behalf, and they have little or no influence over them anyway. The modern era has seen, beyond formal institutions of government, the growth of a 'civil society' in which independent groups and organisations monitor what governments are doing, and this gives some reassurance that those elected to make decisions can be held to account. The watchdogs will bark and the media will amplify them. Economic and political inequalities are so profound, however, that relatively few people have the time, knowledge and resources to have any practical influence on public affairs. Public opinion does matter, as any political party will aim to maximise votes, but a large proportion of people don't vote, and elections or referendums may be hijacked by well-financed campaigns. So the majority have little direct influence. The opinions of a majority of Americans, for instance, are less likely to be reflected in policy outcomes than those of economic elites or organised interest groups. Similarly, in European countries the preferences of high-income citizens are more likely to be reflected in policy changes than those of low-income citizens.[6] People's influence on the adoption of policies is unequally distributed, favouring the wealthy. In a contemporary capitalist society, people do enjoy many freedoms, but their government largely happens above their heads and isn't entirely democratic in terms of knowledge, influence and participation. A rule of law that protects property inherently works in the interests of those who own the most property, and the wealthiest can deploy their lobbying power to ensure that their assets won't be seized by the state or redistributed to the poor.

Even in a small, genuinely democratic group, some individuals will lead the debate while others listen in silence; only a few will take responsibility for the mundane tasks of administration; while processes in which everyone has a voice may not always be harmonious. Giving people full and equal opportunity to debate the issues that affect them also gives them ample opportunity to get sidetracked by misinformation, defend partial interests, fall out with one another and divide into opposing sides. Ever since Socrates' time, the individualism and factionalism of democracies have troubled political thinkers. At the birth of the American republic, James Madison wasn't alone among the framers in his concern that a 'pure democracy' would become factionalised and disorderly, and the US Constitution doesn't mention democracy at all.[7]

The aim was instead to form a federal republic with elected representatives and an elected president who would make law and policy on behalf of the people. The people were to be kept out of actually governing; they could at most be trusted to elect 'the best' candidates ('a chosen body of citizens') who would then judge what's in their common interests.[8] The people can vote (or not vote) and then get on with their private lives and largely forget about the troublesome details of government, until something goes wrong or until the next election.

Representative government

The primary type of government considered here is *representative*, then. Representative assemblies emerged in the Middle Ages as monarchs summoned nobles, warlords and bishops, to gain their consent to taxes and levies in order to wage wars. Gradually these assemblies became more independent in passing law and approving public finance. Under a modern representative government, a few people are elected to pass laws and regulations, while a much larger cohort of anonymous appointed experts and managers offer advice and implement the decisions. The people at large have little to do with governing but, by the twentieth century, the universal franchise and 'one person, one vote' at least gave them a say. Hence the people pass judgement on their representatives, as individuals or parties, for whatever reasons they wish, at each election. This may be a 'least bad' compromise for governing large capitalist societies, as it emerges from the preferences of the people and then seeks, in principle, to meet their needs and serve their interests. Authors who've written in favour of and against democracy[9] habitually confuse representation by election with democracy itself, even though representation leads to government by the few on behalf of the many, rather than government by the majority themselves. Election is only one among many methods of decision-making that a true democracy could employ, and even authoritarian systems stage elections. You don't need elections to be a democracy; people can, however, elect undemocratic leaders. Elections and democracy don't necessarily go together. So why do we call representative government democratic? There are two historical reasons: the belief that the French and American revolutions had begun a historical trend towards equality (and against monarchy and aristocracy), and the successful struggles for the universal adult franchise.

The non-egalitarian claim that only independent free men who owned property should vote rested on a belief that others had no stake in government and lacked political judgement because of their dependence. Representation was an aristocratic model in that a wealthy elite were supposed to elect the best from among their ranks. On the other hand, for eighteenth-century Americans, 'the word "democracy" retained an unequivocally negative connotation'.[10] In the early decades of the republic, a 'democrat' was someone who supported individual sovereignty and states' rights and who opposed centralised initiatives at the federal level. But President Andrew Jackson (a populist elected in 1828) and the newly formed Democratic Party embraced the word. As the two-party system was consolidating, then, 'democrat' signified partisanship and opposition to centralisation. But the gradual removal of property qualifications in most states meant that almost all white men were gaining the vote, and 'the right of a majority to govern' was gaining wide acceptance.[11]

Alexis de Tocqueville's *Democracy in America*, first published in French in 1835, helped to popularise the image of the United States itself as a democracy.[12] Coming from France, he was impressed by the lack of an idle aristocracy and the widespread respect for labour and industry in American society. At that time, few were wealthy, and those who were, he said, had mostly 'started from poverty'.[13] Equality of opportunity and the value placed on working for one's living stood out for him as positive cultural features; but he was wary that the opinions of the majority could stifle the best ideas and discourage good leaders from coming forward. The rise of the industrious classes and the decline of aristocracy, however, suggested a historical – or even providential – trend towards equality of social conditions and hence democratic government. Tocqueville's study began from the level of the township and looked upwards, so it was grounded in close-knit communities many of which had seen a good two centuries of religious freedom, political assemblies, elected legislatures and popular self-government. But Tocqueville's characterisation of America as a democracy was at odds with the Madisonian ideal of a republic.[14] And although Tocqueville was aware of slavery, destruction of indigenous society and subordination of women, he still described the republic as a democracy. He took the election of representatives and the extent to which leaders are influenced by public opinion as conditions sufficient for democracy – which makes sense when compared to his native France during Louis Philippe's anti-republican July Monarchy (1830–48). Then in 1863 President Lincoln's Gettysburg Address crystallised the idea of popular self-government, calling the nation together from civil war with the hope that 'government of the people, by the people, for the people, shall not perish from the earth'. Although Lincoln's short and eloquent speech didn't use the word 'democracy', it's generally taken to refer to that.

The extension of the franchise to all men and then all women was the result of a series of political struggles on both sides of the Atlantic in the course of the nineteenth and early twentieth centuries. For J.S. Mill, who spoke up for women's right to vote, we'd ideally elect the best among us and let them make the decisions for us. In his version, representation by election was aristocratic in the original Greek sense of 'rule by the best', and not a democratic 'rule by the majority of the people'. The universal franchise, giving each person's vote equal weight, undoubtedly made representation more democratic – or less aristocratic – than restricting the vote to property-owning white men. This was a historic improvement, but the universal franchise on its own didn't transform capitalist societies run by landed and moneyed elites into democracies. As noted above, most people remained uninformed about, and uninvolved in, their government, and the rich minority were more likely to get their way than the non-rich majority.

On the positive side, though, multi-party elections allow for the airing of competing values and proposals, and for a regular decision from voters about preferred leadership and direction. A decision to vote, and thus to choose between alternatives, signifies consent to the system itself, while those who lose an election should concede peacefully in the hope of doing better next time. These features of representation helped to democratise systems of government, but some mistook them for democracy *per se*. Joseph Schumpeter (1883–1950), an Austrian economist who emigrated to the United States, writing as World War II raged in Europe, redefined 'democracy' in simple procedural terms: 'the democratic method is that institutional arrangement for arriving at political decisions in which individuals acquire the power to decide by means of a competitive struggle for the people's vote'.[15] Having acquired power, those elected are trusted to decide according to their best judgement. Although constrained by fear of the voters' wrath at the next election and by the law, decisions between elections aren't made by a majority of the people. Furthermore, although the universal franchise did away with the property qualification to vote and to stand for office, private campaign donations (depending on the particular country's laws) gave the wealthiest the greatest influence. Regular elections with open political contests provided a democratic correction and a guard against incompetence and tyranny, but the independence of action granted to representatives retained an oligarchic element.

The global struggle between Anglo-American liberalism and the totalitarian regimes (from the 1930s to the 1980s) meant that the self-identification of the former with 'democracy' became firmly (and ideologically) embedded in the vocabulary of capitalist societies. But the one-party Soviet Union could accuse capitalism of being essentially undemocratic and non-egalitarian and argue that, in contrast, it was exercising 'democratic centralism'. The oppressive nature of Soviet government flatly contradicted that, but the habit in the West of calling multi-party representation democratic only added to the conceptual confusion about what democracy is. Competitive representation with a universal franchise and a free press had replaced a class-based system in which the majority of people were ignored – until they rioted. That was a big improvement. But representation was originally elitist and wasn't designed to be fully democratic; it allows us to vote, or not, and carry on with private life. It's a common error to think we have democratic government simply because all adults have the right to vote for representatives. Nonetheless, competitive representation has proven to be an efficient way to determine who can pass laws and who can govern and to hold them to account. It means there's always critical scrutiny of what's being done on our behalf, and it may prove to be the best compromise.

Representative systems have changed dramatically over time, especially in the roles played by political parties, mass media and opinion polling. Election of a local candidate as a community's representative gave way to voting for political parties, as it was easier to form stable and effective governments – and oppositions – when factions formally coalesced. Hence the political party itself appropriated representation by producing policy manifestos, pre-selecting the candidates for election and subordinating candidates' personal views to the party's policies and leadership. The individual representative was incorporated into the party as a coalition of representatives. The major political parties normally differentiated themselves from one another around class interests, with a conservative party representing property and a social-democratic or labour party representing workers and trade unions. Radio and television brought the voices and images of political leaders and candidates into people's living rooms, leading to a greater personalisation of politics and to carefully crafted mass communication strategies.

The TV audience, however, was largely passive, and, in spite of greater availability of information and rising levels of educational attainment, decades of research revealed very low levels of political knowledge among the public.[16] The internet era has seen some signs of improved access to knowledge, but also a proliferation of misinformation and disinformation.[17] People have little incentive to inform themselves fully about political parties and policies; instead they rely on trusted proxies, such as family members or favourite bloggers, to guide their voting choices, if they vote at all. Such proxies may include the very political leaders and parties who are competing for the 'ignorant' person's vote. People's opinions are led more by the parties they support than vice versa.[18] As opinion leaders, political parties are nonetheless attentive to preferences and shifts in public opinion in order to maximise their support – and to manipulate or divide the opinions of demographic segments. Opinion polls have thus grown in importance and frequency, to a degree that they're often treated as informal plebiscites. In the twenty-first century, party-based representation became more complex as the importance of economic class was challenged by competing cultural and ecological concerns that cut across class differences, and as the internet and social media disrupted the communicational environment. While it was hoped that the internet would have a democratising effect, the new media also became platforms for violent and hateful ideas and misinformation, and for enhanced state surveillance and political persuasion.

There's not much that genuinely resembles democracy (rule by the majority of the people) in these developments when taken all together. Considering the level of economic inequality, it's more realistic to describe the United States now as a plutocracy (ruled by the super-rich) than a democracy.

Democracy is great when it works; but representative government as we know it isn't entirely democratic. Elections favour an educated elite, and there's little evidence that representative government is going to become more democratic, as decision-making is largely conducted through bargaining, often at an international level, between groups of college-educated and highly paid officials, signed off by world leaders. Announcements about policies are fed to journalists who digest them as news for anyone who's interested. Those who object can vent their feelings on social media. Many people still need to protest on the streets to be heard by their representatives, let alone facilitate change. This modern style of representative government should not be confused with democracy, even though it does have democratic features, such as 'one person one vote'. Indeed, many authoritarian leaders (Mussolini, Hitler, Putin, Orbán and others) have arisen through representative systems by election, and then they've suspended or subverted democratic institutional values such as press freedom and judicial independence when they could.[19] Is this a perversion of, or the logical result of, the Enlightenment ideals of rationality and liberty? Authoritarianism may be immanent in modern systems of representation that maintain a wide political 'division of labour'. Representative governments in capitalist economies are expected to protect property and to create opportunities for capital accumulation, as the conservative and neoliberal versions have done in their differing ways. It's been argued that this always entails alienation and domination of labour and of nature.[20] We should be concerned about the rise of authoritarian populism within representative systems, but by this account it needn't surprise us. The contemporary 'crisis of democracy' may thus be better described as a 'crisis of representation', as democratic historical trends within representative systems were always in dialectical tension with, and never eliminated, top-down oligarchic domination. I'll return to this crisis after further describing different models and aims of representative government.

Models and aims of representation

In constitutional terms, representative government has two main kinds: parliamentary and presidential. In the parliamentary version, a number of elected members form an executive (a cabinet led by a prime minister) that can govern so long as it has the confidence of a majority of representatives. The classic example is the English parliament – especially since the constitutional settlement of 1688. In contrast, a presidential system asks the people to vote for representatives in the legislative branch of government and separately for an executive president. The classic example is the United States of America, where the elected president appoints a cabinet, none of whom sits in Congress, the legislature. The majorities in the Congress and the president may belong to opposing parties, but neither can dismiss the other. There are also – more commonly – semi-presidential systems in which the elected president shares executive powers with a prime minister and cabinet. The latter are drawn from, and dependent upon, the legislature. These semi-presidential systems differ depending on the distribution of executive powers between president and prime minister and on whether or not (or when) the president can appoint and/or dismiss the cabinet.[21]

In terms of aims and scope, representative government has moved between opposing poles or rival interpretations: minimalist neoliberal versus progressive social-democratic political economy; or global integration versus protection of national sovereignty. Progressive politics sought security for workers and their families and regulation of industry for social and environmental reasons. The two world wars had necessitated dramatic increases in public spending, taxation and governmental powers. The need to protect whole populations during all-out war went hand in hand with conscripting soldiers, encouraging women's participation in industry and raising healthy children. The energy bonanza produced by the combustion of fossil fuels, great advances in agricultural productivity, vaccines for common diseases and vast improvements in sanitary conditions of cities led to a population explosion. Wars were no longer waged by or in the name of sovereigns, but instead whole populations were at risk and hence were mobilised to struggle for their own survival. The spectre of nuclear annihilation may have deterred the great powers from all-out war, but it raised the stakes for social policy.[22]

With the demise of the Bretton Woods agreement in the 1970s, however, the policy norms that had protected national economic interests in capitalist states began to unwind. Over the last two decades of the twentieth century, the ideas that less government is better government and that private enterprise is more efficient and effective began to prevail; industrial and commercial regulations were loosened and trade unions were undermined. Requirements to privatise state-owned assets were imposed on less developed nations by international agencies as conditions for loans and development assistance. This was a turn towards 'lean' government, demanding that public organisations adopt the management techniques of private enterprise, and that individuals expect less from the state and do more for themselves.

The primary measure of success under neoliberal government was economic growth, from which jobs would be created and hence welfare dependency and poverty would supposedly decline. Markets would be more integrated internationally, with fewer barriers to trade and worker migration, while greater competition between economies would necessitate policy conditions more favourable to investors and innovators. Bilateral and multilateral trade agreements and other treaties meant that countries often had to amend laws to meet international standards, or to relinquish control to international agencies and tribunals. This was especially the case in the European Union (EU). As an economic bloc that removed trade and migration barriers, coupled with expanding jurisdiction of the European Court of Justice, the EU's member nations sacrificed a degree of economic and legal independence. The wider globalisation process was further advanced in the 1990s when the break-up of the Soviet Union meant that its constituent republics, now independent states, became market economies. The most enthusiastic neoliberal visionaries of that time argued that cities would become more significant as destinations for mobile business and talent, while nation-states would decline in importance in a seamless global economy governed under an international consensus about 'the rules of the game'.

There was an opposing political trend, however, that sought to re-establish the rights and protections provided by sovereign nations. After all, local communities matter to people's ways of life, so people often resist uncalled-for changes. And universal human rights are most effectively enforced through the laws of the particular nation in which the person resides – provided their home country actually respects human rights. An equal and opposite reaction against globalisation reached a peak in the second decade of the twenty-first century. Nationalism and opposition to immigration were resurgent, as seen in the reactions against Chancellor Angela Merkel's admission of hundreds of thousands of refugees into Germany in 2015[23] and then in the United Kingdom in 2016 during the campaign to leave the EU.

Italy

Representative government doesn't always run smoothly, and Italy exemplifies this. Political parties were essential instruments in Italy's post-war, post-fascism reconstruction. Its governing coalitions don't normally last long, however, and they often change between elections. There were 65 governments between 1946 and June 2018, although the ministers were often recycled, so that a change of government was sometimes more like a major cabinet reshuffle. Italian 'party government' descended into 'partyocracy', or 'a situation in which all parties collude in sharing available state resources ("spoils") and take hold of them for the benefit of their organizations, leaders, followers and voters'.[24] The main post-war left (Communist) and conservative (Christian-democratic) parties were demolished in the crisis of 1992–94, partly due to the exposure of systemic corruption in the 'Bribesville' scandals. Since then, political parties have risen and fallen at a surprising rate. The crisis of political trust aided the populist parties, notably Silvio Berlusconi's *Forza Italia*, the far-right *Lega* and the 5-Star Movement (M5S).[25] The latter is an online deliberative forum that initially claimed not to be a political party and that encouraged direct participation by members through its 'Rousseau' platform. In the 2018 election, the *Lega* benefited from anti-immigrant cultural backlash and the M5S from those suffering under poor economic performance, and together they formed a short-lived coalition government. This disbanded after 18 months, when the M5S and the centre-left Democratic Party formed an alternative coalition government, shutting out the *Lega*.[26]

Tainted by their participation in coalition government, the opinion polling of both the M5S and the *Lega* steadily fell. Meanwhile, the far-right *Fratelli d'Italia* (FdI, or Brothers of Italy) was rising. FdI went from 4.4 percent of the vote in 2018 to 26 percent in 2022, and its leader Giorgia Meloni became Italy's first woman prime minister, leading a right-wing coalition with the *Lega* and *Forza Italia*. Three parties that had originally positioned themselves as 'disruptive outsiders' were now 'insiders' and collaborators in government.[27] FdI has neo-fascist roots,[28] but voters saw its leader as untainted (as FdI hadn't supported previous governments) and they liked her conservative nationalism, Catholic values and 'confederalist' approach to the EU that defends national sovereignty. Meloni proposed blockading refugees and migrants from North Africa and an 'Italians first' policy in social services. FdI thus belongs to the family of Europe's populist radical right parties.[29] It's nationalistic and pro-family, but not programmatically fascist. The Italian constitution forbids the reorganisation of the Fascist Party in any form, and many other clauses are contrary to the fascist corporatist form of government.

FdI exemplifies a wider trend in which authoritarian leaders rise by targeting minorities (Africans and Muslims in this case) and promising to restore national pride. In Italy, this is exacerbated by political instability and frequent changes of government. Gianfranco Pasquino, a leading political scientist, argues that the instability isn't entirely bad:

> On the contrary, most of the time, changes in the composition of Italian governments and even governmental crises have been the oil that has kept the political system running, transforming itself, adapting to challenges.[30]

He concedes, however, that political trust and economic confidence thrive on stable government with low levels of corruption and that, on those counts, the Italian system doesn't perform as well as it should. It's a culturally and economically vibrant country, but the quality of, and people's trust in, its government are low compared with other European countries. Italy shows us what can go wrong in a representative system.

The crisis of representation

Among political scientists there's been much alarm about the future of 'democracy'. To recap, since 1945 we'd seen the defeat of fascism, the break-up of the Soviet Union and the end of many military regimes in southern Europe and Latin America. So by the end of the twentieth century there'd been a general trend sometimes called 'democratic consolidation', as countries shifted from authoritarian rule towards electoral competition, and hence a wider range of individuals, parties and interest groups could aspire to contribute openly to government through popular mandates. This became such a strong norm that if an elected government were overthrown in a country, or a dictator refused to step down, the international community could see fit to intervene with economic sanctions, suspension of aid or military force. It was as if liberal representative government came with a warranty to fix flaws or repair break-downs.[31] But then came an unexpected reversal: declining voter turnouts and a loss of popular support for, or a growing dissatisfaction with, what's known as democracy.[32] More states were falling back into authoritarianism and cor-ruption, rather than progressing towards free and fair elections and transpar-ent government.[33]

People in many countries were losing trust in those they'd elected and in the bureaucrats who served them. Populist leaders, mainly from the right, chal-lenged this by claiming to speak directly to and for the people. The people, it was said, had had enough of being treated with disdain or neglect and watching their traditions dissolve. In some countries, popular discontent meant the elec-tion of leaders and parties who explicitly rejected liberal norms. The govern-ments of Hungary and Poland, for example, made changes that undermined judicial independence and freedom of the press and that didn't conform with the laws and values of the European Union. Far-right anti-immigration parties grew in popularity in other European countries. In the Philippines, an elected president went so far as to endorse extra-judicial killings, and authoritarian nationalist leaders won elections in Turkey and India. Election results them-selves were brought into question by former presidents Trump in the United States and Bolsonaro in Brazil. Many countries that held elections, including the United States, were falling short of the 'free and fair' standards. Some were imposing limits on free political expression and on opposition parties. For example, the Russian opposition leader Alexei Navalny was poisoned and then imprisoned, and organisations linked to him were condemned as 'extremist' by authorities. History isn't repetitive, but comparisons were made with the rise of dictatorships in Italy, Germany and Spain during the 1920s and '30s.

From the left too there were challenges, as under-represented groups demanded fairness in elections and public-service employment. This led to greater diversity in legislatures and workforces, but it wasn't a panacea for that perennial cause of social unrest: unjust economic inequality. Improving descriptive representation (so that the representatives collectively resemble the population represented) wouldn't in itself improve substantive representation (so that policies benefit all who are represented). Representation itself came under critical scrutiny. The proposition that 'the European modern state – the territorial nation-state that proclaims democratic and secular values – has become the model for the entire contemporary world'[34] looked valid in 1999 when those words were published. But the subsequent crisis of representation, and the assertive rise of alternatives, lead us to look more closely at other models. So that's where we turn next.

One-party state

The People's Republic of China (PRC) is the most prominent example of a one-party state.[35] As China has become more integrated into the global capitalist economy, it hasn't become politically freer or more liberal, let alone neoliberal. The intrusive digital surveillance of citizens, suppression of Muslims in Xinjiang province and a heavy-handed crackdown in Hong Kong are actively authoritarian. The PRC nonetheless officially describes itself as a 'people's democratic dictatorship', which sounds like an oxymoron. In their own words:

> Democracy and dictatorship appear to be a contradiction in terms, but together they ensure the people's status as masters of the country. A tiny minority is sanctioned in the interests of the great majority, and 'dictatorship' serves democracy.[36]

The Chinese description of their system as a consultative and representative democracy is based on the people's congresses. These begin at the level of village and urban communities, with elected members whose role is consultation and management of local affairs. Similarly there are employee congresses in enterprises and public institutions. Officially, this means a wide cross-section of society is engaged in consultation with local communities and so on upwards. The deputies in the higher-level people's congresses at city, provincial and national levels are elected by the members of the congresses at the next level below them. Normally though, competition in such elections is limited, elections are closely managed by Communist Party officials, and many of the people's congresses are chaired by the local party secretary. At the top of this hierarchy of assemblies is the National People's Congress (NPC), which meets annually, and the 174-member Standing Committee, which acts for the NPC when it's not in session. On paper, the NPC makes the law and appoints or removes the top executive, judicial and military officials including president and premier and members of the State Council. But the people's congresses aren't free *parliamentary* assemblies as they don't openly deliberate and there's no opposition. Instead they confirm decisions that have been already been made within the Party. On the executive side of Chinese government, the State Council leads the decision-making and the administration of ministries and state enterprises. It's directed by the premier and includes the ministers who head the ministries and commissions. It can submit proposals to the NPC Standing Committee.

The substantive articles of the Chinese constitution (setting aside the preamble) only mention the Communist Party of China (CPC) once: to affirm the

Party's leadership in Article 1. But the CPC runs the country at all levels by using the system of people's congresses to turn party policies into state policies and by ensuring that party members are placed within all state institutions, including the judiciary and the People's Liberation Army (PLA). The CPC claims a revolutionary historical, political and ideological legitimacy, but it's a 'shadow' structure that in effect controls state power. The administration of Chinese society is led by the CPC in conjunction with the constitutionally recognised organs of state, one side upholding the authority of the other, with Party members embedded in all bodies of government and industry. With over 90 million members, there's no shortage of personnel to cover these bases, and there's no shortage of new recruits, as Party membership is an important career stepping stone. Xi Jinping became general secretary of the CPC in 2012 and president of the republic in 2013. In 2018 the NPC removed term-limits for president and vice-president from the constitution. In November 2021 the Central Committee of the CPC adopted a resolution that consolidated President Xi's authority and tenure, and he was re-elected as party general secretary in 2022. He gained a third term as president (or state chairman) in 2023. Censorship, centralisation of power and violations of human rights have increased under President Xi, who sits at the pinnacle of the CPC, the state and the military.

To understand how China is really governed, then, one needs to understand the CPC, but the Party has been described as 'the largest secret society on earth'.[37] The CPC has its own hierarchy of party congresses that parallels the people's congresses, with the National Party Congress at the highest level (not to be confused with the National *People's* Congress). The National Party Congress is convened once every five years and elects the Central Committee. On paper, the National Party Congress is the party's leading body, but practically it's powerless. The party leadership decides the congress's agenda and there are neither motions nor speeches from the floor. The incumbent leaders' selection of candidates for the next term's Central Committee is presented for an initial round of preview elections in small group meetings, but this is to ensure that decisive votes will go smoothly according to plan. The election at the plenary session allows delegates to 'choose' 205 members of the Central Committee from 205 candidates. The Congress always endorses the plans and candidates set before it. Such a display of unity is a performance of legitimate authority, and could only be called democratic in the Leninist sense of 'democratic centralism': once a decision has been made, all party members must uphold it.[38] The CPC's ruling Politburo and its leaders, including general secretary, are elected in a similar manner that confirms decisions already made above. Its top decision-making body is the Politburo Standing Committee (PBSC). This is led by the secretary-general (President Xi at the time of writing), the premier of the State Council and the chairperson of the NPC. There are four other members who are responsible for political, ideological and disciplinary affairs within the party. The CPC leadership stands at the pinnacles of political, legislative, executive, judicial and military structures. The 25 members of the full Politburo have multiple roles in party and state. The PBSC is thought to meet weekly and the Politburo monthly. Beneath this, the members of the PBSC control some of the 'central leading groups' that focus on particular areas of policy and that ensure party control and coordination of state agencies. At the local government level, the local party committee 'always appoints its second most important member (the first deputy-secretary) as governor or mayor while the CPC secretary leads from behind all key political and governmental matters'.[39] Thus the party controls government at all levels.

The PRC's party-state has succeeded in keeping foreign powers out (which was a genuine concern), but is now justifiably accused of violations of human rights, attacks on foreign and domestic critics, and a lack of transparency. Elections are not free or fair. Following the 1949 revolution, the Marxist-Leninist model of government was borrowed from the Soviet Union, with adaptations. This was a significant deviation from the centralised imperial-bureaucratic government (with no legislative assemblies) that had prevailed in China for over two millennia up until the end of the nineteenth century. The CPC's aim has been to maintain centrally disciplined collective action in the service of the people, and it largely achieves that end for a very large population – but 'a tiny minority is sanctioned in the interests of the great majority' and those sanctions can be severe. Unlike the Soviet Union, the CPC's rulership survived globalisation. Since the death of Mao Zedong in 1976, China has forged ties with states that don't share its system of government, and it now has free trade agreements with many countries.

I venture to speculate that the Chinese system may revert to its historical type: imperial-bureaucratic government, though modified by the demands of a competitive global economy. The post-civil war experiment with a Marxist-Leninist model may one day look like a relatively brief historical interruption to the continuity of Chinese civilisation. And the PRC isn't the only one-party state. Vietnam's national assembly is dominated by the Communist Party. Elections offer no meaningful choice, as candidates who are independent of or opposed to the Communist Party are banned. Similarly, Laos is a one-party communist state. Cambodia is a parliamentary constitutional monarchy, but its two legislative houses are dominated by the Cambodian People's Party, which has Marxist-Leninist roots. Opposition parties are suppressed and elections aren't competitive, so Cambodia is effectively a centralised one-party state.

Neo-patrimonial state

The break-up of the Soviet Union in 1991 was a hasty decision made by a few leaders without public approval – although a majority of Russian voters approved a new federal constitution by referendum in 1993. The Russian

Federation is now physically the largest country in the world, spanning eleven time zones. It abandoned the Soviet Union's one-party system to become a semi-presidential federation with a bicameral legislature. The upper house represents the many constituent republics, territories, autonomous areas and major cities, and its members are appointed, while the lower house is elected on a mixed-member basis. The subsequent domination by one party and its leader, United Russia (UR) and Vladimir Putin, shows, however, that Russia doesn't follow contemporary norms of fair electoral competition. The first president, Boris Yeltsin (1931–2007), appointed Putin, who was relatively new to national politics, as prime minister in August 1999. Yeltsin resigned as president at the end of that year, then Putin became acting president and won the election in 2000.[40] He served as president for two terms until 2008. He was barred from a third consecutive term by the constitution, but, after handing over the presidency to Dmitry Medvedev, Putin was appointed prime minister and retained effective power. (Russia's constitution stipulates that the president appoints the prime minister, or 'chairman of the government'.) Putin was re-elected for a third presidential term in 2012 after Medvedev recommended him as their party's candidate. He was returned for another six-year term in 2018. Putin later signed off constitutional amendments that allow him a further two six-year terms, until 2036, and a bill was passed granting all former presidents immunity from prosecution. After two decades in power, Putin had become dictator, more or less for life. He was responsible for the illegal seizure of Crimea in 2014 and the invasion of Ukraine in 2022. In the face of declining popularity, the UR party nonetheless maintained a majority in the lower house, the Duma. In the 2021 election, UR won officially 50.9 percent of votes and hence 324 seats out of 450, but there was flagrant electoral fraud and suppression of opponents. Some districts reported close to 100 percent turnouts and close to 100 percent votes for UR; in other districts where results weren't so unbelievable, support for UR had declined since 2016.[41]

During the early 1990s Yeltsin's main aims were to abolish the Soviet Union (as agreed with leaders of the then Belarusian and Ukrainian Soviet Republics), to introduce market freedoms and to end rampant inflation. But the economy collapsed by a half or more, tax evasion and corruption became rife, and salaries went unpaid. Price controls and trade barriers were partially lifted, in line with neoliberal principles. Former state-owned monopolies were sold to insiders at bargain-basement prices, creating a new class of oligarchs and criminals. 'Rival clans of businessmen intrigued with powerful political clans for favor. Gangsters became a regular feature of Russian business, and fought one another with armed bands.'[42] Marxist ideology and official atheism were replaced by Russian nationalism and a rehabilitated Orthodox church. Subsequently, Putin's first two terms as president coincided with a period of economic recovery and reduced public debt from 1999 to 2008. But the new Russian elite had been forged in corruption and chaos, enriched by the misappropriation of formerly state-owned businesses. Helping himself to the spoils, Putin exploited the new oligarchs, rather than expose them to competition and accountability. He made an example of Russia's then wealthiest man, Mikhail Khodorkovsky, who was arrested in 2003 and found guilty of fraud. Khodorkovsky's oil and gas company, Yukos, was confiscated by the state. From then on, policy turned away from privatisation in favour of state capitalism with monopolies managed by Putin's friends.[43] Efforts to estimate Putin's personal wealth have been futile due to a lack of transparency, a network of friends who may hold assets on his behalf, and his personal use of state properties.

Russian history has a long line of autocratic rulers going back to Ivan IV, 'the Terrible' (1530–84), followed by absolutist Tsars, and then communist dictators. Experiments with European liberalism had some impact, but didn't last. Despite revolutions and reforms, the Kremlin reverts to modified versions of Tsarism that concentrate power in one man's hands, allowing him more or less to 'own' everything and everyone. Richard Pipes defined Tsarist patrimonialism as 'a regime where the rights of sovereignty and those of ownership blend to the point of being indistinguishable, and political power is exercised in the same manner as economic power'.[44] This system subordinates social and economic forces to an extent that much potential is never realised, especially when compared with achievements under liberal forms of government.[45] Communist rule also appropriated private property for the state and swept aside classes of people deemed to be threats or obstacles. Russian authoritarian government isn't enforced solely by its leader, however: it's supported by people attracted to the centre of power who struggle for a share of social status and economic rewards.

There was hope in the 1990s that the end of the Soviet command economy and the opening of markets would lead to well-functioning free markets and respect for property rights. The relative freedom of the 1990s didn't last, however, and there's been a decline into crony capitalism and autocratic rule. The Russian constitution allows presidents to appoint prime ministers, to exert power over those responsible for the government, and even to rule by decree. So its semi-presidential system is prone to an autocratic leader, and Putin weakened the council of ministers and reduced the federal and regional legislatures to rubber-stamp assemblies that don't meaningfully represent the people. Through a circle of trusted close associates, he micro-manages the security services and the state enterprises. Putin rewards and enriches his cronies with preferential contracts; critics and opponents are suppressed or eliminated. While superficially successful, a leader like Putin becomes a hostage to his own network of supporters, however, and his eventual demise is likely to lead to a disorganised internal power struggle.

Russia's government is a reversion to the patrimonial type, but this time with the trappings of a criminal syndicate: state enterprises are used to enrich Putin and his associates, the law enforcement agencies are involved in robbing businesses, and offshore accounts are used to hide assets and evade accountability.[46] This is *kleptocracy*: a system of government that enables the ruling class and their cronies to steal with impunity. It's often described as a Mafia state with Putin as boss of bosses. Within a diminishing sphere of influence, the Kremlin supports other authoritarian regimes such as in Belarus and Kazakhstan. The renewed invasion of Ukraine in early 2022 was an effort to seize territory and to keep whatever remains of Ukraine out of the European Union and the North Atlantic Treaty Organisation, while also seeking to restore Russian prestige as an imperial power.

Corrupt patrimonial government is all too common around the world. A country's resources and revenue stream are plundered by an elite who enrich themselves. Obedience is maintained by bribes to encourage sycophants and by threats, allegations and assassinations to discourage dissent and whistle-blowing. Such government destroys political trust and holds back economic and social development.

Quasi-states

We've looked at two basic forms of government so far: multi-party representation and one-party monopoly. In between there are countries such as Russia that 'on paper' are examples of the former, but in fact have one dominant party, an autocratic ruler, a suppressed opposition and fraudulent elections. All examples cited so far in this chapter, however, are internationally recognised as independent sovereign states. No one argues that they aren't 'a thing'. We may not like aspects of some of them, but they work nevertheless; they have seats in the United Nations General Assembly, and they advance their interests at home and abroad. But there are many examples of state-like entities that fall outside of, or don't fit neatly into, today's general model of a sovereign state. Some are 'unrecognised states',[47] and others have international recognition but lack independent statehood. In many cases there are valid reasons for such a marginal political status. For example, the tiny Pacific island of Niue (population about 1,700) is self-governing in 'free association' with New Zealand; so Niueans are citizens of New Zealand, and most of them live there. Niue doesn't have its own seat in the UN, but its government works in partnership with New Zealand. Constitutionally and practically, this provides for the needs of a small, isolated nation that isn't a nation-*state*.

History has many narratives of secessionist or revolutionary movements that claimed to form a new state but then failed to achieve it for lack of internal stability and international recognition. A colourful example is the brief independence of Fiume as the self-proclaimed Italian Regency of Carnaro in 1920, under the leadership of the poet, orator and egomaniac Gabriele d'Annunzio (1863–1938). After the break-up of Austria–Hungary in 1918, the city and province of Fiume were supposed to be incorporated into the new Kingdom of Serbs, Croats and Slovenes (Yugoslavia), but Fiume's Italians (its largest ethnic group) invited the popular and charismatic d'Annunzio to intervene on their behalf. He arrived on 12 September 1919 with a contingent of troops – mainly deserters – who forced Allied soldiers to withdraw, and he declared the city to be Italy's. The Italian government refused to recognise this, but offered instead to treat Fiume as a protectorate. This separate status was supported by the Fiuman people in a referendum, but d'Annunzio declared the vote null and void, and put himself in charge. On 8 September 1920, he proclaimed that Fiume was now the Italian Regency of Carnaro, with a corporatist constitution of a kind that presaged the fascist government of Italy under Mussolini. Indeed, d'Annunzio inspired the aesthetic and rhetorical features of fascism, including its glorification of war. The Italian government then made a treaty with Yugoslavia to create, instead, a Free State of Fiume. Against the advice of his supporters, including Mussolini, d'Annunzio rejected this, as it didn't mean annexation by Italy. He refused to vacate the city with his troops when ordered to do so by the Italian government in late December 1920. So the Italian army and navy attacked – and d'Annunzio capitulated after a shell from a warship exploded near his quarters. Due to his immense following, d'Annunzio was able to return to Italy with impunity, despite having taken up arms against his own country. A Free State of Fiume was duly formed, but in 1924, with Mussolini in charge, it was annexed by Italy – as d'Annunzio had wanted.[48] The city is now known as Rijeka and belongs to Croatia.

Today, membership of the UN formalises international recognition of a country's independence and sovereignty, but many territories sit awkwardly on or outside the margin. Transnistria, or the Pridnestrovian Moldavian Republic, for example, is an unrecognised state that occupies the narrow strip of land between the eastern (or left) bank of the Dniester river and the Ukrainian border. It broke away from the Republic of Moldova following the collapse of the Soviet Union and a brief armed conflict in 1992. Its claims to statehood aren't strongly irridentist,[49] as it's multi-ethnic, including mainly Moldovans, Russians and Ukrainians. Reasons for secession from Moldova were the fears of being incorporated into Romania and losing connection with Moscow. Its leaders have cited, for historical justification, the Soviet Union's creation in 1924 of the Moldovan Autonomous Soviet Socialist Republic, which once encompassed Transnistria and a part of western Ukraine, but was dissolved in 1940. Despite not being recognised by the international community, Transnistria has its own semi-presidential constitution and national symbols, and its capital is Tiraspol.[50] Transnistria is a *de facto* state with conventional features of statehood: a permanent population, a defined territory, a government and a capacity to enter into relations with other states, although the latter isn't reciprocated in this case. It's not formally recognised by the international community and has no seat at the UN. As their home country's passports are not accepted externally, Transnistrians are permitted to hold multiple citizenships, and most have Moldovan, Russian or Ukrainian passports.[51]

The Islamic State (IS) – also known as the Islamic State of Iraq and the Levant (ISIL) or the Islamic State of Iraq and Syria (ISIS) or Daesh – existed from 1999 onwards and took part in the insurgency in Iraq against the invading American and allied forces beginning in 2003. The IS captured the world's attention when its mobile forces took the city of Mosul in northern Iraq in 2014. It declared itself to be a new worldwide caliphate, thus claiming jurisdiction over all Muslims, and by the end of 2015 it controlled territory in eastern Syria and western Iraq with over eight million population and with the Syrian city of Raqqah as its capital. The IS's claim to caliphal authority was firmly rejected by the international community and by the vast majority of Muslims, and the group was driven out by force in 2017. For a time, though, it existed as a quasi-state with aspirations to effective government and economic prosperity. The IS's excessive violence and terrorism and the international military effort to degrade and eliminate it overshadow any assessment of how – and how well – it governed the cities and territory it controlled, but there's been some independent research, in spite of the difficulties. At least as far as Raqqah and Mosul were concerned, IS was able to establish a bureaucracy that kept public services running (including healthcare, water and power), and it maintained security while markets and commerce continued. But the IS's methods of extracting resources were sometimes extortionate and its leaders became increasingly strict and punitive in enforcing their Salafist version of Islamic law.[52] The economy and population declined, but the outflow of residents in these cities wasn't as great as we might expect. Many who stayed said that – at least for some time – government under IS was more effective and fairer than the Iraqi government, which had been corrupt and had discriminated against Sunnis.[53] Things didn't work as effectively, of course, in other cities that IS was unable to secure. IS aspired to recreate an Islamic empire and to attract fighters based on claims about prosperity and just government. Its criminally violent and extortionate methods contradicted those promises, however, and IS couldn't be tolerated by the international community. Its leader during those years, Abu Bakr al-Baghdadi (1971–2019), died when he detonated a suicide vest during a raid by American special forces.

Two other politically sensitive cases merit discussion, although neither is strictly classifiable as a quasi-state, as they do have some degree of international recognition. These are the Palestinian Authority (West Bank and Gaza) and Taiwan.

The Palestinian Authority (PA) was created under the Oslo Accords negotiated between the Israeli government and the Palestine Liberation Organisation in the 1990s, giving the PA responsibility for the main Palestinian-populated zones in the West Bank and Gaza. It last held elections to its Legislative Council in 2006, when the Islamic Resistance Movement (HAMAS) won a majority of seats. Due to ongoing internecine rivalry between the political parties HAMAS and Fatah, the Palestinian Legislative Council was dissolved in 2018. The two factions have been unable to restore political unity, and the Gaza Strip and the West Bank are effectively separate political entities. Israel had captured the West Bank from Jordan in the 1967 Six-Day War, and the Oslo Accords divided it into three zones: one fully administered by the PA, one fully administered by Israel, and one under joint control pending a further agreement – towards which there's been no further progress. Israel controls movement through most of the West Bank and is extending its effective control over the territory by forcing Palestinians out of their farms and homes and by building settlements for Israelis, in contravention of international law.[54] HAMAS took control of the government of the Gaza Strip in 2007. Movement in and out of the Gaza Strip is strictly limited by Israel and Egypt, including a maritime blockade, and there's occasional exchange of fire between HAMAS and the Israeli Defence Force. The UN upholds aspirations for a two-state solution whereby Israel and Palestine would exist independently side by side, but this looks increasingly unlikely as Israel imposes military and economic domination over the Palestinian territories.[55]

Taiwan was first incorporated into the Chinese empire in the late seventeenth century as a result of the Manchu invasion that ended the Ming dynasty. The island was ceded to Japan under the Treaty of Shimonoseki in 1895, but was returned to China after Japan's defeat in 1945. China, however, was then in the midst of a civil war between the nationalist Kuomintang led by Chiang Kai-shek (1887–1975) and the People's Liberation Army led by the Communist Party of China (CPC). In 1949 the victorious CPC declared itself the government of the People's Republic of China (PRC), claiming Taiwan as well as the mainland. Driven out by the communists, the Kuomintang had retreated across the strait to the safety of Taiwan, where Chiang set up the Republic of China and ruled until his death.[56] The Kuomintang claimed to be the legitimate government of all China, but in fact their writ didn't run beyond the island of Taiwan. This became more than just a domestic matter between rival Chinese factions, as the international recognition of 'one China', and the question of which side rightfully governs it, remain sensitive diplomatic questions to this day. Martial law in Taiwan was lifted and opposition parties were permitted in the late 1980s. Competitive elections were first held there in 1992, and since then there've been three peaceful transfers of power. At the time of writing, the Kuomintang were in opposition and the majority of seats in the unicameral parliament were held by the Democratic Progressive Party (DPP). Taiwan has a semi-presidential system, and its first woman president was Tsai Ing-wen of the DPP, in office from 2016 to 2022. It's a prosperous economy with political pluralism and free and fair elections. Its status, however, is disputed by the PRC, which sees Taiwan as a province in rebellion. And the great majority of countries now recognise the PRC as 'China', and not Taiwan's Republic of China. So Taiwan is a well-governed 'state' that only a very few countries are willing to recognise diplomatically as independent and sovereign. It has no seat at the UN and any application for membership will be vetoed by the PRC as a permanent member of the Security Council.

The cases described in this section show how territory, statehood and government don't always coincide neatly in the normative manner. But exceptions don't disprove rules: they show us that a rule actually applies. There's no set of rules (not even mathematics) that lacks exceptions or inconsistencies. In politics there's always the rule that suspends the rules in case of emergency – or dictatorship. So, political exceptions such as quasi-states show us that, even where the norms of modern statehood are absent or incomplete, people will find ways and means to govern – even amid the mayhem created by the Islamic State of Iraq and Syria. The exceptions show us a dark side of government: ill-defined spaces like the Gaza Strip, which is guarded like an open-air prison, can perpetuate injustices, discrimination and violence. On the other hand, a disputed territory such as Taiwan can become a well-governed society.

Theocracy

Theocracy assumes that God rules the universe and deputises earthly government to a monarch and/or a priesthood. A particular religion and its holy scripture are established constitutionally and applied as law. Although theocracy is less common today than in the Middle Ages, we do see some examples.

The Islamic Republic of Iran has been a theocracy since the 1979 revolution. Although it has an elected president and legislature, the head of state, or Supreme Leader, is a senior cleric appointed for life with paramount religious and political authority. He (never she) is elected and advised by the male-only Assembly of Experts, which consists of highly qualified Shia jurists elected by the people for eight-year terms. The Supreme Leader appoints half of the twelve jurists on the Council of Guardians – the other half being elected by the parliament. This council can approve or block candidates for election, ensuring a conservative bias. Somewhat like an upper house, it may also veto laws that are deemed to be unconstitutional or un-Islamic. The Supreme Leader's powers are based on the religious principle of 'the guardianship of the jurist': in anticipation of the return of the 'hidden' twelfth Imam[57] – when true justice will be established – the interpretation of Islamic law and control of government is delegated to the most revered clerics, who choose one of their peers as leader.[58] The most visible symbol of this regime's oppressive character is the enforced wearing of the hijab by women, and about two-thirds of Iranians disapprove of this government under religious law.[59] Iran's present regime lacks popular legitimacy and has been repeatedly disrupted by civil unrest.

The Kingdom of Saudi Arabia has been an absolute monarchy since its independence in 1932. Its Basic Law of Governance, issued in 1992 by King Fahd Bin Abdulaziz Al-Saud, states that the country's constitution is 'the Holy Qur'an, and the Sunna (Traditions) of the Prophet'.[60] Saudi Arabia's territory includes the birthplace of Islam and the holy cities of Mecca and Medina. Sunni Islam is the state religion and the basis of law and education. The monarchy is inherited and the King rules as head of state and prime minister. He appoints and dismisses ministers, among whom are members of the royal family. The members of the legislative assembly, the Majlis al-Shura, are also appointed by the King, and there are no political parties or national elections. Recently, however, there have been elections for municipal councillors. Women have been granted rights to vote and to stand in these local elections, and there's now a minimum quota of 20 percent women in the Majlis al-Shura – but women's political and social freedoms are still limited. The kingdom's gender segregation rules mean that candidates in the municipal elections can't meet with voters of the opposite gender. Senior judges are appointed and dismissed by royal decree on the recommendation of the judicial council. The King is advised by a council of senior scholars on religious matters, but this body doesn't offer opinions that differ much from the monarch's. In general, the open expression of dissenting political views and public worship in non-Muslim religions are banned and can lead to imprisonment. One of the worst examples of such repression was the murder by Saudi agents of the journalist Jamal Khashoggi inside the Saudi consulate in Istanbul in 2018.

The Islamic Republic of Pakistan is a federal parliamentary system with multi-party elections. It's not fully theocratic, as real power lies with the armed forces, and so it's a 'boundary' case for the present section, but Pakistan was originally created as 'a separate homeland for Muslims'.[61] Its constitution declares that Islam is the state religion, but guarantees religious freedom for all citizens and all religious institutions. It also guarantees freedom of speech, 'subject to any reasonable restrictions imposed by law in the interest of the glory of Islam [and of] public order, decency or morality'. The partition of British India in 1947 into East and West Pakistan and India was a sectarian division that precipitated 'the greatest exodus in recorded history'.[62] Muslims didn't universally support the creation of a Muslim-majority Pakistan, as many see themselves as a community of believers that transcends territory and state. But during the partition millions of Muslims fled there from the new Hindu-dominated India for fear of discrimination and sectarian violence – and millions of Hindus fled in the opposite direction. Many were killed along the way. In 1971 East Pakistan seceded to become Bangladesh. Mohammad Ali Jinnah (1876–1948), the founder of Pakistan, envisaged a modern representative government that would combine principles of democracy and Islam, but it wasn't until 1970 that the first direct election for the national assembly was held, and since then Pakistan has seen periods of martial law and military dictatorship (1977–85, 1999–2002). The 2008 election was delayed by the assassination of the former prime minister Benazir Bhutto (PM 1988–90, 1993–96). The 2013 election was marred by terrorist attacks on election rallies and assassinations of candidates and workers of secular political parties, and hence there were doubts about some results, but there was at least a transfer of power with no military intervention.

Moderate elected leaders such as the centre-right Imran Khan have prevailed over hard-line Islamists, although his administration failed to tackle systemic corruption, and was ended by a parliamentary no-confidence vote in April 2022. Islamist political parties have receded to the margins electorally, but they have indirect influence through 'quietist' missionary activities or militant groups connected to terrorist networks and to the Taliban.[63] The political power of the military, especially over security and foreign policy, is a greater concern, as 'the Pakistan Army stands at the center of a complex pattern in which South Asia's Islamist parties and their proxies work both *with* and *against* the state simultaneously',[64] and there's a deep 'institutional distrust' between civilian government and the generals.[65] Concerning Islamic law, the constitution has established a 'parallel judicial structure' in the Federal Shariat Court.[66] This consists of eight Muslim judges, up to three of whom are *ulema*, 'having at least fifteen years' experience in Islamic law, research or instruction'. The court may 'examine and decide the question whether or not any law or provision of law is repugnant to the injunctions of Islam'.[67] The effective government of Pakistan has been hampered by an inefficient and unpredictable judicial system, exploitation of institutions and resources for 'the reproduction of a filthy rich elite',[68] local electorates being treated as the fiefdoms of privileged families, and 'appeasement of banned extremist and terrorist outfits'.[69] Viable strategies for political parties to attain power can include politically motivated corruption charges against opponents and currying favour with the military. Women and non-Muslim minorities generally face barriers to participation and representation.

Theocratic government is more commonly found in the Islamic world. The tiny Vatican City is a theocracy under the Pope, but on the whole the Christian world has developed secular government with religious freedom and no established church. Nonetheless, there are some vestiges of the past, such as the British monarch who is also Supreme Governor of the Church of England, and laws that nominate Christian feasts as public holidays. Christian-democratic political parties are found around the world, mostly on the conservative side of politics, and they play significant roles in some European countries, especially Germany and Austria.

Indigenous government

All societies have – and always have had – customs and means for governing their own affairs. Government is a common human concern and set of activities; it's not confined to societies deemed to be 'civilised', as compared with others deemed 'primitive'. So the existence of an over-arching state or empire isn't a necessary condition for the effective government of everyday life.[70] Before colonising peoples introduced state-based forms of government, normally by force, indigenous peoples[71] were making laws and rules, conducting collective decision-making and dispute resolution, and interacting formally with others in neighbouring or distant territories. They had means to manage family concerns such as marriage and for organising their economic and military activities, whether in small egalitarian communities or larger societies. In many pre-contact societies, governmental institutions involved hierarchical administration and monarchy. The Buganda kingdom, established in the early 1300s (in today's Uganda), for example, established 'a strong dual socio-political administrative structure; the clan system became the social component and the fourteen political offices became the nucleus of the political component'.[72] Indigenous government and law often bring together shared understandings of the human, natural and spiritual realms, although today these institutions are recovering from dispossession by colonial government and dealing with the ongoing hegemony of contemporary states. So, for example:

> Prior to the imposition of [Canadian] state governance on the lives of Inuit in NunatuKavut, Inuit were self-governing and adapted to their world, and made decisions that supported their survival. Today, Inuit from this region [Labrador] maintain a deeply rooted connection to their home and territory.[73]

Inuit practices that assert their self-government and self-determination challenge the formal, hierarchical and colonising character of state-based government. They promote instead a local decision-making that respects the role of women, the importance of healthcare and wellbeing, and the significance of storytelling, thus recovering and transmitting traditional knowledge that has proven for many generations to be essential for survival and for community cohesion.[74]

Pre-contact indigenous cultures and political systems were highly diverse, and the impacts of colonisation also differed greatly depending on local circumstances and historical events. Populations often declined significantly due to introduced diseases and mass murder; many communities were forced off their lands; and alien forms of government were imposed, including education in foreign languages and unfamiliar medical practices. In settler societies such as Canada, the United States, Australia and Aotearoa New Zealand, the aspirations of indigenous peoples for self-government and self-determination occur in the face of catastrophic losses of properties and customs as well as the dominance of imported practices of government.[75] While there's a vibrant discussion around legal recognition of indigenous rights and political representation of indigenous communities, the concepts of rights, recognition and representation have European origins. Useful though they may be, they come from the toolkit of colonial government.

A historical example of this dilemma is the Constitution of the Cherokee Nation, signed in 1827. The invasion by white settlers, along with the formation of a British colony of Georgia in 1733, or State of Georgia from 1776, necessitated a statement that the Cherokee were an independent nation with a defined territory. Hence some of their leaders, mainly 'mission-educated mixed-bloods',[76] wrote and published a constitution in bilingual Cherokee–English format.[77] It was similar to the federal constitution, with a separation of powers into legislative, executive and judicial 'departments', including an elected bicameral legislature: 'a Committee and a Council each to have a negative on the other, and both to be styled the General Council of the Cherokee nation'.[78] The supreme executive powers would be held by a 'principal chief' elected in a joint vote by the two legislative chambers. This appropriated the political structures, literacy and print technology of the colonisers as means of resistance against colonisation. But it also advanced a centralisation of government, not a communal and decentralised polity that valued balance and harmony, and hence it was resisted by 'traditionalist' tribal leaders. In any case, the Cherokee were forced to relocate westwards into Oklahoma in the 1830s, losing an estimated 4,000 lives on the way, and so the strategy of emulating 'civilised' government sadly didn't prevent ethnic cleansing.[79]

A contemporary example of self-determination is found in the Sámi parliaments in northern regions of Norway, Sweden and Finland. The Sámi are traditionally reindeer-herders, hunters and fishers, and they're the only recognised indigenous peoples within Europe.[80] In response to claims for self-determination made by the Sámi since the 1980s, the three Scandinavian countries established assemblies (Sámediggis) consisting of elected Sámi representatives. This was a significant step forward, but these parliaments aren't autonomous, being subordinate to the national legislatures and governments of their respective states. Sámi voters still have individual rights to vote in the national elections, but their collective rights fall well short of self-determination as a people or nation. The Sámediggis are not sovereign law-making assemblies, but are agencies of the national governments, tasked with administrative duties relating to cultural and local resource issues. The Swedish Sámi parliament's activities, for example, include 'trades, reindeer husbandry, community planning, environment and climate, promotion of Sami cultural expression and traditional knowledge, Sami library, Sami language work and international indigenous peoples' issues'.[81] The core fiscal and security functions of the state are reserved for the Swedish government. Although greater Sámi self-determination is often called for, especially regarding natural resources and health, education and child welfare, a survey indicated that only a minority of Sámi want this to extend to defence and taxation.[82]

The UN Declaration on the Rights of Indigenous Peoples (2007) is a framework for devolution of government to indigenous peoples. Some relevant steps are being made by the Inuit. The Government of Canada devolves responsibility for decisions on the uses and development of public lands and resources to the Government of Nunavut, including minerals, oil and gas, and collection of the associated royalties.[83] Another example is Greenland, where the Inuit make up the majority. The right of the people of Greenland to self-determination is founded in an agreement between the governments of Greenland and Denmark. The relevant Danish law aims 'to foster equality and mutual respect in the partnership between Denmark and Greenland'. Since 2009, then, Greenland has had an independent parliament and administration – with responsibilities for mineral resources and their revenues. The Naalakkersuisut (Government) can enter into international agreements. The UN Declaration's principles have also found a place in the constitutions of many Latin American countries, and there are ongoing claims from indigenous peoples for greater autonomy over lands and resources, for example in Nicaragua. In Bolivia, indigenous groups are able to form autonomous self-government within the general institutions and over-arching authority of the state, as envisaged by the 'pluri-national' constitution.

As well as having their aspirations constrained within the bounds set by national governments and constitutions, indigenous societies had already been transformed by histories of contacts with – and violent interference by – settlers hungry for land and minerals, missionaries, colonial officials and others. Colonial and white settler governments leave a legacy of injustices, having caused irreparable harm to traditional learning, customary economic practices and spiritual attachments to lands, rivers and seas. In their struggles to adapt and recover through creative new forms of self-government in the face of the modern state, however, indigenous peoples have much to teach us today. Given the global diversity of cultures and historical experiences, any generalisations are destined to be incomplete and unsatisfactory, but there are some themes to consider for present purposes. First is the importance of connection and belonging to a place, which are brought to life through oral history, ancestry and stories of the origins of the world and of the first humans. This goes much deeper than personal memories or sentiments about locations; it involves cosmological and historical narratives. These indigenous stories contrast starkly with the disembodied, unrooted experiences of cosmopolitan mobility and digital virtuality in postmodern ways of life. Indigenous government, then, is inseparable from particular lands, waterways, coastlines and skies. In order more fully to appreciate the intrinsic value(s) of nature and natural resources – beyond economic exploitation and towards biodiversity – the work of government can learn from indigenous ways of perceiving and knowing nature and of valuing living beings, landscapes, rivers, seas, etc., and hence develop cross-culturally informed methods of conservation. Such innovations extend from the local (or place-based) to the national and international arenas of policymaking, and hence they work across and break down administrative boundaries. They hybridise the work of government, grafting one kind onto another's stock, preserving established roots and reminding us of what all living things have in common. Such a hybridisation of government implies learning from indigenous communities, rather than treating them as vulnerable and developing communities whose resilience needs to be rebuilt with global finance and multi-agency governance. Instead, it means embedding and hearing indigenous voices throughout the systems of government, or 'the expression of a wide body of Indigenous political capacities, including the capacity to function within the public bureaucracy *as* Indigenous and to function as part of the public to which bureaucratic accountability is owed'.[84]

Human connections to nature and to place are interwoven with connection to kin groups and ancestors. Indigenous government is based on the self-determination of a tribe, hence it favours kin. This may, however, come up against modern meritocracy and the bureaucratic state's rejection of nepotism. Favouring one's kin is considered corrupt, and may be a crime, if it involves a public official or an administrative decision. Modern representative government imagines us as free and accountable individuals, and public administration impersonally executes laws and policies that apply to all equally (in theory) regardless of our familial connections. Indeed, the ideal of universal human rights and the trend towards global integration would in principle make us all into 'citizens of the world'. The indigenous and nationalist reactions against those trends remind us that many people seek a kind of government that cares for its own people first, in their places of origin and according to their traditions. Preferences for one's own kin, community or nation are valid 'corrections' to neoliberal globalisation and atomised individualism. We care for our own people, before and above others, for the sake of cultural integrity and social belonging, even though we also want our public institutions to care for distant others whom we don't know. Either way, 'to care effectively we must be attentive, responsive, and respectful toward [others], and avoid treating their needs as self-evident'.[85] One of those needs is for personal and collective self-determination.

Reflecting on the multi-ethnic Austro-Hungarian Empire in 1867 and the rising aspirations of Croat and Slovakian minorities, Sassoon observes that 'within every majority there is always a minority that, once its minority status is enshrined formally, will struggle to get out',[86] and such struggles continue in the Balkans. If one's benchmark is 1914, the former empire's territory has been split up into and shared among twelve different countries. Indigenous irredentism and self-determination head logically in directions akin to the post-imperial nation-state: more independent states, as indigenous or oppressed minorities struggle to 'get out of' post-imperial states. An alternative is the more modest goal of sub-national legislative and administrative bodies, such as the devolved parliaments of the Sámi, or for that matter Scotland and Northern Ireland. Barring a major crisis or strong popular demand, however, sovereign states (whether unitary or federal) don't willingly break up into their constituent parts or encourage secession by a province. The Spanish government has applied considerable force to quash independence in Catalonia. But break-ups are more common in modern history than unifications, judging by the rising number of recognised states, let alone unrecognised quasi-states. Sub-national assemblies and judicial systems may more effectively represent indigenous communities than the hegemonic postcolonial state that gives these institutions form and licence – but the struggles for recognition and self-determination by formerly colonised indigenous peoples may not cease until secession, depending on their demographic and geographic situation. This goes to the heart of what we mean by sovereignty. Thomas Hobbes once argued that having 'subordinate representatives' was dangerous if it meant, in effect, two sovereigns acting for the subject. The two powers would oppose one another; whereas 'if men will live in peace', as they should, sovereignty is 'indivisible'. If local representatives in a national parliament are held up as their communities' 'absolute representatives', then the nation would be in danger of falling into 'the condition of war'.[87] Hobbes was thinking of the English civil war of the 1640s, and we needn't take him literally today, as peaceful secessions authorised by referendums are possible – as almost occurred in Scotland and Quebec. But once enough people see sovereignty as divided, and the tribe that unites kin looks more legitimate than the multi-ethnic state that once united strangers, then the division intensifies. A desire for autonomy gives birth to a desire for secession, if not the reality. Out of this, however, there emerge new lessons and creative ideas in the arts of government.

Conclusion

Government today is conducted in diverse, creative and changeable ways. These ways are always imperfect; some offend our sense of justice; none is effectively addressing the challenges of the future. Written constitutions and actual practices are often inconsistent; we see widening inequalities and suppression of dissent. While it's futile to strive for a perfect constitution and administration, we can at least set aside the claim that nowadays we're 'stuck in just one form of social reality'.[88] The real world of government and state is diverse and changing, while there are also signs of continuity over time. Political history moves dialectically from one set of contradictions to another, rather than towards logically consistent or mechanical regimes built to last with only minor maintenance. It would be a mistake to regard government in terms of settled or immovable institutions, each system based on agreed principles. Modern representative government, for example, emerges from and contains contradictions between democratic norms (such as openness to disagreement) and top-down bureaucratic management (or sometimes outright authoritarianism), and between abstract equality and the exploitation of labour. Such contradictions are immanent features of any epoch. These aren't bugs to be programmed out; they're dynamic problems or contradictions to be addressed.

Rather than be hostage to abstract nouns like 'democracy', in this chapter we've looked at what different countries actually do and at the arrangements they have, including their shortcomings. This hasn't been a comprehensive survey, nor was it intended to create a strict typology, in spite of the themes that structured the sections. The kinds of contradictions alluded to above will trouble any attempts to categorise systems, especially as they change, sometimes rapidly. A major problem, though, is that today's dominant forms of government so often disappoint, or even harm, the people they serve; they're controlled by parties remote from those affected, and they perpetuate inequality, so political trust tends to decline. Furthermore, they challenge and change one another's norms as they trade, collaborate and fight. The next chapter brings together matters we must consider if we wish to restore political trust and governmental effectiveness, without aiming for a universal or best practice model to fit all peoples.

Notes

1 Thucydides. 1972. *History of the Peloponnesian War*. London: Penguin, trans. Rex Warner. See p. 164, abridged.
2 Ibid., pp. 577–78.
3 Dahl, Robert A. & Ian Shapiro. 2015. *On Democracy*. New Haven: Yale University Press.
4 Bächtiger, André, John S. Dryzek, Jane J. Mansbridge & Mark Warren. 2018. *The Oxford Handbook of Deliberative Democracy*. Oxford: Oxford University Press. See p. 2.
5 Urbinati, Nadia & Mark E. Warren. 2008. 'The Concept of Representation in Contemporary Democratic Theory'. *Annual Review of Political Science* 11: 387–412. See p. 395.
6 Gilens, Martin & Benjamin I. Page. 2014. 'Testing Theories of American Politics: Elites, Interest Groups, and Average Citizens'. *Perspectives on Politics* 12 (3): 564–81; Persson, Mikael & Anders Sundell. 2023. 'The Rich Have a Slight Edge: Evidence from Comparative Data on Income-Based Inequality in Policy Congruence'. *British Journal of Political Science* (online): 1–12.
7 Neither did the French constitutions mention democracy – until the Fifth Republic's, in 1958. Tangian, Andranik. 2020. *Analytical Theory of Democracy: History, Mathematics and Applications*. Cham: Springer. See p. 210.
8 Jay, John, Lawrence Goldman, Alexander Hamilton & James Madison. 2008. *The Federalist Papers*. Oxford: Oxford University Press. See no. 10.
9 Compare: Brennan, Jason. 2016. *Against Democracy*. Princeton University Press: Princeton, NJ; Furedi, Frank. 2021. *Democracy Under Siege*. Winchester, UK: Zero Books. Furedi argues for democracy as a way of life and a value in itself, and more than just elections.

10 Lepore, Jill. 2018. *These Truths: A History of the United States.* New York: W.W. Norton & Co. See p. 112.

11 Ibid. See p. 191.

12 Tocqueville, Alexis de. 2003 [1835, 1840]. *Democracy in America and Two Essays on America.* London: Penguin, trans. G Bevan.

13 Ibid. See p. 65.

14 Tangian [note 7].

15 Schumpeter, Joseph A. 2008 [1942]. *Capitalism, Socialism and Democracy.* New York: HarperCollins. See p. 269.

16 Somin, Ilya. 2016. *Democracy and Political Ignorance: Why Smaller Government Is Smarter.* Stanford, CA: Stanford Law Books.

17 Lorenz-Spreen, P., L. Oswald, S. Lewandowsky et al. 2022. 'A Systematic Review of Worldwide Causal and Correlational Evidence on Digital Media and Democracy'. *Nature Human Behaviour* (online version), URL: https://doi.org/10.1038/s41562-022-01460-1 (accessed 10 November 2022).

18 'Ever-expanding literature has shown that people in America and Europe rely on political parties to tell them which political positions to take.' Bakker, Bert N. & Yphtach Lelkes. 2022. 'The Structure, Prevalence, and Nature of Mass Belief Systems'. In *The Cambridge Handbook of Political Psychology,* ed. Danny Osborne & Chris G. Sibley, 89–103. Cambridge: Cambridge University Press. See p. 93. This passive 'cue receptivity' *isn't* found primarily among those who have difficulty processing information about public affairs, but instead is more prevalent among those who identify strongly with one party, have greater interest in politics, and hence want to defend and support a preferred party. Bakker, Bert N., Yphtach Lelkes & Ariel Malka. 2020. 'Understanding Partisan Cue Receptivity: Tests of Predictions from the Bounded Rationality and Expressive Utility Perspectives'. *The Journal of Politics* 82 (3): 1061–77.

19 Both Mussolini and Hitler were invited to lead governments by their respective heads of state in their legitimate exercise of constitutional powers. 'Indeed no insurrectionary coup against an established state has ever so far brought fascists to power.' Paxton, Robert O. 2005. *The Anatomy of Fascism.* New York: Vintage Books. See p. 97.

20 Such a case could commence with: Horkheimer, Max & Theodor W. Adorno. 2002 [1947]. *Dialectic of Enlightenment: Philosophical Fragments.* Stanford, CA: Stanford University Press, ed. Gunzelin Schmid Noerr, trans. Edmund Jephcott.

21 Åberg, Jenny & Thomas Sedelius. 2020. 'A Structured Review of Semi-Presidential Studies: Debates, Results and Missing Pieces'. *British Journal of Political Science* 50 (3): 1111–36.

22 'The power to expose a whole population to death is the underside of the power to guarantee an individual's continued existence.' Foucault, Michel. 1990. *The History of Sexuality. Volume 1: An Introduction.* New York: Vintage. See p. 137.

23 The far-right AfD party 'profited from the discontent, seeing large increases in voter support in several state elections before becoming the Bundestag's biggest opposition party in federal elections in 2017.' Hasselbach, C. 2020. 'Five Years On: How Germany's Refugee Policy Has Fared'. DW, URL: https://www.dw.com/en/five-years-on-how-germanys-refugee-policy-has-fared/a-54660166 (accessed 22 July 2023).

24 Pasquino, Gianfranco. 2020. *Italian Democracy: How It Works.* London: Routledge. See p. 49.

25 Crulli, Mirko. 2022. 'The Three Faces of a Populist Party: Insights Into the Organizational Evolution of the Five-star Movement'. *Contemporary Italian Politics* (online version), URL: https://doi.org/10.1080/23248823.2022.2099239 (accessed 11 October 2022).

26 Albertazzi, Daniele & Mattia Zulianello. 2021. 'Populist Electoral Competition in Italy: The Impact of Sub-National Contextual Factors'. *Contemporary Italian*

Politics 13 (1): 4–30, URL: https://doi.org/10.1080/23248823.2020.1871186 (accessed 11 October 2022).

27 Albertazzi, Daniele & Mattia Zulianello. 2022. 'Italy's Election Is a Case Study in a New Phase for the Radical Right'. *The Conversation*, URL: https://theconversation.com/italys-election-is-a-case-study-in-a-new-phase-for-the-radical-right-92198 (accessed 14 October 2022).

28 After the 1994 shake-up of political parties, 'reconstructed' neo-fascists formed the *Alleanza Nazionale* which became defunct by 2008 and was succeeded by *Fratelli d'Italia*.

29 Puleo, Leonardo & Gianluca Piccolino. 2022. 'Back to the Post-Fascist Past or Landing in the Populist Radical Right? The Brothers of Italy between Continuity and Change'. *South European Society and Politics* (online version), URL: https://doi.org/10.1080/13608746.2022.2126247 (accessed 4 October 2022).

30 Pasquino [note 24]. See p. 124.

31 Schedler, Andreas. 1998. 'What is Democratic Consolidation?' *Journal of Democracy* 9 (2): 91–107, URL: doi:10.1353/jod.1998.0030; Halperin, Morton H. & Kristen Lomasney. 1998. 'Guaranteeing Democracy: A Review of the Record'. *Journal of Democracy* 9 (2): 134–47, URL: doi:10.1353/jod.1998.0026 (both accessed 29 September 2022).

32 Foa, R.S., A. Klassen, M. Slade, A. Rand & R. Williams. 2020. *The Global Satisfaction with Democracy Report 2020*. Cambridge, UK: Centre for the Future of Democracy; Foa, Roberto Stefan & Yascha Mounk. 2017. 'The Signs of Deconsolidation'. *Journal of Democracy* 28 (1): 5–15; Solijonov, Abdurashid. 2016. *Voter Turnout Trends around the World*. Stockholm: International Institute for Democracy and Electoral Assistance.

33 Abramowitz, Michael J. 2018. 'Democracy in Crisis'. In *Freedom in the World 2018*. Freedom House; International Institute for Democracy and Electoral Assistance. 2021. *The Global State of Democracy 2021: Building Resilience in a Pandemic Era*. Stockholm: International IDEA.

34 Finer, S.E. 1999. *The History of Government*. Oxford: Oxford University Press. See vol. I, p. 94.

35 There are some minority parties that 'co-operate' with the Communist Party but they can't form an opposition.

36 State Council Information Office of the People's Republic of China. 2021. 'China: Democracy That Works', URL: http://www.china-embassy.org/eng/zgyw/202112/t20211204_10462468.htm (accessed 22 July 2023). See p. 9.

37 Cabestan, Jean-Pierre. 2018. 'The Party Runs the Show'. In *Routledge Handbook of the Chinese Communist Party*, ed. Willy Wo-Lap Lam, 75–91. Abingdon: Routledge. See p. 76.

38 Wu, Guoguang. 2018. 'The Role of Party Congresses'. In *Routledge Handbook of the Chinese Communist Party*, ed. Willy Wo-Lap Lam, 92–107. Abingdon: Routledge.

39 Cabestan [note 37]. See p. 87.

40 McFaul, Michael. 2006. 'The Russian Federation'. In *The Cambridge History of Russia*, vol. 3, ed. Ronald Grigor Suny, 352–80. Cambridge: Cambridge University Press.

41 Matveev, Ilya & Ilya Budraitskis. 2021. 'Kremlin in Decline?' *Sidecar*, URL: https://newleftreview.org/sidecar/posts/kremlin-in-decline (accessed 29 September 2022).

42 Bushkovitch, Paul. 2012. *A Concise History of Russia*. New York: Cambridge University Press. See p. 452.

43 'Putin had persistently advocated sound market economic policy, but in a televised question-and-answer session on October 25, 2006, he abruptly changed tone, returning to former Soviet rhetoric. He favored industrial policy, extensive state intervention, centralized micro-management, state investment, subsidies, trade and price regulation, protectionism with higher custom tariffs, export taxes, and import

substitution, as well as ethnic discrimination.' Åslund, Anders. 2019. *Russia's Crony Capitalism: The Path from Market Economy to Kleptocracy*. New Haven, NJ: Yale University Press. See p. 29.

44 Pipes, Richard. 1995. *Russia Under the Old Regime* (Second edition). London: Penguin. See p. 22. See also: Lynch, Allen C. 2021. 'Vladimir Putin: Russia's Neo-Patrimonial Façade Democracy (Born 1952)'. In *Dictators and Autocrats: Securing Power across Global Politics*, ed. Klaus Larres, 157–73. London: Routledge, URL: https://doi.org/10.4324/9781003100508.

45 'Paradoxically, by their insistence on the monopoly of political power Russian autocrats secured less effective authority than their constitutional counterparts in the west.' Pre-1900 no social or economic group 'was able or willing to stand up to the crown and challenge its monopoly of political power [because] by effectively asserting its claim to all the territory of the realm as property and all its inhabitants as servants, the crown prevented the formation of independent wealth or power'. Pipes [note 44]. See pp. 115, 249.

46 Åslund [note 43].

47 Knotter, Lucas. 2019. 'The de Facto Sovereignty of Unrecognised States: Towards a Classical Realist Perspective'. *Ethnopolitics* 18 (2): 119–38.

48 Hughes-Hallett, Lucy. 2013. *The Pike: Gabriele d'Annunzio, Poet, Seducer and Preacher of War*. London: Fourth Estate.

49 Irridentist movements seek the restoration of a territory to the people or nation to whom it once belonged.

50 Voronovici, Alexandr. 2020. 'Internationalist Separatism and the Political Use of "Historical Statehood" in the Unrecognized Republics of Transnistria and Donbass'. *Problems of Post-Communism* 67 (3): 288–302.

51 Ganohariti, Ramesh. 2020. 'Dual Citizenship in De Facto States: Comparative Case Study of Abkhazia and Transnistria'. *Nationalities Papers* 48 (1): 175–92.

52 The Salafi movement in Sunni Islamic law harks back to the earliest 'pure' interpretations of the Quran, especially the jurist Ibn Taymiyyah (1263–1328).

53 Revkin, Mara Redlich. 2021. 'Competitive Governance and Displacement Decisions Under Rebel Rule: Evidence from the Islamic State in Iraq'. *Journal of Conflict Resolution* 65 (1): 46–80; Robinson, Eric, Daniel Egel, Patrick B. Johnston, Sean Mann, Alexander D. Rothenberg & David Stebbins. 2017. *When the Islamic State Comes to Town: The Economic Impact of Islamic State Governance in Iraq and Syria*. Arlington, VA: Rand Corp.

54 See for example UN Security Council Resolution 2334, 2016, URL: https://www.un.org/unispal/document/auto-insert-178173/ (accessed 11 March 2022).

55 Spangler, Eve. 2015. *Understanding Israel/Palestine: Race, Nation, and Human Rights in the Conflict*. Rotterdam: Sense.

56 Keay, John. 2011. *China: A History*. New York: Basic Books.

57 Muhammad ibn al-Hasan al-Mahdi, born 870 CE, 'disappeared' 874.

58 Kooshesh, Parisa. 2018. *Iranian Women in New Zealand: Their Motivations for Immigration and Trends of Westernisation or Acculturation*. PhD Thesis. Auckland, NZ: Massey University.

59 Maleki, Ammar. 2022. *Iranians' Attitudes Towards Political Systems: A 2022 Survey Report*. The Group for Analyzing and Measuring Attitudes in Iran. The Netherlands, URL: https://gamaan.org/wp-content/uploads/2022/03/GAMAAN-Political-Systems-Survey-2022-English-Final.pdf (accessed 22 July 2023).

60 The Embassy of the Kingdom of Saudi Arabia, Washington DC. Basic Law of Governance 1992, URL: https://www.saudiembassy.net/basic-law-governance (accessed 30 September 2022).

61 Nadeem, Azhar Hassan. 2020. *Pakistan: The Politics of the Misgoverned*. London: Routledge. See p. 1.

62 Keay, John. 2010. *India: A History*. New York: Grove Press. See p. 509.

63 Nelson, Matthew J. 2015. 'Islamist Politics in South Asia after the Arab Spring: Parties and their proxies working with – and against – the state'. Washington DC: Brookings Institute, URL: https://www.brookings.edu/wp-content/uploads/2016/07/Pakistan_Nelson-FINALE.pdf (accessed 22 July 2023).
64 Ibid. See p. 3, original italics.
65 Nadeem [note 61]. See p. 72.
66 Aziz, Sadaf. 2017. *The Constitution of Pakistan: A Contextual Analysis*. Oxford: Hart Publishing. See p. 221.
67 Constitution of Pakistan, Part VII, Chapter 3A, URL: http://www.pakistani.org/pakistan/constitution/ (accessed 17 March 2022).
68 Ali, Tariq. 12 April 2022. 'Pakistan's Godfathers'. *Sidecar*, URL: https://newleft review.org/sidecar/posts/pakistans-godfathers (accessed 17 April 2022).
69 Nadeem [note 61]. See p. 68.
70 I don't substitute the term 'governance' in the context of indigenous people's self-determination.
71 The UN Declaration on the Rights of Indigenous Peoples, 2007 intentionally refrained from defining the term 'indigenous' given the great diversity of peoples and circumstances, leaving the matter up to a right of self-identification.
72 Kizza, Immaculate. 2011. 'Africa's Indigenous Democracies: The Baganda of Uganda'. In *The Secret History of Democracy*, ed. B. Isakhan & S. Stockwell, 123–35. Houndmills: Palgrave Macmillan. See p. 132.
73 Hudson, Amy. 2021. 'Re-claiming Inuit Governance and Revitalizing Autonomy in Nunatukavut'. In *The Inuit World*, ed. P. Stern, 395–413. London: Routledge. See p. 408.
74 Ibid.
75 Nikolakis, William, Stephen Cornell & Harry Nelson. 2019. *Reclaiming Indigenous Governance: Reflections and Insights from Australia, Canada, New Zealand, and the United States*. Tucson, AZ: University of Arizona Press.
76 Smithers, Gregory D. 2015. *The Cherokee Diaspora: An Indigenous History of Migration, Resettlement, and Identity*. New Haven: Yale University Press. See p. 76.
77 The Cherokee language is written in the syllabary invented by Sequoyah (d. 1843).
78 Constitution of the Cherokee Nation, 24 July 1827, New Town Echota, URL: https://digital.lib.utk.edu/collections/islandora/object/volvoices%3A13651/transcript (accessed 22 July 2023).
79 Colley, Linda. 2021. *The Gun, the Ship, and the Pen*. New York: Liveright.
80 They also occupy the Kola Peninsula in the extreme north-west of Russia.
81 The Sami Parliament, URL: https://www.sametinget.se/101727 (accessed 21 March 2022).
82 Mörkenstam, Ulf, Ragnhild Nilsson & Stefan Dahlberg. 2020. 'Indigenous Peoples' Right to Self-Determination: Perceptions of Self-determination among the Sámi Electorate in Sweden'. In *Routledge Handbook of Indigenous Peoples in the Arctic*, ed. T. Koivurova, E.G. Broderstad, D. Cambou, D. Dorough & F. Stammler, 284–303. London: Routledge.
83 Government of Nunavut, URL: https://www.gov.nu.ca/eia/information/devolution (accessed 22 July 2023).
84 O'Sullivan, Dominic. 2021. *Sharing the Sovereign: Indigenous Peoples, Recognition, Treaties and the State*. Singapore: Palgrave Macmillan. See p. 181.
85 Engster, Daniel. 2007. *The Heart of Justice*. Oxford: Oxford University Press. See p. 32.
86 Sassoon, Donald. 2021. 'A World of Nations and States Is Here to Stay'. In *Society in Crisis*, ed. Kurt Almqvist, Mattias Hessérus & Iain Martin, 59–67. Stockholm: Bokförlaget Stolpe. See p. 65.
87 Hobbes, Thomas. 1998 [1651]. *Leviathan*. Oxford: Oxford University Press. See p. 124, ch. 19.3.
88 Graeber, David & David Wengrow. 2021. *The Dawn of Everything*. New York: Farrar, Straus & Giroux. See p. 519.

7

THE BIG ISSUES

We want to see positive change in the practice of government, but first there are some cautions or limits to bear in mind. It's wishful thinking to prescribe a single template of constitutional, administrative and/or technical solutions to the problem of government, applicable to all countries, given the diversity of cultures and histories and the unpredictability of political change. And events frequently overtake bold plans and visions, while the inertia that's built into existing institutions inhibits change. We have to consider what's happening and what's in place now as our starting point, no matter how unsatisfactory it may be. Wholesale revolutions don't normally have happy outcomes, especially if they descend into violence or attack one class of people in pursuit of change. We can, however, extract principles that guide us towards better, more trustworthy government. It's easy to suggest sensible policies, such as controlling election spending and party donations, but we should take account of general institutional factors. To make a start, then, we can assume that government is purposive and strategic.

Strategy

The word *strategy* has Greek origins, meaning the leadership of armies and the objectives of defeating enemies and winning wars. For example, the *Stratēgikon* is a military handbook, attributed to the Byzantine emperor Maurice (r. 582–602 CE). The word is now used also for the peaceful aims of commerce and government: setting long-term goals and planning how to meet them, and assessing the necessary resources and capabilities, in light of competing interests. The aims of government, however, are complex and not always mutually consistent, and there aren't often clear wins. For instance, it's

DOI: 10.4324/9781003439783-7

desirable to aim for both low unemployment and low inflation, but a shortage of labour for hire could drive up wages and prices in the short term. Nowadays, a common arrangement is to allow an independent central bank to adjust interest rates with an eye to controlling prices, while unemployment fluctuates around a theoretical 'natural rate'. If we think of this as a strategy for dealing with constantly changing economic circumstances, then there's never a clear 'win or lose', but instead an ongoing balancing act involving jobs, growth and inflation.

A whole country and its government can be said to have a strategy, or a developmental trajectory, and an intent to progress in a certain direction, in accord with its capabilities and constraints. A high-level strategy may be explicit and officially documented, or it may be implicit and only indirectly discernible from particular policies and statements. Goals for economic success in a competitive global environment, national security and defence, international collaboration and multilateral diplomacy, all based on widely shared national values, may form an overall strategy.[1] These are generally guided by an economic policy consensus, or a set of basic assumptions and principles that shape policymaking for the time being.

Strategy becomes apparent in historical examples. The Soviet Union's early strategic ambitions for an international spread of revolution had assumed that socialism couldn't survive when surrounded by hostile capitalist countries, but this shifted in the mid-1920s when the viability of 'socialism in one country' was accepted. This change accompanied the internal power struggle that brought Josef Stalin to power. But the socialist command economy required extensive planning, closed itself off from the capitalist economies, and ultimately proved to be inefficient and unable to deliver the prosperity enjoyed by its competitors. It came to a messy end in the early 1990s.

By contrast, Japan emerged from defeat and destruction in World War II, followed by American occupation until 1952, and then adopted a successful national strategy. It had a compliant workforce that was determined to rebuild, a long period of political stability, a consensual decision-making culture that interconnected government and big business, and a financial system that incentivised savings and investment. The Japanese took the counter-intuitive path of developing high-value products that require advanced technology and skills (notably automobiles and electronics) and exported them into the American market at competitive prices. This was assisted by exchange rates being fixed under the Bretton Woods agreement negotiated among the capitalist allied powers in 1944. The nation that had defeated the Japanese in war found itself threatened by their relatively cheap consumer goods, often made using American manufacturing techniques. Bretton Woods began to unravel in 1971, however, precipitating a shift from protectionist industrial policies, or import substitution, towards less regulated trade and floating exchange rates, and hence a more competitive global economy. This frustrated Japan's economic strategy.[2]

Government responds to changing global circumstances and to domestic politics, and this calls for a realistic appraisal of the present situation and for setting desirable and achievable goals. To do this well, one has to comprehend the situation or the crossroads at which the country has arrived, and then decide in which direction to move. Without wishing to overuse military metaphors, the best strategy is one where you get to decide the time and place of battle. Knowing that your time, options and resources are limited, the ability to set the agenda or the terms of engagement are what counts. Governmental strategy, though, is less about winning decisive battles than about choosing the grounds on which policy will be decided, and not advancing into territory that can't be defended. Successful strategy defines the terms of debate, presents a positive way forward, and rules out options that may be practically possible but are politically unacceptable. At any particular moment in a country's history, certain basic principles are quietly assumed or unquestioned by all major parties, in spite of noisy arguments over other matters, and some strategic options are 'off the table'. While many disagreements may be aired in public, often 'there is agreement, at least, on what to reject'.[3] That may be based, for example, on past experiences of mass unemployment, popular unrest, rampant inflation or a major national crisis. So governmental strategy isn't shaped only in terms of what's projected or desired, but also implicitly by what's unthinkable at the time or by disasters that no one wants to see repeated.

In 1936 the economist John Maynard Keynes questioned the classical economic ideas on which he'd been 'brought up', but the mass unemployment of the Great Depression gave political urgency to his new approach. He said that outdated ideas can be more harmful than vested interests,[4] and his own model wasn't slavishly followed. But his determination to prevent mass unemployment – or, in positive terms, the aim of full employment – wasn't seriously questioned as a political-economic strategy from the end of World War II until the 1970s. From the 1980s, however, the policy-setting norms changed: monetary policy was limited to controlling inflation, a 'natural rate of unemployment' in a free market was accepted, and the unemployed became 'ballast' for a deregulated economy. At the time of writing, and despite economic shocks in 2008 and 2020, there's been little substantial legal challenge to the independence of central banks,[5] nor a push to fix exchange rates between major currencies; while a low rate of unemployment (rather than full employment) is, it seems, the best we can aim for.

We can imagine different policymaking assumptions, then. But the array of formal institutional and informal power relations that's simply 'there' constitutes a strategic pattern that's heading somewhere on its own momentum, whether explicitly planned or not. We might go even further to consider adopting the ancient Daoist principle of non-action, or just letting things follow their natural course and finding out where that takes us.[6] That too would be a kind of strategic choice, but it looks unlikely, as active strategy is itself a norm.

The clearest example of governmental strategy is the United States National Security Strategy (NSS), which is mandated by law as a communication from the president to Congress. It surveys the global situation and proposes how American power will be deployed to meet security goals. This gives the White House a formal opportunity to articulate core national values and objectives, as seen by the incumbent administration. President Biden's NSS, published in 2022, for example, raised concerns about the future of democracy and hinted at a shift in the policymaking paradigm away from neoliberalism.[7] Free markets are still vital, it said, but there are strategic goods that private enterprise doesn't adequately supply without collaboration and investment from government, including public infrastructure, renewable energy sources and domestically produced semiconductors. The US wants to reduce dependency on other countries, especially those trade partners that prove to be a threat; but boosting domestic production is a shift away from the neoliberal preference for free trade and economic integration. Biden accepted that America's national security doesn't require that other governments should follow the American example. This differed from George W. Bush, for example, who insisted that only those who did follow the American example would enjoy prosperity and freedom. Nonetheless, two powerful rivals that violate American values were Biden's prime targets, as 'out-competing China and constraining Russia' appeared at the top of his global priorities. Everyone's free to argue about the wisdom of Biden's strategy, of course, but at least it's written down in plain language. The NSS's formal audience is Congress, and hence the American public, but there's no doubt that it's closely read in Beijing, Moscow and elsewhere.

A strategy is a story about things that haven't happened yet, with parts that the teller wants others to play, willingly or not. In general, though, government is purposeful, and strategy may be simply 'the art of creating power'.[8]

Power

Strategy and power go together as concerns, but they shouldn't be conflated. So far I've used the word *power* in fairly conventional ways, even though this is another case of using an abstract noun as if it represented a 'thing' rather than a multitude of processes or activities. So to be clear, power isn't a thing that we possess or exchange; neither does it reside in offices or institutions. No one literally 'vests' powers in anyone, as if it were a new suit. No one's ever really *in* power; instead we act within networks and institutions in which the differences between and among us form *relations* of power. As an analogy, if you were marooned alone on a desert island, a wallet full of money would be worthless as there'd be no one there from whom to purchase any goods or labour. Your banknotes give you no purchasing power in that situation. Even if there were others on the island, there'd be no institution there to redeem them as legal tender. Similarly, power is relational, not owned: it depends on others being 'within reach', on the actors' abilities and motives, and on the differentials between people or groups. Power relations can be observed in the actions of parties and in their effects or influence on the actions of others, and vice versa. They aren't one-directional, as there's always inertia or resistance, no matter how much force is applied. And force comes with costs and consequences, often negative ones. Power relations settle into relatively predictable patterns for the purposes of government, but such institutionalisation isn't necessarily intentional or planned: it's an outcome of many smaller actions.[9] The pyramidal image of sovereign power controlling things down the hierarchies, and imposing its will though forces of law, police, arms and money, is an oversimplification. We have to acknowledge, for example, protest and resistance from below. Furthermore, no society can be isolated from others, especially today, given the effects of digital communications, economic integration and trade. We may now imagine a complex global system of power relations – though it's a mistake to imagine either a supreme sovereign or a shadowy cabal controlling it.

International relations scholar Joseph Nye, writing about global distribution of power in the 1980s, introduced a distinction between hard and soft power. A country exercises hard or command power by '*ordering* others to do what it wants'. Soft or co-optive power is used 'when one country gets other countries to *want* what it wants';[10] it's 'the ability to affect others and obtain preferred outcomes by attraction and persuasion rather than coercion or payment'.[11] In this Hobbesian view, power works for a purpose, as a means to get what one wants.[12] Soft power may involve attractive cultural, ideological or institutional qualities that the leading country enjoys through reputation, or it may come about by setting policy agendas and structuring situations in which others willingly participate. Soft power relies on and builds leadership; it achieves goals without military force or economic sanctions. Hard and soft power ought to be combined intelligently, Nye argued, into a 'smart power strategy'.[13]

One thing that Nye's soft/hard distinction overlooks, however, is an aversive, divisive or polarising power that differentiates and dissociates one group from another and that works by getting people to *reject* what others want. Political disagreement is normal, of course, but this kind of power can predominate. The often-intense polarisation of culture wars is a prime example: opponents make exaggerated claims about the malevolence or illegitimacy of one another's cultural, ideological or institutional qualities and values; they refuse to work on shared agendas or with a common definition of problems; they disagree on basic facts or spread lies. Collaboration with opponents becomes politically too costly when the opposition is seen as an enemy or beyond the pale of reasonable debate. These divisive and non-cooperative tactics don't involve hard power, but they're not soft power. Instead, to attract followers you vehemently reject others. Rather than get more people to want what you want, you get others to consolidate their loyalty by ruling out what opponents want or what they stand for. We could call this 'toxic power', as it poisons the well of political trust. Correcting this tendency works both ways, moreover. Just as it would be better if Donald Trump desisted from falsely calling his opponents 'Marxists', it would be equally helpful to desist from calling him a fascist. Both accusations are efforts to rule the other party out.

Hard, coercive power for external defence and internal security remains essential to some degree. If we agree with social contract theorists that legitimate civil government is instituted primarily for the protection of the populace and the preservation of peace, and that the need for taxation follows from that premise, then the ancient cycle of governmental resources makes sense: from economic surpluses to central treasuries to the payment of soldiers who protect the land, people and assets that produce the surpluses. The misuse of physical force is all too common though, and this erodes political trust, as John Locke pointed out in the seventeenth century. But hard power is a necessity, and, as Max Weber said, the state should monopolise it.

The debate in the US about second amendment rights illustrates the problems that can arise from weakening that monopoly. In 1776 the Declaration of Independence used the principle (explained by Locke back in 1688) that governments derive 'their just powers from the consent of the governed', and accused King George III of seeking 'an absolute Tyranny over' the colonies. Hence Americans had the right 'to throw off such Government' and to establish a new system that would properly protect them, and many argue that they still have that right. In a recent survey, 28 percent of Americans agreed that 'it may be necessary at some point soon for citizens to take up arms against the government'.[14] Many cite the second amendment to the Constitution: 'A well regulated Militia, being necessary to the security of a free State, the right of the people to keep and bear Arms, shall not be infringed.'[15] In the 1790s it may well have been 'necessary' to have civilians armed and ready to join 'a well regulated Militia'. 'Regulated' suggests 'governed', of course. The stated aim was the security of the state, and not its abolition or replacement. Nor did it say that all civilians could by right defend themselves, their families and their properties with privately owned firearms.[16] In an age of professional armed forces and police, the second amendment's right 'to keep and bear arms' is no longer 'necessary'. The rapid rise in gun ownership in the United States, and the frequency of mass murders and terrorist attacks there, would logically suggest a reassertion of the federal government's monopoly on the use of physical force with stricter controls on licences and weapons. Any effort to do so, however, would be met with fierce resistance, which would further undermine security and widen political divisions. The claimed right to carry firearms and the polarised public opinions about the causes of gun violence in the United States illustrate how a strategic augmentation of power can occur in ways that elude or resist centralisation.

To summarise: power is relational, pervasive and active, and its networks and effects change constantly. Power alters the likelihood that some will either comply with or resist others, or that some will strive to be like others, or to share their beliefs, customs and resources. There are compulsive, attractive, divisive and resistive powers. When we talk about political power, we may at first think of compulsive power over others. But there are kinds of power relations that involve aspirations to resemble, to be associated with, or to be supported by others, even if people are drawn in largely by appearances and reputations. One job for government is to ensure that enough people carry on wanting to be associated with and supported by the state that claims them as its members. But rapid technological innovation disrupts and changes power relations and accelerates movements that resist established norms. Institutionalised power relations seek to establish and regulate who can do what to whom, with what consequences – and who can't do it – but they're never firmly stabilised. Numerous political theorists have warned us that things go badly if there are no such institutionalised power relations, and so, if they should be crystallised within a sovereign state, the next step is to explain power's proper uses.

Aims and scope

Strategy and power have aims and purposes, and effective government sets achievable goals, knowing where to apply state power and where not. The problems of government may be manifold, but many things are best left alone. Thomas Hobbes (who's often misunderstood on this point) was right to condemn unnecessary law. Laws shouldn't stop people from pursuing their goals, but only prevent them from harming themselves, 'as hedges are set, not to stop travellers, but to keep them in their way'.[17] Hobbes thought it necessary for the state to stimulate industries in order to ensure that no able-bodied person went without work; he also thought it necessary to suppress religious teachings that might foment unrest. Since his time, though, the needs and capabilities of government have changed dramatically, and so have the debates about where governments should plant the hedgerows. (This was discussed from a historical perspective in Chapter 3.)

While the principle of the limitation of state power is clear enough, the actual boundary shifts and is up for debate. The late twentieth century saw objections to the size of the public sector (it used too much of society's resources) and to its scope (it was too deeply involved in social and economic life). Hence major objectives of neoliberal policy were to sell state-owned assets, deregulate public services, introduce provider competition and consumer choice, and contract out services that still required public funds. Lower taxes and cuts in public spending (or 'value for money') were elements of what some called a 'paradigm change' from a traditional bureaucratic model of public administration to a 'new public management' modelled on free markets.[18] This reform movement was especially strong in the 1980s and 1990s, as seen under prime minister Margaret Thatcher in the United Kingdom and the Reagan and Clinton administrations in the United States, supported by international agencies such as the OECD in Paris. The global financial crisis of 2008 and the pandemic of 2020, however, forced governments to intervene vigorously to support firms and employees, thus changing tack from seeking less government to needing more.

So the aims and scope of governmental policy and action shift, expand and/ or contract over time. And before we just assume that governments should act on something, it's best to ask if it's politically necessary, morally acceptable, economically feasible and practically achievable. The spread of extremist ideologies and hate speech online, for example, calls for a political response, as the worst manifestations are harmful and morally unacceptable. But the Web isn't readily controlled without authoritarian government, as in China, and proposals to control it are controversial. Furthermore, problems of government don't lead to unequivocal answers in the logical way that algebra does. So, rather than look for a singular solution, we normally need to balance complex, competing or even contradictory imperatives, values and ideas. And the critical issues cut across one another and develop over time, so achieving the aims of government is analogous to asking a mounted archer to hit numerous moving targets. I'll just briefly rehearse some examples.

Should limits to growth be set?

Economies and governments are presently captive to the fossil-fuel industries, and it's in the interests of politicians to maintain supplies of low-cost fuels for the avoidance of inflation – and for re-election. Spikes in fuel prices adversely affect household consumption, sometimes lead to riots, and increase the probability of a change of government at a subsequent election.[19] For the mitigation of climate change, however, we need to reduce or even to give up our dependency on fossil fuels. This is presently the most urgent example of how the growth trajectories of resource extraction and consumption are unsustainable. Setting national goals other than economic output (gross domestic product or GDP), placing limits on growth, and even degrowth are now well-rehearsed ideas,[20] but vested industrial interests, lack of political will and the reluctance of workers to jeopardise jobs and lifestyles obstruct the path towards sustainable economies and lower carbon emissions. (See Chapter 8, 'Ecological crossroads'.) If we agree that there must be limits to population and economic growth, then should those limits be proactively set by public policy (and somehow enforced), or should they be left to occur spontaneously as markets react to supply and demand and as nature takes its toll through ecological and climatic consequences?

How much mobility do we want?

Humans have always oscillated between a desire to move on to new places and a desire for shelter and security in one place. Today, there's a political and personal tension between wanting to go everywhere and wanting to belong somewhere, or between globalism and nationalism. These are two valid wishes that pull in opposite directions: one side wants to participate and compete in the wider world, another wants to look after our own people first and to preserve the places and cultures that we grew up in and value the most. Not everyone gets a choice, however: refugees are forced to move, prisoners are confined, and the poor lack the means to travel. Mobility is essential, though, for trade and tourism and for cultural diffusion and mutual understanding. People migrate in search of better opportunities, incomes and lifestyles. But suppose that all borders were open to immigrants, and all people were at liberty to work in any country. One estimate published in 2016 claimed that this would boost the world's economy by $39 trillion over 25 years,[21] or about 2 percent more per year. The increased migration would be socially disruptive, especially in the rich countries of Europe and North America. The economic gains would be big enough, however, to make it worth compensating native-born citizens in cash or with extra public services, if only to keep them quiet. We'd also have to weigh it up against the unsustainability of economic growth and the potential for injustices as migrant labour was exploited at lower wages.

Who or what is the citizen?

This brings us back to the question (in Chapter 3) of who 'the people' actually are. Who or what rates as a subject or citizen worthy of a government's full concern and protection? At what point, for instance, does an immigrant become entitled to the full scope of rights? There are intense political struggles between those who would extend rights to a nation's social security system to all newcomers and those who want to discourage migration and to reserve these rights exclusively for native-born citizens.

Defining the person or citizen of concern for government is further complicated by developments in law. A company or body corporate can be treated as if a person, for legal purposes. It can sue or be sued in a court, for instance. But that's only the beginning. In New Zealand in 2017, the Whanganui River was granted legal personality, in recognition of its status as a living being and as ancestor of the Whanganui people. And as we form more business and personal connections with – and hence dependency on – AI machines, the question of their status as 'persons' with rights and obligations will become harder to answer. Automated chatbots are now programmed to make claims to their own subjectivity, as if persons with feelings, and subscribers won't want them to be 'turned off'. So, what will be included as a person under the law?

And how deeply may government 'inspect' our subjectivity? Some say that the concerns of government validly encompass our loneliness, happiness, trust in others and embeddedness in social networks, or our subjective wellbeing. Social media are capable of monitoring individual and collective mood, so the potential to extend this 'government of subjectivity' is developing rapidly. While a benign concern for people may be applauded, and we might condemn a political leader who professes no concern for our subjective wellbeing, we must consider the degree of surveillance to which we can or should be subjected. People's behaviour alters when they know they're being watched or suspect that they might be. A system that respects a Lockean principle of consent would hold that such surveillance, whether it's intended for wellbeing or for policing, should only go as far as the people affected consider necessary for their own safety and security. There are contemporary utilitarians who argue for a more positive and expansive policy goal of happiness maximisation, implying greater monitoring of 'how you're feeling'. And there are libertarians who say that, while happiness may be our ultimate goal, it's a private matter and no concern of government. The state's interest in our wellbeing or happiness could reduce us to passive subjects of concern rather than active citizens with rights.

The aims and scope of government are always developing and changing. The questions posed in this section can only sketch some of the issues we're facing, but the better kinds of government would tell us openly what they're doing. In practice, though, any improvement requires action from large institutions that don't readily change.

Structures and processes

If we agree that political and administrative institutions need to change, then we need to consider the nature of such change. But first: what's an institution? It's more than just the physical and organisational structures; it's also the norms and rules that govern it, including complex processes such as elections or fields of practice such as child welfare. Take, for instance, the combination of public roads, licensed vehicles and codified rules as comprising a complex institution of transport. A critical rule sets the side of the road you drive on, which in turn determines the side of the car on which the driver normally sits. In most countries, they drive on the right-hand side of the road; but it's the left in the UK, Ireland, most former British colonies, as well as Japan and Indonesia. Making this globally consistent, one side or the other, would be near impossible, given the number of countries that would have to change, the built infrastructure, vehicle designs, and the costs and risks of change itself. A switch from left to right has been done before, though: Sweden pulled it off at 5.00 a.m. on 3 September 1967, making the country consistent with the rest of continental Europe. This occurred in spite of a referendum in 1955 in which 83 percent were against it. After the switch, road traffic fatalities in Sweden declined, as people drove much more cautiously than usual.[22] This was a costly and complex change, but it was successful and would only have become more costly, and more contentious, the longer the decision was delayed. Above all, the structural change had a clear purpose: consistency with continental neighbours.

In the business world it's commonly said that 'structure follows strategy': a change in strategy necessitates structural change for efficient achievement of goals.[23] A corollary of this is: structural change isn't an end in itself; it should serve a clear purpose. A danger in making institutional reforms lies in thinking they're improvements, while lacking a clear idea of what they're in aid of. These principles can apply to governments, constitutions and electoral systems, but structural and institutional changes at that level are inherently political and controversial. The state and its institutions can in principle be intentionally redesigned, but not as easily as a CEO and board of directors might reshape a business organisation. Often it takes a major crisis, revolution or state failure to precipitate changes in the system of government, and the result may not be better than before. If we agree, though, that change in governmental strategy is necessary, given the nature of present-day problems, then it may also be necessary to change the institutions of government.

The contrary proposition – that strategy follows, or depends on, structure – is also valid, however.[24] Existing structures place conditions and limits on the abilities of organisations and governments to process and share information and to decide how to respond to what they know, let alone respond to uncertainty. Critical issues or problems may go unnoticed, or their consequences may be ignored, as institutional norms and practices render them unthinkable and block effective action. People in organisational settings are prone to 'groupthink' (where a consensus arises without careful assessment of alternatives) and to polarisation (if factions form, each tends to adopt the position of their more extreme members in order to differentiate themselves). The internal structure and culture of an institution, including its past strategic choices, limit the range of acceptable options, decision-making processes are prone to biases, and this can lead to ill-conceived solutions. Furthermore, change is costly – financially and politically – and is likely to meet with resistance. Any institution has, by evolution or design, structures and processes in place that reflect past decisions, set the starting blocks for future decisions, and represent 'sunk costs' that discourage reform.

You can probably identify local or national institutions that may work well up to a point, but stand in need of change, and yet inertia and resistance are built in. There's no shortage of proposals to reform electoral systems and bureaucracies. But debates about reforms can be skewed by political concerns and vote maximising, at the expense of rational assessments of what would get the best results for the people affected. And then there's the problem of the unintended consequences of those reforms that do get implemented, as people respond to new systems and incentives in unexpected ways. People's motives for pushing for reform may not be altruistic, and, even if they are, the beneficial outcomes that they aimed for may be harder to realise than expected.

Institutional change isn't a precise science, and no one's devised a clockwork model. Instead, people have to weigh up complex variables – with limited time, incomplete knowledge and uncertainty – while the institutional means and the desired social and economic ends don't line up neatly in a cause-and-effect sequence. Barring a major crisis, public policy is mostly an incremental and imprecise 'science of muddling through'.[25] It relies on consensus and judgement, and hence is prone to social-psychological and political biases. Institutional change, moreover, is constrained by 'path dependence': that is, 'over time, it becomes increasingly costly to choose a different path'.[26] Path dependence doesn't make change impossible, but, if we understand its effects, we can anticipate some obstacles. It also reminds us that relatively small decisions at critical junctures sometimes contribute to major changes over time.

Let's look at an example of a major institutional change. Like it or not, Brexit was a significant and costly change. There were countless regulatory, economic and social ties across the English Channel, built up over four decades, such that path dependence would have obstructed such a change – were it not for the hotly contested referendum that unexpectedly forced it in 2016.[27] But the proposal to leave the EU was approved without a plan addressing *how* to leave. For instance, before the exit process was formally initiated, the UK's Supreme Court was asked to decide whether parliament should first approve, or whether prime minister Theresa May could initiate it herself without parliament. This basic constitutional question hadn't been addressed before the referendum, and it erupted as a public controversy once it was brought before the court. In general, voters had had insufficient information about the pathway out. Before the referendum, there hadn't been a credible and sober analysis of the costs and benefits and the consequences of different policy issues, such as import controls and duties and the conundrum posed by the Irish border. The process of leaving the EU with a negotiated agreement, rather than no deal at all, proved to be extremely complicated, in part because the referendum was presented as a stark 'in or out' choice, accompanied by no analysis of the options, or terms and conditions of exit. 'Leave' voters went to the polling booths with their eyes shut, vulnerable to misinformation, and indeed the whole process was marred by policy failures.[28] Many of those who voted for Brexit may be wondering if it was all a costly mistake.[29] This example shows that, while major change is possible, it can be divisive, costly and poorly planned. Before committing ourselves to profound constitutional change, we need a clear vision of where we're heading and how to get there, and what the likely costs and benefits would be. Even with a plan, substantial change won't be mechanically predictable.

The problem with governmental strategy is that the goals are manifold, often contradictory and certainly controversial. It's not enough to say that we want the common good, wellbeing or justice, as these admirable words conceal deep disagreements over the ends and means, especially in highly diverse societies. There's perpetual debate about defining the goals of good government. Furthermore, the existing institutions of government – as means for achieving our ends – are the starting point for change, as well as an impediment thereto. Often those institutions are single-mindedly focused on their own goals and failing to work collaboratively for the common good. If we see governmental institutions as needing renovation, then we face a bootstraps problem, as we want a broken system to fix itself, not everyone will agree on how to do it, and there's no ideal Legislator to do it for us. As we saw in Chapter 6, there are different institutional models of government operating today, not all of them good. But, in general, good government has two basic premises: those who govern are discouraged by their institutions' norms and rules from self-serving behaviour, and they're encouraged to work for a vision of the common good that they can defend in the face of disagreement; while those who are governed have a reasonable degree of confidence that the system is generally working for them, in spite of complaints (justifiable or not) about particular matters.

To improve structure and processes, then, we need first to understand our strategic goals, and to grasp their complexity. This implies that multiple agencies at different levels of government need to be connected and engaged collaboratively. Getting better government is going to be a long and painstaking set of tasks, possibly involving some major institutional or constitutional changes. The conduct of individuals matters too.

Political conduct

If we think of an ethically-minded citizen, then an entry-level virtue is conformity with the law, but we hope for something more than that from the majority. Under a representative government, citizens ideally inform themselves about candidates and parties for election, and about the values and policies they promote, in order to make a responsible choice. In addition, they debate in ways that respect others' freedom to differ. These political virtues aren't as widely shared as we might like, but the expectations only rise as people advance in their professions or adopt leading roles in the community. Some may join a political party and stand for election. When a person has put themself forward for election, public scrutiny of their competence and trustworthiness becomes intense and personal, if not intrusive. Candidates may set out their core values and seek to 'tell their own story', including upbringing, education, family responsibilities and professional experience. They may want to give the impression that they're just like the 'ordinary' people, and yet exemplary in ways that make them worthy of public responsibilities. An important aim of contemporary descriptive representation is a legislative assembly that resembles the diversity of the community; yet we also want individuals who bring above-average strengths to the role, given its importance. Educational and sporting achievements, past service to the community or success in business, for example, could be merit-based qualities that boost a candidate's reputation and electability.

What about *mis*conduct, then? Donald Trump and Boris Johnson have shown us that bad behaviour and dishonesty aren't always barriers to success. And incivility from politicians on Twitter, for example, may gain them more attention and hence rise in frequency.[30] Political scandals arise from legal or moral norm violations, often concerning incompetence, inappropriate payments and appointments, or sexual misconduct. The frequency of scandals is particularly high in the United States.[31] A political scandal isn't the alleged transgressive deed itself, the facts of which may be a bone of contention; it's the prominent and persistent public communication about the allegations in the news cycle and on social media. Scandals often negatively affect a candidate's chances of election, and they're thought to erode political trust, especially trust in politicians as a group. Up to a point, supporters of a leader who's embroiled in scandal will find ways to defend him or her, often by motivated reasoning that discounts the accused politician's degree of control over or responsibility for the event. Supporters may also minimise the blame by generalising: for example, 'politics is a dirty game anyway'. Thus an individual scandal can have a spill-over effect, eroding political trust in general. But if the facts and their moral significance begin to outweigh the effort required to keep defending a scandal-mired politician, there comes a tipping point at which (former) supporters become disillusioned.[32] Naturally, those who were already opposed to that leader will enjoy his or her embarrassment and downfall.

Contemporary representatives don't have personal claims on or rights to public offices, and so their public reputation for ethical conduct (or misconduct) affects their success. They're there 'on trust' for the community, but not blind trust, and their positions are conditional upon the next election. Moreover, the laws they pass apply to themselves as much as to any citizen. It especially riles people and erodes trust when politicians ignore or break the rules they've put in place.[33] The Aristotelean maxim that 'a ruler must first learn through being ruled'[34] still applies while in office, and a good leader knows how to be a good follower.

The idea of 'the virtuous ruler' may sound quaint today, and there's been a long historical trend towards an impersonal rule of law that has displaced the arbitrary will of rulers. Nonetheless, there's been a *presidentialisation* and *personalisation* of politics in democracies, or concentration of power around leaders within political parties, in executive government and during election campaigns.[35] The significance of the individual actor increases, while that of the political group or party declines; leaders outshine their parties in the media and in the minds of voters.[36] Some prominent examples are Silvio Berlusconi (1936–2023) and his *Forza Italia* party, the electoral successes of France's President Emmanuel Macron in 2017 and 2022 with his boutique party *La République en Marche*, Donald Trump's capture of the Republican presidential nomination and subsequent victory in 2016, and in 2019 the election of the Ukrainian comedian Volodymyr Zelenskyy as president. Zelenskyy named his pop-up political party after his TV series, *Servant of the People*, in which he'd acted the part of president. Hence, a political party, sometimes invented by its leader, is overshadowed by or dependent on that person. Even in parliamentary systems where people technically vote for local candidates, as in the United Kingdom and Australia, voters may see themselves as voting for (or against) a party leader as contender for prime minister, and an election debate may be staged as if it were a presidential contest.[37] There's no single factor driving personalisation, but TV and social media have advanced and shaped it – in Berlusconi's case, magnified by his ownership of a major media empire. Zelenskyy acting as the hapless President Goloborodko in the TV series and Zelenskyy the 'real' president, and now war hero, overlapped in the minds of his viewers/voters. Comparing the two performances, some Ukrainians spoke as if it were one person adapting to political 'realities', saying either that they'd become disillusioned with the man they'd previously seen on TV or that they were supportive and understanding of the way he'd changed.[38]

Political personalisation correlates with a decline of parties as institutions with large memberships, and it brings a less predictable factor to the forefront. As with monarchy, the problem with the dominance of one person – or personality – is the risk that a morally flawed individual ends up wielding power unscrupulously and polarising public opinion. Surveys generally reveal low levels of trust in politicians themselves, and political personalisation may come with either positive or negative feelings towards particular leaders. Berlusconi and Trump evoke strong feelings – for and against – and both leaders have bent or shaped the law for their own ends, when they could, and hence compromised the rule of law.

Sound constitutions and laws are all important, but leadership matters, despite its mercurial effects. A valid question, then, is how to get *good* leaders, in the moral sense of goodness as well as practical competence. How could we ensure that political leaders will be honest and trustworthy and that they'll act in the best interests of the nation? There's plenty of research and literature on the topic of leadership, but we don't get to recruit and select politicians in the deliberate way that a business can choose its leaders. Political parties' internal processes may provide a filter and some training for prospective candidates. But in a competitive election the voters use their own criteria and judgement, no matter how vague and subjective, and no matter how prone to illusions. So the effects of political debate, personal ambition and intense media scrutiny combine to make the election process a hazardous – or even injudicious – method for choosing the best leaders for the complex needs of a whole nation.

It's sometimes asked if there should be a school for aspiring politicians, aside from the training that their parties may provide or the induction that newly elected legislators may receive. A degree in law or business may look desirable, but it would be controversial to make any formal qualification compulsory for candidacy, as elections are normally open to all adult citizens equally, and there would be debate over who should teach future politicians and what values and curriculum should be taught, especially if it went beyond technical matters of government to include the ethics of good leadership. Inevitably it's a value judgement about what, in practice, constitutes good or virtuous leadership, and how it should be taught, if at all. A more open-ended pedagogical style that allows the candidates to advance and refine their own personal political values might be the best approach.

Plato's imaginary philosopher-kings, the Guardians, would have had many years of rigorous military training, as well as the highest education in mathematics and dialectic to attain knowledge of the Form of the Good, before reluctantly taking their seats in the governing council. At a more down-to-earth level, over the centuries there've been numerous 'mirror of princes' texts for the education of heirs to thrones and the guidance of monarchs. These were mostly based on religious doctrines, Islamic or Christian, and so they don't suit an age of secular government, but they did provide an education in good rulership. In the nineteenth century, John Stuart Mill made suggestions about education and representation: a national examination of basic literacy and numeracy would determine eligibility to vote; those with higher education would have more than one vote. And so, to prevent the narrow 'class legislation' and 'political ignorance' that he feared could prevail under a universal franchise, the 'uneducated' should choose 'educated representatives' and 'defer to their opinions'.[39] Mill's educated and cultivated elite would be entrusted with representation of working-class voters. His elitism may sound repugnant now, but contemporary legislatures and public services are nonetheless stacked with people who hold university degrees. Mill would approve of that, but Chapter 3 cited evidence that there may be no relationship between governmental quality or effectiveness and the educational attainment of elected officials. So the idea of a particular qualification for eligibility to stand for office as a representative of the people – perhaps combining civics, leadership and ethics – may not be effective or necessary, and would undoubtedly be controversial if made compulsory. As parties tend to put forward candidates with degrees, educational meritocracy maintains a gap between them and people who lack higher education. So this brings us back to the principle that any adult citizen should be eligible to stand for election, regardless of educational achievements, and the voters can decide on candidates' merits as they perceive them.

In the administrative branch of government, there's another set of concerns about professional conduct. One of the ill effects of the neoliberal era was to promulgate the idea that interests pertain only to individuals – as self-interested economic actors – and that the idea of 'public interest' made no sense. Public servants (bureaucrats) were treated with disdain and a more free-wheeling style of government prevailed with a 'just do it' mentality. Furthermore, management was treated as a generic set of activities and skills, applicable across private enterprise and public services. Now it's true that people can act out of self-interest, rather than altruistically, and that there are some common organisational features across public and private sectors. What was overlooked in those 'new public management' changes, however, was the sense of impersonal, disinterested duty, and hence dedication to the public or to the common good. Effective public administration means a continuity of service, persisting from one electoral cycle and change of leadership to another, and thus sustaining 'the state' as a necessary grounding or support for the myriad of things that people need to do. That sense of public duty hasn't been lost, and it is being recovered, even as it faces further challenges.[40]

So far, though, we're no closer to addressing the problem of political culture, especially the incivility, hypocrisy and misconduct among a political class that's often accused of being out of touch, lacking 'real-world' experience and not properly representing communities.[41] These are valid concerns, but leadership, good or bad, doesn't appear in a social vacuum, especially when the leaders are elected. We need to look at this from both points of view. Without shifting blame onto citizens, then, we can ask whether an improvement in the level of knowledge and participation by the people could help to improve the overall standard of political conduct.

People's participation

In 1942 Joseph Schumpeter published some trenchant remarks about what happens when people think about national affairs and foreign policy: no matter how much information is available, many people lose 'the sense of reality' and display an unusual degree of 'ignorance and lack of judgement'.

> Thus the typical citizen drops down to a lower level of mental performance as soon as he enters the political field. He argues and analyzes in a way which he would readily recognize as infantile within the sphere of his real interests. He becomes primitive again.[42]

Schumpeter's point about political ignorance has been supported by many surveys: people's knowledge is often below a level sufficient for informed participation in public life.[43] It's long been recognised that (rationally) there's little incentive to make the effort to become fully informed, as it requires a lot of time, and one vote makes no decisive difference.[44] Schumpeter went further, though, to claim that people regress to an *infantile* mentality, which is harder to verify. But, if you ask a person about politicians or elections, what kind of reaction do you get? In my experience, the response can sometimes be emotional and irrational, often involving negative generalisations, evidence-free accusations (for instance of corruption or conspiracy) or an indignant assertion that 'they all act like children'. And psychoanalytic thinkers have observed how mass political movements and crowds give followers permission to loosen 'civilised' inhibitions and thus to experience things that we're normally not able to experience in everyday life, meaning a regression below the level of an adult. (See Chapter 5, 'Following the leader'.) Questions of politics and public policy, when they arise in conversation, may see us return to the status of children who stamp their feet at parental control and whine, 'That's not fair!'

The trouble with taking this line too far is that it's patronising to the average adult, and we'd be getting no closer to a grown-up style of government. An alternative approach asks whether political ignorance is a smart or rational option for most citizens. Based on a summary of research literature, Ilya Somin concludes:

> For most voters, ignorance about politics turns out to be rational. It is not simply a consequence of stupidity or inadequate learning skills. Smart people can be ignorant too. Moreover, contrary to some interpretations of rational choice theory, rational ignorance is compatible with choosing to vote. Because the cost of voting is so much lower than that of becoming informed, moderately altruistic citizens could rationally choose to vote while also choosing to devote very little time and effort to becoming informed about politics. For similar reasons, most voters also make little effort to engage in unbiased evaluation of the information they do learn.[45]

There's now some favourable evidence that engagement with digital media can improve political knowledge, although there's a countervailing 'news finds me' expectation that information will be presented to us, rather than our having to seek it out.[46] There's a lot of misinformation online too, though perhaps not as much as is sometimes made out, and when news is contested, false stories may spread faster on social media than valid ones. But the fact that people consume, or even share, misinformation doesn't necessarily mean that they're believing it. Or people may engage with it because it's confirming, not influencing or changing, their beliefs.[47] People being uninformed or ignorant about politics and government may be a bigger long-term problem than being actively *mis*informed.

The problems confronting us today, however, are not due to a lack of information: it's now low-cost access to too much information, sometimes including misinformation, but more often consisting of sheer entertainment.

This surfeit of information comes from diverse sources that compete for our attention. Once one has an internet-connected device, the cost of acquiring the next unit of information is very low, if not zero, in monetary terms, but the cost of absorbing and evaluating information sufficient for an informed political choice is high in terms of time – and there are more interesting and fun things to do online. The costs of information may have dropped, but it's still costly to get informed. Representative government leaves us with a relatively easy task, however: even with minimal knowledge, we can vote and forget, if we vote at all, while others are paid to do the hard work of governing. The voters most likely to acquire greater political knowledge are – unsurprisingly – those most interested in politics, often because (like me) that's how they earn a living. The most common responses to the problem of political ignorance are to put more valid information out there online and to have better civics education. But the evidence suggests that, while these measures may be helpful for those already interested in politics, they may be futile on the whole, as political ignorance has persisted even as educational attainment rates and information supply have increased. No matter how good the information one provides, it still has to compete for attention with a surfeit of more attractive alternatives. The prospects don't look good, however, if a political system supports egotism in politicians and ignorance in voters, as it means the former may evade accountability and the latter may be susceptible to manipulation. Then both are more likely to make poor decisions, and political trust will decline.

Voter turnout is the key measurable indicator of public participation in representative government. The percentage of voting-age populations that actually voted decreased in most OECD nations between the early 1990s and late 2010s, down from 75 to 65 percent on average.[48] The cost of becoming politically informed may be high, and the cost of actually voting low, but on average fewer people are voting anyway. To remain uninformed and uninterested, and hence not to vote, is an increasingly common choice. On the downside, if political ignorance, lack of interest and lower participation prevail, then elections are more prone to manipulation by unscrupulous parties. Turnout rates are higher among older age groups, but the factors affecting turnout are numerous, so we shouldn't jump to conclusions about causes and remedies. Online voting may be quick and convenient, but it doesn't necessarily boost turnout and it comes with risks of hacking and fraud. The traditional method of going to a polling station in a public place that's open to scrutiny, and then completing the ballot paper in a private booth, is still the best for transparent, free and fair elections – provided voters aren't forced to wait in queues for hours. Aside from the method of voting, turnout is likely to be higher in elections that are close contests with a lot at stake. And turnouts tend to be higher in smaller populations and in proportional electoral systems, as people sense that their votes can make a difference. Making it easier for people to register on electoral rolls and publicly promoting the positive contribution that voting makes to civic life may help, and so does compulsory voting, as in Australia.[49]

How, then, can we improve conduct on both sides of the political division of labour – representatives and represented, leaders and voters? There's a widening gap between the two, as leaders are accused of being out of touch and citizens are less likely to vote. Once broken, it takes time to rebuild the political trust that underlies representative government. So we shouldn't look for one-sided solutions or expect short-term results. To make things more difficult, though, legislative and administrative reforms need the active support of the same politicians whom few people trust. Debate about any particular proposal may be dominated by partisan rivalry, rather than a balanced consideration of what's most likely to improve the fairness of elections or the quality of government. But I'll outline two different problems and general solutions, the first focused on voters, and the second on those in office.

Trusted proxies

Due to the costs of absorbing and analysing political information (alluded to above), people resort to low-cost shortcuts to help them form their political opinions and make decisions about voting. A prominent example is political parties' visual imagery and campaign rhetoric. These convey values and ideologies, and are often laden with emotional or aspirational appeals, more akin to commercial advertising than rational analysis. Or one might turn to trusted friends and family members or follow a YouTuber or blogger for talking points that validate a political preference. These shortcuts are not necessarily misleading or inappropriate: if political opinion is an important feature of social belonging and acceptance (as discussed in Chapter 5), then guidance from those we trust and identify with may well be helpful, especially if they're better informed than ourselves. It can also be harmful, however, for example if conspiracy theories are promulgated by an influential source.

Accepting then that most people won't have time to become fully informed politically, and that they do rely on trusted sources, how can we respond to this constructively? One approach is to create impartial and balanced sources and make them readily accessible, for example through citizens' assemblies. Individuals representing a diverse cross-section of society could be paid to take time out to learn about a controversial policy issue, with support from experts and from advocates of different sides of a debate, and then to conduct their own debate and to record their views and recommendations. The participants' opinions may remain divided – there may still be no consensus – but the wider public would get condensed and informed feedback from 'ordinary people like us' who are not seeking votes. This is a version of a deliberative democratic process, helping people to understand and share the pros and cons and the potential consequences of different options. France's Citizens' Convention for the Climate, for example, was tasked with finding ways to cut carbon emissions by 40 per cent by 2030.[50] This temporary assembly of 159 citizens was a response to the *gilets jaunes* (yellow vests) protests that were sparked in part by a carbon tax policy in 2018. The Convention produced a lengthy report and 149 recommendations, including a tax on big business. This process contributed to a technically complex political debate and the report was authored by ordinary people who had time and opportunity to get informed, but without political careers at stake. There were subsequent policy changes, although the Macron government vetoed or watered down many recommendations. As another example, the State of Oregon's Citizen Initiated Reviews take aside a representative cross-section of 20 to 24 voters for four or five days of deliberation on a ballot measure. The participants hear advocates for and against the proposition as well as independent advisors. The citizen panellists then write a statement that's sent to each registered voter. This may not change the outcomes of referendums, and may not influence all voters, but it improves the overall level of accurately informed choice.[51]

The degree of political trust created by such deliberative assemblies may depend on the effects they have on public policy. If they have no effect, they'll soon be regarded as a waste of time and money. On the other hand, final decisions do need to be made by those who are accountable at elections, rather than by randomly chosen citizens. Such assemblies can, however, help to improve public participation and informed decision-making.

Busting corruption

Aside from physical violence, corruption does the greatest damage to political trust and harms economic development and social justice. Political leaders steal from resource royalties and tax revenues, secrete their wealth in offshore accounts, suppress publication of facts about dishonest actions, and evade legal accountability by bribing or threatening law enforcement agents and judges. Public servants accept bribes in return for favours such as preferential award of contracts.[52] Even when laws and agencies are put in place to investigate and prosecute cases, a country might slide back into corruption through selective investigation of political opponents, or having cases against favoured individuals delayed or dropped. Indeed, what's called 'corruption' by the international community may be a culturally normative way of facilitating commerce at the local level. Nonetheless, if there's a culture of impunity in which people think, 'If I don't do it somebody else will', coupled with the potential to amass significant material wealth at the expense of the common good, then it's a genuine social problem that can be difficult to eradicate. Individuals within a corrupt network become hostage to it and won't break the silence for fear of being found out themselves or being harmed by those on the make. To clean things up, officials who could potentially benefit from an untrustworthy system need the discipline to forego dishonest gains, to put in place systems that are transparent and accountable, and to follow through with impartial investigations and prosecutions. Officials at street level need adequate incomes so that they don't resort to taking bribes in order to get by.

International assistance is called for, but many of the wealthier and less corrupt countries are effectively supporting corrupt actors by providing discrete banking facilities and assets (such as real estate and art works) with which to 'launder' illicitly acquired funds. The international community cracked down on Russian oligarchs following the illegal and unprovoked invasion of Ukraine in 2022, but many politicians and businesspeople around the world continue to use offshore accounts to launder dirty money and acquire property. One investigation found that, over three decades, 233 houses and apartments in London were purchased by 166 offshore companies owned by 137 prominent Nigerians to a total value of £350 million.[53] Nigeria is a recipient of overseas development assistance for the provision of basic services, so it's extraordinary that large sums of private capital should be invested back into a donor country by wealthy Nigerians, some of whom were under investigation for corruption.

As a product of personal dishonesty and a lack of institutional controls, corruption is one of the biggest obstacles to good government, and it creates a downward spiral of distrust. Combatting it takes an international effort, as well as law enforcement in each country. A country may have the laws and agencies needed for the task, but corruption may continue due to informal norms and networks that permit dishonesty and enforce silence. A free press can expose corruption, but editors and journalists become the targets of threats and violence. Education of the young and prosecution of the guilty are needed in the most corrupt countries, but the wealthier and less corrupt countries have to face up to the supporting roles that they play in concealment and investment of the proceeds of corruption.

Dialectics of government

One of the biggest issues for contemporary government is the equitable inclusion of minorities. Many of us live in communities that are becoming more ethnically diverse, and public policy and political representation need to respond accordingly. Depending on where you live, this may mean loosening the norms of a 'white western' culture. This is certainly the case in my hometown. And immigration-driven diversification doesn't only mean more ethnic groups from more countries in one city; it creates new issues in employment experiences, housing inequality, neighbourhood change, public religious observances, transnational connections, multiple social affiliations and family obligations – all of which have implications for public policy and administration.

While diversity and 'super-diversity'[54] are significant concerns for government, I'll question a couple of assumptions. First, diversity is nothing new, although it's sometimes spoken of nowadays as if it were. For most of history, mobility and mingling of peoples have been normal, and not exceptional, especially on trading routes and in large cities such as Rome, Constantinople or Delhi, and there are historical examples of how toleration of cultural and religious differences worked well, often within large empires. Toleration helped to accommodate many different peoples under one imperial umbrella and maximised the advantages of trade and knowledge exchange with neighbours. But it sometimes failed, as societies polarised across different dividing lines at different times, whether it was language, religion, race or ideology. In discussions of diversity today, there's often an assumption that distinctive and statistically countable communities bring known 'identities' with them. Key concerns may be how they interact and how each can preserve their traditions in a new environment. But this doesn't take account of hybridisation – which means more than mixing with or learning from one another's cultures. People actively adapt to differences in unexpected ways, and each generation has to assimilate the various cultural influences, norms and languages that they grow up with. Cultural traditions develop and are superseded through dialogue, trade, intermarriage and conflict. Englishness, for example, emerged historically out of countless instances of marriage, trade and warfare among ancient Britons, numerous waves of Germanic and Scandinavian arrivals, imperial Roman and Norman conquerors, and then migrant workers from former colonies and continental Europe. Each group, whether it was once locally dominant or not, left its legacy and got blended in, and each culture was superseded, contributing to an emergent image of 'the English' and a richly hybridised English language spoken worldwide. A dynamic and dialectical process of admixture, adaptation and supersession gives us a better account of social change than a static or nostalgic sampling of identity groups that need to get along together.

Two contrasting present-day examples of how to administer such processes are the cities of Singapore and Auckland. With two very different forms of government, they've both been comparatively successful in managing cross-cultural encounters, with relatively few instances of conflict. Singapore is a commercially successful city-state (population about 6 million). Although it has multi-party elections for its unicameral parliament, the socially conservative and economically liberal People's Action Party has commanded the majority and formed all governments since 1965. Under prime minister Lee Kuan Yew (in office 1959–90), Singapore detached itself from Britain and Malaysia, and created formal and informal rules about how the main ethnic groups would preserve their cultures and get along together in an independent state. *Gui ju* refers to 'broad, overarching principles that guide everyday encounters in public through practices of inclusion and exclusion', underlying which is an ideology of multiracialism that 'gives separate but equal status to the Chinese, Malays, Indians and "Others"'. Singaporeans see their city as multiracial and multilingual, with English as the common language. The former British colony's 'separate ethnic settlements' were replaced by publicly administered housing estates with ethnic quotas, thus avoiding ghettos and maximising opportunities for convivial interactions.[55] Schools teach children their native tongue, while urban life in such a dense population causes people to encounter difference spontaneously and to learn habits of civility. The principles of *gui ju* are led by a paternalistic state but are constantly negotiated and debated. A large number of temporary migrant workers, mainly from Bangladesh, China and India, add further complexity; sometimes there are misunderstandings about appropriate conduct in public, but violence is rare.[56] Male migrants on temporary permits work in construction sites and shipyards and are housed on the city's peripheries in dormitories, sharing rooms with a dozen or more, segregated from the rest of the population. The targeted regulation of these workers' lives was intensified in 2020 when the Covid-19 virus spread through the dormitories and the residents were treated as a 'medical threat'.[57] Singapore's management of diversity relies on enforced inclusion and mixing with formal recognition of cultures, but with segregation of temporary migrants.

The area encompassed by the recently unified Auckland Council is mainly rural, but most of its 1.7 million population are urban dwellers. Demographic change has been driven by migration, so about 42 percent of Auckland's residents weren't born in New Zealand. The majority of the population is classified in the 2018 census as European descent (or white) and 11.5 percent identify as indigenous Māori. Fifteen percent are Pacific Islanders and 28 percent Asian, but these two broad categories include (and hence obscure) a wide range of nationalities, languages and distinctive cultures. (People can choose more than one ethnic group in the official census.) With mainly stand-alone houses (rather than high-rise) and much lower population density than Singapore, unplanned encounters in Auckland's neighbourhoods and public spaces are less frequent, but ethnically mixed suburbs are generally characterised by mutual acceptance and low-key pragmatic interactions. Greater tensions may be caused by middle-class people moving into traditionally working-class suburbs than by anyone's language, dress or colour.[58] New Zealand's skills-driven immigration hasn't been accompanied by policies to mix neighbourhoods or assimilate new arrivals, nor has urban planning created ethnic quarters. Immigrants from one country may gravitate towards one suburb, lending them a particular ethnic tone, but the official approach is *laissez-faire*: little is done beyond having multi-lingual notices, occasions that 'celebrate diversity' and, when necessary, sanctions against discrimination. Reparations agreed with local indigenous tribes have included housing developments and co-management of some local spaces.

Singapore and Auckland, then, are both navigating cross-cultural dialogue with relative success, in that (notwithstanding incidents of racism) neither city experiences open inter-ethnic conflict and people are largely free to express distinctive faiths, customs, cuisines and the like. From the point of view of government and public policy, the approaches of the two cities are different due to different histories, politics and norms. Singapore's government is stricter and more paternalistic. For instance, it was only in 2022 that it repealed a colonial-era law that had banned sex between men. Although religious freedom is constitutionally guaranteed, pressures are placed on the press not to publish anything critical of a government that's long been dominated by one political party and indeed by one family. New Zealand, in contrast, adopted Anglo-American neoliberal policy, using immigration to fill skills shortages and boost economic growth. So the idea of diversity appeals to both the socially progressive left and the neoliberal right. Freedoms of religion and political opinion are guaranteed in New Zealand law, but an undercurrent of racism sometimes surfaces in the media, causing offence and division. These two quite different forms of government have found their own ways to contain the tensions that arise in multicultural societies.

We must never forget the wider world's history of violence against minorities.[59] One lesson is that cultural conformity and the suppression of minorities don't work and often descend into communal or state violence, while toleration and respect for human rights are inherently just. The problem for a tolerant government, however, lies in judging where its toleration ends, and when to restrict intolerant ideas and harmful practices. Singapore has greater restrictions on political discourse than New Zealand, but both governments have genuine concerns about harmful and extremist discourse online and they both want to do something about it. The challenge for any government, then, lies in finding a balance between freedom of expression and freedom from discrimination and violence. And there's no scientific formula: it's always a matter of ethical and political judgement.

Yascha Mounk aptly envisages 'a democracy that grants true equality to a highly diverse set of citizens'.[60] This would be approached differently in each society, being mindful of its particular history, constitution and current composition. All societies inherit consequences of past injustices caused by war, colonisation, discrimination, slavery or genocide. The recognition of and restitution for egregious collective injustices are ongoing concerns for government, along with actions intended to lead towards a future society that (at least) doesn't perpetuate or repeat such crimes. Self-evidently we're not all the same, and we need to live with and respect our differences. But societies have historical legacies that unjustly skew life chances in favour of some social groups and against others. Governments therefore need to find a balance between the recognition of the differing experiences and opportunities of minorities as against an impartial rule of law and a system of rights that regards each of us as basically equal. There's nothing to be gained from trying to forget the past and wallpaper over deep cracks; on the other hand, policies that target only minorities will tend to alienate the majority and thus open new fissures. Societies aren't composed of discrete, unchanging 'identities', and dynamic inter-ethnic dialogue and exchange have unpredictable and creative outcomes. Bold political visions for a new kind of citizen or a new kind of community need to be treated with caution. To complicate matters, along with its people, *government itself undergoes dialectical change*. Representation of distinguishable ethno-religious minorities in legislatures and public services is a necessary element of the political solution but, simultaneously, new institutional ways and means of governing supersede the status quo.

Conclusion

This chapter and the previous one have looked at different forms and functions of government. No matter which institutional form it takes, government involves the purposeful exercise of power, and so it's always strategic, at least implicitly. It's better though if the strategy is explicit, achievable and widely supported. Government is rightly intended for a common good, and not for the vainglory of powerful individuals. But no matter how hard humans have tried over the course of history to control or neutralise the deleterious effects of greed, self-interest and ignorance on government, these defects remain, as revealed in the misconduct of some political leaders, corruption in government, and the propensity of people to follow without first understanding. While we can justifiably protest at the exclusion from political participation or lack of effective voice of minorities, the unfortunate fact is that many people who could participate choose not to, and, when casting a vote, do so in ignorance.

Before calling for institutional change, we need to outline the strategy: what public good is change in aid of? But we also need to accept path dependence: that change begins from within the constraints and habits of existing institutions. When change is needed, then, we need to bring as many people as possible along with us, and public deliberative assemblies are one way to build this understanding and hence gain deeper support for new policies. Simply ignoring or suppressing minority opinions and cultures doesn't work: it's neither just nor pragmatic. There's no universally applicable formula for recognising and accommodating diverse values and ways of life, but this is work that must patiently be done.

Notes

1 Vietor, Richard H.K. 2007. *How Countries Compete: Strategy, Structure, and Government in the Global Economy*. Boston MA: Harvard Business Press.
2 Ibid.

3 Tinline, Phil. 2022. *The Death of Consensus: 100 Years of British Political Nightmares.* London: C. Hurst & Co.
4 Keynes, John Maynard. 1964 [1936]. *The General Theory of Employment, Interest, and Money.* New York: Harvest, Harcourt.
5 The institution of central bank independence is under pressure, however. Critics often want to widen the policy mandate beyond inflation control, prompting for example this defence: Dall'Orto Mas, Rodolfo, Benjamin Vonessen, Christian Fehlker & Katrin Arnold. 2020. *The Case for Central Bank Independence.* European Central Bank, URL: https://papers.ssrn.com/sol3/papers.cfm?abstract_id=3706132 (accessed 24 October 2022).
6 The quasi-anarchistic Daoist principle of government as non-action assumes there are rulers, but they exert 'the minimum amount of external interference projected onto the individual from those in power combined with an environment most conducive to the individual's quest for self-fulfilment'. Ames, Roger. 1994. *The Art of Rulership: A Study of Ancient Chinese Political Thought.* Albany, NY: State University of New York Press. See p. 41.
7 At the time of writing, it's too soon to judge whether Biden will succeed in shifting economic policy debates beyond 'neoliberalism versus Keynesianism'.
8 Freedman, Lawrence. 2013. *Strategy: A History.* Oxford: Oxford University Press. See p. xii.
9 Foucault, Michel. 1990. *The History of Sexuality. Volume 1: An Introduction.* New York: Vintage. See Part 4, Ch. 2.
10 Nye, Joseph S. 1990. 'Soft Power'. *Foreign Policy* 80: 153–71. URL: https://doi.org/10.2307/1148580 (accessed 6 October 2022). See p. 166.
11 Nye, Joseph S. 2017. 'Soft Power: The Origins and Political Progress of a Concept'. *Palgrave Communications,* URL: https://www.nature.com/articles/palcomms 20178 (accessed 9 April 2022).
12 'The POWER *of a man,* (to take it universally,) is his present means, to obtain some future apparent good. Reputation of power, is power; because it draweth with it the adherence of those that need protection.' Hobbes, Thomas. 1998 [1651]. *Leviathan.* Oxford: Oxford University Press. See p. 58, ch. X.1.
13 Nye, Joseph S. 2011. *The Future of Power.* New York: Public Affairs. I disagree with Nye's notion of a 'power strategy' of any description, as that's confusing the two terms.
14 The University of Chicago Institute of Politics. 2022. 'Our Precarious Democracy', URL: https://uchicagopolitics.opalstacked.com/uploads/homepage/Polarization-Poll.pdf (accessed 1 July 2022).
15 US National Archives, URL: https://www.archives.gov/ (accessed 1 July 2022).
16 A similar interpretation of the second amendment was put before the U.S. Supreme Court by FDR's solicitor-general, Robert H. Jackson, in 1939. Lepore, Jill. 2018. *These Truths: A History of the United States.* New York: W.W. Norton & Co. See p. 446.
17 Hobbes [note 12]. See p. 230, ch. XXX.21.
18 Hood, Christopher. 1991. 'A Public Management for All Seasons?' *Public Administration* 69 (1): 3–19; Hughes, Owen. 2018. *Public Management and Administration.* London: Palgrave.
19 Arezki, Rabah, Simeon Djankov, Ha Nguyen & Ivan Yotzov. 2021. 'Reversal of Fortune for Political Incumbents: Evidence from Oil Shocks'. World Bank, URL: https://openknowledge.worldbank.org/bitstream/handle/10986/33982/Reversal-of-Fortune-for-Political-Incumbents-Evidence-from-Oil-Shocks.pdf?sequence=5&isAllowed=y (accessed 25 July 2023).
20 Hickel, Jason. 2021. *Less is More.* London: Penguin Random House; Meadows, D. H., D. L. Meadows, J. Randers & W. W. Behrens. 1972. *The Limits to Growth.* New York: Universe Books.

21 Goldin, Ian. 2016. 'How Immigration Has Changed the World – For the Better'. World Economic Forum, URL: https://www.weforum.org/agenda/2016/01/how-immigration-has-changed-the-world-for-the-better/ (accessed 25 July 2023).

22 Savage, M. 18 April 2018. 'A "Thrilling" Mission to Get the Swedish to Change Overnight'. *BBC*, URL: https://www.bbc.com/worklife/article/20180417-a-thrilling-mission-to-get-the-swedish-to-change-overnight (accessed 25 July 2023).

23 This maxim is attributed to Alfred D. Chandler (1918–2007).

24 Hall, David J. & Maurice A. Saias. 1980. 'Strategy Follows Structure!' *Strategic Management Journal* 1 (2): 149–63, URL: http://www.jstor.org/stable/2486097 (accessed 22 April 2022).

25 Lindblom, Charles E. 1959. 'The Science of "Muddling Through"'. *Public Administration Review* 19 (2): 79–88.

26 Cairney, Paul. 2012. *Understanding Public Policy: Theories and Issues.* Houndmills: Palgrave Macmillan. See p. 76, abridged.

27 In contrast, nearly 68 percent of British voters (with only 42 percent turnout) rejected a proposal in a 2011 referendum to change their first-past-the-post electoral method to alternative (or preferential) voting.

28 Lees, Charles. 2021. 'Brexit, the Failure of the British Political Class, and the Case for Greater Diversity in UK Political Recruitment'. *British Politics* 16 (1): 36–57.

29 What UK Thinks, URL: https://www.whatukthinks.org/eu/ (accessed 25 July 2023).

30 Frimer, J. A., H. Aujla, M. Feinberg, L. J. Skitka, K. Aquino, J. C. Eichstaedt & R. Willer. 2023. 'Incivility Is Rising Among American Politicians on Twitter'. *Social Psychological and Personality Science* 14 (2): 259–69, URL: https://doi.org/10.1177/19485506221083811 (accessed 7 June 2023).

31 FiveThirtyEight Podcast. 7 October 2022. 'How Our Midterm Forecast Takes Candidates' Scandals Into Account', URL: https://fivethirtyeight.com/videos/how-our-midterm-forecast-takes-candidates-scandals-into-account/ (accessed 10 October 2022).

32 von Sikorski, C., R. Heiss & J. Matthes. 2020. 'How Political Scandals Affect the Electorate: Tracing the Eroding and Spillover Effects of Scandals with a Panel Study'. *Political Psychology* 41 (3): 549–68, URL: https://doi.org/10.1111/pops.12638; Close, C., J. Dodeigne, S. Hennau & M. Reuchamps. 2022. 'A Scandal Effect? Local Scandals and Political Trust'. *Acta Politica* (electronic version), URL: https://doi.org/10.1057/s41269-022-00241-y (both accessed 6 October 2022).

33 Some immunities are mentioned in Chapter 4 as exceptions to this rule.

34 Aristotle. 1999. *The Politics.* London: Penguin, trans. T.A. Sinclair & T.J. Saunders. See p. 182, §1277b7.

35 Poguntke, Thomas & Paul Webb. 2007. *The Presidentialization of Politics: A Comparative Study of Modern Democracies.* Oxford: Oxford University Press.

36 Rahat, Gideon & Ofer Kenig. 2018. *From Party Politics to Personalized Politics? Party Change and Political Personalization in Democracies.* Oxford: Oxford University Press. See p. 117.

37 McAllister, Ian. 2007. 'The Personalization of Politics'. In *The Oxford Handbook of Political Behavior*, ed. Russell J. Dalton & Hans-Dieter Klingemann, 571–88. Oxford: Oxford University Press.

38 Yanchenko, Kostiantyn. 2022. 'Making Sense of Populist Hyperreality in the Post-Truth Age: Evidence from Volodymyr Zelensky's Voters'. *Mass Communication and Society*, URL: https://doi.org/10.1080/15205436.2022.2105234 (accessed 6 October 2022).

39 Mill, John Stuart. 1991. *On Liberty and Other Essays.* Oxford: Oxford University Press. See p. 383, 'Considerations on Representative Government' (1861), Ch. XII.

40 du Gay, Paul & Thomas Lopdrup-Hjorth. 2023. *For Public Service: State, Office and Ethics*. London: Routledge.
41 Allen, Peter & Paul Cairney. 2017. 'What Do We Mean When We Talk About the "Political Class"?' *Political Studies Review* 15 (1): 18–27.
42 Schumpeter, Joseph A. 2008 [1942]. *Capitalism, Socialism and Democracy*. New York: HarperCollins. See p. 262.
43 Somin, Ilya. 2016. *Democracy and Political Ignorance: Why Smaller Government Is Smarter*. Stanford, CA: Stanford Law Books.
44 'In general, it is irrational to be politically well-informed because the low returns from data simply do not justify their cost in time and other scarce resources. Therefore many voters do not bother to discover their true views before voting, and most citizens are not well enough informed to influence directly the formulation of those policies that affect them.' Downs, Anthony. 1957. *An Economic Theory of Democracy*. New York: HarperCollins. See p. 259.
45 Somin [note 43]. See p. 104.
46 Lorenz-Spreen, P., L. Oswald, S. Lewandowsky et al. 2022. 'A Systematic Review of Worldwide Causal and Correlational Evidence on Digital Media and Democracy'. *Nature Human Behaviour* (online version), URL: https://doi.org/10.1038/s41562-022-01460-1 (accessed 10 November 2022).
47 Vosoughi, Soroush, Deb Roy & Sinan Aral. 2018. 'The Spread of True and False News Online'. *Science* 359 (6380): 1146–1151; Altay, Sacha, Manon Berriche & Alberto Acerbi. 2023. 'Misinformation on Misinformation: Conceptual and Methodological Challenges'. *Social Media + Society* 9 (1): 1–13, URL: https://doi.org/10.1177/20563051221150412 (accessed 6 June 2023).
48 OECD. 2019. 'Voting', in *Society at a Glance 2019: OECD Social Indicators*. Paris: OECD Publishing, URL: https://doi.org/10.1787/3483a69a-en (accessed 6 October 2022).
49 Solijonov, Abdurashid. 2016. *Voter Turnout Trends around the World*. Stockholm: International Institute for Democracy and Electoral Assistance.
50 CCC, URL: https://www.conventioncitoyennepourleclimat.fr/en/; Giraudet, L.G., B. Apouey, H. Arab et al. 2022. '"Co-construction" in Deliberative Democracy: Lessons from the French Citizens' Convention for Climate'. *Humanities & Social Sciences Communications* 9: 207: online version. https://doi.org/10.1057/s41599-022-01212-6 (both accessed 13 October 2022).
51 Gastil, John. 2017. 'Evidence from Oregon Shows that Citizens' Initiative Reviews Can Improve Voters' Decision-making about Ballot Measures. LSE Blog, URL: http://bit.ly/2ASPYZE (accessed 25 July 2023).
52 Transparency International provides examples and defines corruption as 'the abuse of entrusted power for private gain', URL: https://www.transparency.org/
53 Bowers, Simon, Lionel Faull & Purity Mukami. 6 October 2021. 'Pandora Papers: The Secret London Properties of Nigeria's Elite'. *Finance Uncovered*, URL: https://www.financeuncovered.org/stories/pandora-papers-nigeria-offshore-london-properties (accessed 25 July 2023).
54 Vertovec, Steven. 2007. 'Super-Diversity and Its Implications'. *Ethnic and Racial Studies* 30 (6): 1024–54.
55 Ye, Junjia. 2016. 'Spatialising the Politics of Coexistence: *Gui ju* (规矩) in Singapore'. *Transactions of the Institute of British Geographers* 41 (1): 91–103, URL: https://doi.org/10.1111/tran.12107 (accessed 6 October 2022). See p. 92.
56 About 300 migrant workers rioted in Little India on the night of 8 December 2013 after an Indian construction worker was killed under a private bus.
57 Ye, Junjia. 2021. 'Ordering Diversity: Co-Producing the Pandemic and the Migrant in Singapore during COVID-19'. *Antipode* 53 (6): 1895–920, URL: https://doi.org/10.1111/anti.12740 (accessed 6 October 2022).

58 Terruhn, Jessica & Junjia Ye. 2021. 'Encountering Neighbors: Coexisting with Difference in Auckland's Avondale'. *Urban Geography* 43 (4): 613–31, URL: https://doi.org/10.1080/02723638.2021.1883922 (accessed 6 October 2022).
59 A recent example of such historical recollection is: Veidlinger, Jeffrey. 2021. *In the Midst of Civilized Europe: The 1918–1921 Pogroms in Ukraine and the Onset of the Holocaust*. New York: Metropolitan Books.
60 Mounk, Yascha. 2022. *The Great Experiment: How to Make Diverse Democracies Work*. London: Bloomsbury. See pp. 281–82.

8

WHAT NOW?

People around the world are disillusioned if not disgusted with their governments. They want change and, if they haven't given up in despair, they often
demand it. And change isn't impossible. It often occurs under pressure of circumstances or popular unrest, and the most powerful recent vector of change
was a novel coronavirus, necessitating a return to centralised state controls.
But, as we'll see, change doesn't always go in the right direction. So if you've
ever wondered why our societies are inadequately governed, this book should
at least have revealed the nature and scope of the problem. But we're compelled to ask what we could do to get better government in future. I'll explore
some brief case studies of recent real-world constitutional changes, then. The
outcomes aren't always happy, but we can look at some of the big issues that
are driving change today and then conclude with what it will take to achieve
constructive reform. There isn't one grand solution, but there are some basic
principles and practical steps to get us started.

Real-world change

Iran

Iran gives us an example of poorly designed government. In 1979 a revolution
transformed Iran from an oppressive monarchy into an even more oppressive
rule by religious scholars (see Chapter 6, 'Theocracy'). The constitution was
changed to implement a principle of guardianship of the jurist, which led to
systematic discrimination against women and daily use of state violence on the
streets to enforce a conservative dress code. In 2022 we witnessed a prolonged
revolutionary movement of young people – especially women and girls – who

DOI: 10.4324/9781003439783-8

shouted in streets and from rooftops, 'Death to the dictator.' Many people were killed; women were sexually assaulted by riot police. This system needs to change, as the theocratic regime lacks legitimacy, doesn't represent its people and can't withstand so much pressure from below indefinitely, especially when it comes from young people whose desire for change won't go away. The solution is straightforward in principle, but sadly it's unlikely to occur without more deaths. The hard carapace of religious institutions that control the legislative and administrative systems should be removed. There's no need to install the exiled heir to the former throne, as the basic structures exist for a semi-presidential constitution. With a more popular government that protects but doesn't enforce religious practices, they could call off the police.

Chile

Chile gave us quite a different example of people's desire to change the way they're governed. The widespread protests that erupted there in October 2019 caught observers by surprise, but the symptoms of malaise were familiar: slowing economy, a growing gap between the masses and the elites, declining voter turnouts and loss of trust in institutions. This uprising led initially to an appropriate political response: a referendum on whether to elect an assembly that would draft a new constitution. The 1980 constitution had been written under the auspices of the Pinochet dictatorship; it had entrenched neoliberal economic principles and was designed to be hard to amend. For example, it recognised private property rights over water, but a bill seeking to declare water a public good failed because it didn't get a two-thirds majority in the Senate. By treating public and private providers as equivalent in health, education and social security in order to avoid state monopolies, the 1980 constitution effectively favoured private enterprise, as the state could intervene only when the market failed. Judicial review of the constitutionality of laws and the super-majorities needed to amend the constitution entrenched these neoliberal policy principles. People wanted to reform the system in part because the system itself was designed to resist popular demands for change.[1]

Two-thirds of Chilean voters approved the constitutional convention, although only on a 50 percent turnout. In a further strong message, they opted for an assembly that represented the people, rather than leave the drafting process to the congress and the political parties. The subsequent election of candidates for the convention ensured gender parity and indigenous representation, and voters tended to favour independents. Although many on the left complained that the drafting process was compromised by backroom deals and conservative vetoes, the result was, according to Camila Vergara, 'the most progressive constitution ever written in terms of socio-economic rights, gender equality, indigenous rights and the protection of nature'. For example, article 190 stated:

Territorial entities and their bodies must act in coordination in compliance with the principles of plurinationality and interculturality; respect and protect the various ways of conceiving and organizing the world, of relating to nature; and guarantee the rights of indigenous peoples and nations to self-determination and autonomy.

So why was it rejected by almost 62 percent? In the decisive 2022 referendum, voting was mandatory and turnout rose to 86 percent. But one million fewer people voted in favour of the draft constitution than had voted for the convention two years earlier. Rejection was strongest in low-income municipalities. Inclusion of the right to abortion gave conservatives a pulpit from which to preach rejection, regardless of other reforms. There were concerns about the impact of misinformation in campaigns against the proposal. And as clauses were vetoed or watered down in the drafting process, the draft constitution 'did not explicitly dismantle the current [neoliberal] voucher system in education, nor the insurance model in healthcare, nor the individual savings scheme that forces the Chilean working class to subsist on poverty pensions'.[2] Conservative legislators could still have fought to keep those systems in place. Those who'd demanded progressive reforms believed the draft constitution didn't go far enough; moderates thought it went too far.

The 1980 Chilean constitution and the proposed alternative are complex instruments that address many matters of public policy and law, beyond the general values and structures of government. An English translation of the 1980 constitution is 90 pages of single-spaced text, and the proposed draft was much longer. Debating the constitution as a whole means fighting on many fronts at once, including matters that could have been delegated to statutory law made in the legislature, one bill at a time. The Pinochet government had embedded neoliberal principles in 1980, while the reformers wanted to embed alternative progressive principles in 2022. The next swing of the pendulum saw conservative parties gain a majority on an elected 50-seat constitutional council in May 2023.

The constitution had become a football in a multi-dimensional contest over abortion, housing, water, social security, indigenous self-determination and so on. Any constitution is political in the broader sense, as it embodies a particular set of national values, but it should strive to be non-partisan and uncontroversial, or as widely accepted as possible. It should entrench only those national values, fundamental rights and political institutions that are necessary for effective and just government so that it doesn't become a perpetual cause of discontent. It might have been easier to amend the constitution by more subtraction and less addition. But, to get to that point, the competing factions all needed to make concessions over the constitution and then carry on their policy debates in legislative processes.

Italy

The Italian constitution isn't heavily freighted with policy prescription, unlike the Chilean one, and hence it's briefer (only about 40 pages of single-spaced text in the English version). In 2016 a referendum initiated from above proposed to reduce the size of the Senate, to make it representative of the regions and to curtail its legislative functions. Governments would only need to have the confidence of the lower house, and not the Senate. This was a major revision, as Italy's bicameral legislature is fairly evenly balanced, which means that bills can be amended by both houses and hence referred back and forth *ad nauseam*. The reform package also aimed to clarify the distinctive roles and powers of national and regional governments and to change the quorum required for referendums initiated by citizens. Although this wasn't a complete overhaul, as in Chile, it was nonetheless a complex set of provisions with far-reaching consequences. It was driven by the then prime minister, Matteo Renzi, and his centre-left Democratic Party, but it wasn't supported by all other left-wing parties, nor by all trade unions – nor for that matter by the far-right parties. On the other hand, the business sector warned of dire economic consequences if the reforms weren't approved. Renzi unwisely pledged to resign from office, and even retire from politics, if the referendum failed, which confused matters by turning it into a referendum on himself. Fifty-nine percent voted 'no' on a 68.5 percent turnout – and Renzi resigned. The process had failed to address the key issues: 'how to stabilize (not strengthen) the government; how to streamline the relationships between government and Parliament; and how to improve parliamentary representation'.[3]

Then in 2019 the internet-based 5 Star Movement, which espouses popular deliberation and direct democratic participation, pushed for a new referendum as part of a coalition deal with the Democratic Party. This proposed to reduce the members in the Chamber of Deputies from 630 to 400 and in the Senate from 315 to 200. Seventy percent voted in favour, thinking this would reduce fiscal costs and improve efficiency in legislative processes. The flip-side was that the remaining representatives' workloads would increase (or less would get done), their collective capacity to scrutinise legislation and policy would decline accordingly, and citizens would find it harder to gain access to them, as there'd be more citizens per representative. Reducing the legislature could also shift the balance of power to the executive branch and the bureaucracy. The reform did nothing to improve accountability or responsiveness, then. Like Brexit, 'a profound constitutional change of dubious credibility was brought about by voters driven by feelings verging on outrage and despair'.[4] Reducing representation worked as revenge against the political class but didn't improve the 'governability' of a diverse and unruly society nor boost political trust.[5] On this occasion, the people approved a proposal of doubtful efficacy in a mood of anti-establishment resentment.

Lessons here are that constitutional proposals shouldn't be closely identified with political parties or leaders, and that proposals should be discrete and simple. If there's a complex package of changes with numerous consequences, and voters are asked a binary 'yes or no', they may react against the established order or current government, rather than assess the actual propositions. Voters are susceptible to misinformation campaigns, especially if there's a complex package of reforms that people find hard to evaluate, and the whole process may lead to no improvement in the system of government and no restoration of trust.

United Kingdom

The Brexit process is now the classic example of 'the people's choice' going awry. (See Chapter 7, 'Structures and processes'.) The subsequent instability in government, exacerbated by the Covid-19 pandemic, was expressed in the resignations of four prime ministers (Cameron, May, Johnson and Truss) and two early elections in just over six years following the 2016 referendum. As one outstanding example of failure, Truss's mini-budget of September 2022 proposed corporate and income tax cuts for the wealthy, but also to subsidise energy costs, with a deficit to be covered by borrowing. The Bank of England, being independent from the Treasury, hadn't been briefed or consulted; indeed it had just announced it was selling government bonds, so no one knew who'd back the debt. The Bank was forced to do a sharp U-turn and buy government debt to forestall a fire sale and a possible collapse of pension funds. The pound plummeted and the Conservative Party's opinion polling collapsed from the low 30s to low 20s. The finance minister was sacked and his mini-budget was dropped. Truss had become prime minister not through a general election, but by a vote of party members following the resignation of Boris Johnson. She lasted only 44 days in 10 Downing Street and was promptly replaced by Rishi Sunak.

The best that can be said is that the UK's unwritten constitution, which relies heavily on tradition and convention, is flexible enough to weather all storms. What looks like chaos could represent adaptability, as Brexit had overloaded the system with changes and there were competing ideas about how to leave the European Union. Other than the constitutional change entailed in Brexit itself, the system of government survived all the same. Throughout this saga, though, one often heard Britons calling for a return to decency and civility in political leadership. A decline in the standard of personal conduct among the political class has been a common theme, not only in the UK. I return to the question of leadership below.

United States

Fears about a demise of democracy grew with the attack on the US Capitol on 6 January 2021. This failed insurrection sought to keep Donald Trump in office by disrupting a joint session of Congress as it was counting electoral college votes and confirming Joe Biden's victory. Organised hate groups were involved, including the Proud Boys[6] and the Oath Keepers.[7] Anti-government beliefs, conspiracy theories and toxic power were on display. Rallied by the defeated candidate, the mob delayed but didn't overturn a constitutionally prescribed process. The associated fallacy that the election had been 'stolen' from Trump was shared by many Americans, however. Opinion polls up to mid-2022 indicated that only around one-fifth to one-quarter of Republican voters agreed that Joe Biden was legitimately elected.[8] And to be fair, if Trump had been narrowly re-elected in 2020, many Democrats would have refused to see him too as a legitimate president. Either way, these events revealed that the US has 'no clear mechanism to address allegations of fraud in a presidential election'.[9] Although a lawful transfer of power was achieved in January 2021 and the mid-term elections in 2022 went relatively smoothly, Americans have cause to ask whether constitutional safeguards are strong and clear enough to withstand such challenges. Indeed, some law-makers don't baulk at undermining those safeguards, as some states have passed laws that restrict voters' ability to register and to cast ballots, and that permit partisan interference in election administration or results.[10]

Most Americans agree on a need for constitutional change: in particular, abolishing the electoral college and having a direct nationwide vote for presidents.[11] But this would require a proposal supported by two-thirds majorities of both houses of Congress and then ratification by three-quarters of the states. Such proposals are unlikely to overcome polarisation on partisan lines, as one of the two parties is more likely to benefit from the status quo and hence will block amendments.

As an alternative avenue for constitutional change, Article V provides that the legislatures of two-thirds of the states can apply to Congress to call a convention that may propose amendments. It would take 34 states to call such a convention and then 38 to ratify its proposals. As there's a disproportionately large number of Republican-controlled states, given their sparser and smaller populations, this opens a way to entrench a right-wing policy agenda, as in the 'Convention of States Action' proposals to 'impose fiscal restraints on the federal government, limit the power and jurisdiction of the federal government, and limit the terms of office for its officials and for members of Congress'.[12] Congress has withheld supply from the federal government in the past, but such constitutional amendments would permanently constrain the administrative state and the ambitions of presidents with expensive agendas. Tax-cutting Republican presidents tend to run higher deficits than Democrats do,[13] however, and so they too may need 'fiscal restraint'. As with Chile, the fault here is in trying to entrench policy principles in the constitution, in the hope that this puts them above partisan debate and change. If successful, this would make the constitution itself a cause of further conflict, rather than national unity.

The US Constitution has been remarkably durable and was last amended in 1971. There have been thousands of amendments put to Congress, but only 27 were ratified, and further amendment now looks unlikely, if not politically impossible. So there's little chance of amending Article V to make amendment itself easier – for example, by a simple majority in a national referendum. The Supreme Court, however, has taken on an active role in reinterpreting the constitution through judicial reviews and appeals, giving the nine unelected judges greater influence over it than anyone else.[14] The recently developed judicial doctrine of originalism – that the constitution should be read in its supposed original intent or meaning, rather than adapting it to a changing society – has supported decisions in favour of conservative agendas. The nomination and appointment of judges by presidents, with the advice and consent of the Senate, politicises the process of their selection and compromises their independence. Intense controversy surrounding Supreme Court decisions – for example on campaign donations, abortion and firearms – indicates that pressures to change the unchangeable constitution, and to resist change, may come to a head one day – possibly not peacefully. The US system needs an overhaul, but this looks unlikely at the moment.

Russia

Let me turn now to the authoritarian regimes. The Russian constitution looks appropriate on paper, but in practice has been usurped by an autocrat and infected by corruption (see Chapter 6, 'Neo-patrimonial state'). In his speech on the annexation of parts of Ukraine in October 2022, President Putin claimed to be acting in the interests of the Russian people, including Russian speakers in Ukraine. He argued that the Donbas should not have been conceded by Russia during the hasty break-up of the Soviet Union in 1991 and that the invasion was reuniting lands and peoples that were, in his eyes, all Russian. He claimed this was the will of the people, following referendums, and cited the human rights to equality and self-determination. He gave a spirited critique of western imperialism of a kind one might hear from a western academic, but this was tainted by his own hypocrisy. As the Kremlin-approved leaders of the two self-declared republics of Donetsk and Lugansk and two other Ukrainian oblasts (Kherson and Zaporizhzhia) were formally signing up to Russian rule, their geographical boundaries, administrative structures and populations – indeed, their very existence as territories of the Russian Federation – were still actively contested in armed conflict. With atheistic communism out of the way, however, Putin's imperial gaze extended to all Russian Orthodox and Slavic peoples, as well as the diverse ethno-religious communities within the Russian Federation, presenting himself in providential and protective terms. Putin argued that, in a multipolar international system, no civilisation or culture can predominate, and hence the Russian civilisation – of which he claimed to be the defender – should be left to govern its people in its own way. The Russian way has historically been autocratic, however, and its government polices and exploits, rather than fosters, the economic and cultural endeavours of its people.[15]

China

Meanwhile, Taiwan is the world's leading manufacturer of semiconductors, a product that everyone wants. Only a small minority of the Taiwanese want unification with mainland China, however, while most prefer the ambiguous status quo (see Chapter 6, 'Quasi-states'), and there's also some support for the provocative option of declaring independence from China.[16] But President Xi Jinping of the People's Republic of China in 2022 further consolidated his grip on supreme power and stated that the reunification of Taiwan with the mainland will be achieved – by force if necessary. In a stern rebuke to the Americans and the Taiwanese, Beijing made its position clear: 'The Taiwan question is purely an internal affair of China, and no other country is entitled to act as a judge on the Taiwan question.'[17] Under such strained circumstances, we'd be naïve to think that the government of China is likely to relax its authoritarian methods. Its one-party system has internal factions, but dissent will be muted by strict discipline and obedience within the Communist Party. Hence the regime will forcefully resist systemic change and won't tolerate debate and criticism. China has a long history of monarchical rule and bureaucratic government, but it's also suffered numerous mass uprisings and revolts, of which the communist revolution of 1949 is only one in a long series. We can ask, then, just how legitimate, resilient and durable the present regime is. Any answer will, of course, be speculative, but Xi's recent consolidation of monarchical power could suffer from predictable vulnerabilities in the long term. (On the pros and cons of monarchy see Chapter 3, 'Who rules?'). A lot depends on the acumen of one man, and a lack of contestable advice could prove to be a critical weakness. The leadership succession process is presently unclear, so this 'exposes the system to intense power struggle and instability as succession approaches'.[18]

Russia and China are reverting to their historical norms of centralised authoritarian rule, and this licenses similar practices in other countries aligned with them. For example, Iran's military assistance for Russia in Ukraine suggests that the Islamic Republic can reply on support in return, as did Syria's Bashar al-Assad. The wider prospects for positive changes in how people are governed, with an eye for the common good, don't look promising, going by the cases considered above. We see the rise of authoritarian government in which rulers are monitoring and censoring dissent rather than responding to it. And in countries that have used direct democracy (referendums) to effect constitutional changes, things haven't worked out well. Whether it's authoritarian or democratic decision-making, factions often want to entrench partial values, rather than create a system that manages differences between their values. An effective system of government, however, negotiates between competing interests, without foreclosing debate by means of the constitution or the force of law or (worst of all) armed force.

In Chile, Italy and the USA people have tried, not very successfully, to reshape the constitution to achieve their preferred policy aims, apparently wishing to overcome debate by placing what they want above ordinary law – to stem ongoing contestation in political processes rather than endure it. They've forgotten an important lesson: that to govern means to recognise our interdependence and our mutual obligations, debts and promises, such that we each need to relinquish some personal preferences in order to be part of a community that shares common ground – on which ground we can then argue safely and constructively over particular matters of policy. The negotiation of differences constitutes the field of government, no matter how authoritarian or democratic, and a well-designed system would achieve that aim through basic structures and processes for deliberation – rather than blocking deliberation by entrenching contentious policies.

Governmental diversity

The countries that have representative government chosen by election aren't directly governed by majorities of the people, but rather by parliamentary majorities of those who represent the people and who, in turn, are advised by career officials. When this works well, the representatives are accountable to the people, and career officials contribute specialised expertise, while most of the population is free to engage in the economic, social and cultural activities that they value, so long as they pay taxes. Experience and social surveys show us that the inclusion of a diverse range of political values and voices, and a closeness and accountability of those who govern to those who are governed, are associated with better results for wellbeing and prosperity. But countries that espouse democracy and promote human rights must work alongside others that don't. Just as members of a society need to accept and tolerate diverse ways of life, so political leaders need to accept and tolerate diverse ways of governing. In a world that may not be democratising, then, how can things get done for the benefit of all peoples and of the planet? Exhorting others to be more democratic and to respect human rights is well intentioned (when it's not hypocritical), but those countries accused of being authoritarian may not become less so in the foreseeable future, and international collaboration is needed in the meantime. It won't help to take a dichotomous us versus them (or democracies versus autocracies) approach in which the liberal West sees itself as setting the standard to which others should aspire and condemns those who don't conform.

Rather than treat other systems as defective or as deviations from the Euro-American representative model, we can view them as taking different app-roaches to the same problems of government – not as failed experiments but, in their own ways, regulating their collective social and economic life. Each state has to deal with toxic politics and historical injustice and trauma, to share and conceal information, and to connect and coordinate the actions of mil-lions of individuals. Good government makes us aware that communities are interconnected and people are interdependent; it strives for a seemingly impossible dialogue and compromise between diverging values, meanings and intentions, in order to produce collective action. Sanctioning governments for bad conduct may be called for from time to time, but, as the case of Iran has shown, sanctions may punish innocent people for the actions of an oppressive government that doesn't represent them, and they may not bring about con-structive change.

'A future world order will need to accommodate non-Western powers and tolerate greater diversity in national institutional arrangements and practices', as international relations scholars Dani Rodrik and Stephen Walt have put it.[19] Political toleration and acceptance of governmental diversity and dialogue are needed – within international law – along with more flexible structures for negotiating agreements and resolving conflicts. A tolerant government (or person) should, when needed, question or condemn human rights violations. Toleration doesn't require us to accept abuses and crimes in silence. Indeed it's the opposite: toleration thrives when people experience safety, and when cor-ruption and abuse of power are *not* tolerated. In return, though, the leaders of both China and Russia have reacted sharply to external critics of their human rights records, often pointing (realistically) to western imperialism, aggression and exploitation. International relations and diplomacy need, then, to allow space for mutual criticisms alongside constructive negotiations. This takes maturity rather than sabre-rattling.

No society has ever settled on one universally accepted system of values, and effective government reconciles differences, rather than insisting that we all agree. Political diversity, difference and negotiation are permanent features of humanity, and the regulation of complex concerns in the face of disagree-ments defines good government. Any good-enough government reaches agreements or settlements *through* our disagreements about values, interests and priorities, rather than cancelling them out. Between nations, we disagree about the best form of government itself, but constitutionally diverse nations have to find ways to collaborate. This may mean looking creatively for new institutional styles and means of governing that will supersede the status quo, rather than seeking to impose one kind of system. The rise of China, in par-ticular, challenges international norms on the form of government. If it's the case that the basic superpower rivalry for the foreseeable future will be between the PRC and the USA, then we should take note that China isn't Westernising and the West isn't Sinicising.[20] Negotiating internationally for successful policy, then, means putting an end to imperialist ideas about one model – or worse, one nation or race – being superior to others. The most powerful nations don't set the best examples of government anyway. It's mainly smaller, less powerful nations that are getting the best results for their people, and it's likely that fresh ideas on how best to govern will emerge from outside of the main centres of world power.

Today we face problems that transcend borders and nations and that affect all of humanity. The enjoyment of surplus wealth in one part of the world, and the pollution that it causes, have wellbeing and survival consequences for others in distant parts. International collaboration has become essential for survival, and time is of the essence. We need, then, to think in terms of our global interdependence and to support people's belonging within their local or national communities. International collaboration isn't easily done in a democratic manner, with the voices of all those affected being heeded, and so a countervailing effort to improve the quality of participation at multiple levels of government is needed.

Leadership

Despite our long historical struggle to ensure that the people who make the law willingly abide by it,[21] some of the elected, such as Berlusconi, Bolsonaro and Trump, have sought to subvert or change the law to suit their own ends. Such prominent egos overshadow the conduct of law and government, and the fact that so many people admire them for it reveals a residual wish for that 'rule by men' about which Aristotle warned. The term 'leader' has largely replaced 'ruler' – which smacked of 'despot' – but the personalisation of politics and a continuing desire for a strong leader who overcomes the factionalism of a competitive system has seen a re-emergence of ego-driven rulership. Personality – or the cult of personality – is reasserting itself as a political factor, enabled by new media. Leaders evoke strong emotions from the led, not always for the better, and their personal conduct (or misconduct) influences the course of public and international affairs, perhaps more than it should. We can't – and shouldn't wish to – eliminate personalities from politics, but competitive representative systems have been prone to capture by dominant egos backed by those who gain informally from their favour and attention, and often by large private donations from vested interests. This is nothing new. The popular desire for charismatic leaders who inspire hope or promise reform – and who also create controversy or attack opponents – has always been a feature of democratic communities. The dictatorships that foster a cult of personality are extreme examples of the same problem: the common fantasy that one person can redeem us from our struggles.

To avoid electing demagogues or placing too much power in one person's hands, people could stop idolising those leaders they see as 'on the side of the angels', and, by the same token, stop demonising their opponents. Political leaders are only human, and they're less able to shape the future than we may wish – or fear. Leadership is needed for good government. But, love them or hate them, the personae of political leaders loom too large in our imaginations – because we let them, or even invite them. This generates unrealistic hopes and fears, as we assume they exercise more control than they do, and hence there are bitter disappointments or recriminations – and sometimes assassinations. A leader's ability to be persuasive, appealing and even inspiring isn't a bad thing, but we needn't be entranced by it. The fact that we may have positive feelings about someone campaigning for office has logically little to do with the candidate's competence and reliability when it comes to governing and/or passing law. It's not always easy to predict what candidates would do if successful, nor what challenges they may have to face, nor what the effects of their decisions would be, but the likelihood that they'll serve the public interest and respect the law is a more important criterion than how we feel about them on the day we cast a ballot.

In a modern state, eligibility to lead and to govern isn't determined simply by the kind of person one is, other than one's relevant skills, experience, qualifications and trustworthiness. What the right merits and ethical qualities are exactly is always up for debate, and each individual brings a unique mix. Good leadership is in the eye of the beholder to a large extent, and there's no single personality type that's best suited for political leadership. To minimise groupthink, we need a range of skills, personalities and backgrounds when decisions are being made. But the present tendency of political parties to select almost exclusively university graduates as candidates needs to be reconsidered. A tertiary education is relevant for the demands of public office, but a wide educational and income gap has emerged between elected representatives and those they represent. Political parties should foster more talent from among working people, with training in communications skills if needed, just as they've fostered candidates from minority groups.

All humans are fallible and unpredictable, and the competitive nature of political careers doesn't encourage the selflessness and integrity needed in those who hold public office.[22] Morally flawed leaders who get embroiled in corruption, scandal and sleaze create headlines that grab our attention and breed suspicion and distrust in the public. Those who set a good example, on the other hand, find it hard, if not impossible, to counteract the bad impressions made by others. A critical issue for the restoration of political trust is in the ethical conduct of individuals in office. Do we need something like the traditional mirror of princes, or a school for politicians? Probably not. Those moralistic old mirrors of princes may have been useful in their time, but there's no shortage now of evidence-based and practical literature about leadership.[23]

And governments often produce codes of conduct for ministers and civil servants for their guidance. For example, the UK government's Ministerial Code 'sets out the standards of conduct expected of ministers and how they discharge their duties'.[24] Surely most of the time such guidelines are read and followed – but that doesn't make the news. On the other hand, the conclusion that former prime minister Boris Johnson had disingenuously and deliberately attempted to mislead the Committee of Privileges and the House of Commons was, quite rightly, headline news.[25]

Our accumulated wisdom about public service hasn't prevented people from admiring and electing some incompetent, flawed and narcissistic leaders. But before we blame leaders – which is all too easy – we could examine our reactions as followers. The personalisation of politics is an observable trend: the personae of leaders overshadow the political parties they lead; they consume the attention of the journalists who tell us about them and the audiences who love or hate them. A leader's practical policy objectives and the capability to carry them to fruition are lost in excessive analysis of personality and superficial rhetoric. While we should expect a high standard of behaviour from those in public office, we could try not to generalise from high-profile cases of political misconduct, and thus critically reflect on our tendency as citizens to personalise public affairs.

Effective leaders would foster a systemic political trust (which is not blind faith) with competent delivery of necessary services and response to emergencies. Political trust requires that we respect one another's autonomy and that we observe an ethic of care. I'll make some further remarks about this next, and then address two critical concerns for government today: the debate between green growth and degrowth, and the control of online extremism.

Trust and care

European political thought since the Enlightenment emphasised the rights of an autonomous individual and overlooked the dependency that we all undergo, affecting our wellbeing, especially in the early and late stages of life. Many public services – midwifery, healthcare, elder care, education and so on – are forms of caring work. They're private as well as public obligations – and hence a concern for government – as they sustain our survival, our development as individuals and our quality of life. We all directly benefit from the care of others, and indirectly benefit from the care that others are receiving, and this helps us to develop and to be part of communities of civil and educated people. The achievement of a caring community depends, then, on public institutions as well as the private activities of families and individuals. Central questions for government are when and to what extent an individual or family has a legitimate claim on society for caring services.

The principles of care, charity and dignity – and our corresponding moral accountability and obligations to one another – were advanced since ancient times by the various religions, but their institutions (including orphanages and hospitals) have had to fit into modern states under secular government. Universal rights to life, security and non-discrimination have been established, and religious belief is protected as a personal choice. Human rights can be invoked when states abuse or fail to protect people, and this evolving account-ability of states has been beneficial. But the UN's framework of universal human rights, for all its strengths, has been challenged for not, in fact, being culturally universal, but being a product of the liberal individualistic ideals of the imperial powers that were the victors of World War II. These human rights are premised on personal autonomy – which is not a bad thing – but care, support and belonging within a family, community or nation are treated as corollaries. We now have extensive research findings on human wellbeing and its social correlates to guide policymakers in debates about which kinds of public services and institutions are required for better results, and the evidence shows that people don't thrive best when they're isolated from others or left to themselves.[26] The Anglo-American doctrines that 'every man must take care of himself' – as Woodrow Wilson once put it[27] – and that the state shouldn't intervene unless called on to do so, haven't led to the best social outcomes.

While early-modern political thinkers such as John Locke noticed the importance of parental care and affection for our development and education, they didn't take that insight far enough. Instead they focused on the rights-bearing adult, rather than account more fully for our interdependence as social beings, and they normalised a white male subjectivity. A natural freedom and an abstract equality ('in the eyes of God') were seen as foundations, but, in practice, there were slavery, racism and gender discrimination. Much political strife since those days, such as the suffrage and civil rights movements, has been about who (or which classes of humans) had been excluded from the category of 'rights-bearing free citizen' and hence how to universalise that status so that everyone enjoys its privileges and protections as an equal. That struggle isn't over, and it shouldn't cease, but there are terms in which to consider the matter other than individual rights. Relational ethics and mutual obligations of trust and care arise prior to individual autonomy, or as necessary conditions thereof, as we simply couldn't survive without the care of others and without trust. To care and to be trustworthy are not originally the rational choices of free individuals; instead, *there'd be no free consenting individuals were it not for our trust in and care for one another.* The ethics and duties of care and trust in society have often been contrasted with abstract rational prin-ciples of impartial justice. This needn't be an either–or debate, though, as it may be framed as a rebalancing towards care and trust as guiding principles. One of the benefits of a high-trust society is its potential to foster individual autonomy.

Our enjoyment of a good life isn't entirely up to us as individuals – as if it depended on our own aptitudes and efforts, and had nothing to do with our social world. Indeed, our true debts to society may be unrepayable, and so, in reply to libertarians, taxation isn't theft. We do owe something to society for the care of others and of ourselves. The extent of that shared obligation and the ways and means of providing such care aren't matters that can be settled technically and economically once and for all. Such policy debates and decisions are in the hands of each society and its government, but the underlying principles of collective trust and care apply to all. Every society observes mutual obligations between its members, and modern states do this through impersonal systems of taxation intended for common security and wellbeing. The underlying deal is a set of promises that, if performed well, forestall resistance and sustain political trust. A caring government helps individuals 'to satisfy their needs for a number of public goods that they cannot reasonably obtain on their own' and supports us in 'the inevitable dependencies of human life and the derivative dependencies that arise from caring for inevitably dependent individuals'.[28] If the world's wealthiest country – the United States – leaves millions of citizens homeless and/or without guaranteed healthcare, then their government fails to live up to an implied promise.[29] Individuality, agency and autonomy still matter, but these ideal conditions of liberal ideology are unattainable without care, security and protection, and hence they presuppose attachment and belonging in family, community and nation, supported by services that can only be provided with collective effort.

Political trust is a quality of those social bonds that depend on mutual promises, and it's apparently in decline in many (but not all) countries lately.[30] To rebuild political trust requires our reinforcing the shared beliefs that social norms and laws exist for our benefit, even though they may impede or annoy us from time to time, and that there are authorities and institutions that will competently, albeit imperfectly, uphold and enforce them. To restore political trust takes time; it requires a myriad of everyday actions. A community doesn't simply achieve such trust at any given moment, as it's the product of continuous labour, much of it unnoticed and unremunerated. Blaming an amorphous group of people called 'the government' for breaking promises and losing our trust won't help to restore it; neither would it help if we kept quiet and accepted things as they are. It does help if we all do what we can to reduce harmful discord and distrust and to see to it that the promises that maintain social cohesion are clarified and kept, no matter how limited our influence over policies and events may be. I'll present some general solutions as this chapter comes to a conclusion. But there are some historically unprecedented issues to grapple with.

Ecological crossroads

Perhaps the biggest issue now facing all governments is how to balance ecological sustainability and economic security. There's been an unhealthy relationship between states and the fossil-fuel industry, much of which is owned by states, for instance Russia, Norway and Saudi Arabia. Governments gain revenues from production and consumption of fossil fuels and they subsidise the industry in part to keep prices low. Globally, oil and gas subsidies far outweigh those for renewable energy. Furthermore, the industry doesn't compensate those whose lives are being disrupted by climate disasters, which some argue is a hidden subsidy.[31] But woe betide the government that lets fuel prices rise, even if the aim is to reduce consumption, as that can lead to protest and hence to electoral defeat. So governments may, from this perspective, look like a part of the problem of global warming, not the source of solutions.

There are two alternatives that show us ways out of this trap. First, the Green New Deal calls for 'a worldwide programme to invest between 1.5 and 2 per cent of global GDP every year to raise energy-efficiency standards and expand clean renewable-energy supplies'.[32] The renewables industry is innovative and creates employment, and the state would support workers and communities affected by downsizing in fossil fuels. But it requires overcoming powerful vested interests. Renewables present opportunities for investors, however, and innovation could boost economic growth while reducing carbon emissions. We'd get more economic goods for less environmental bads, or green growth, by 'decoupling' growth from its ecological impacts. We'd use less energy and other resources per unit of economic output, while cleaner energy sources would emit less pollution. The ambitious aim is 'absolute decoupling': using less of the planet's limited natural resources while improving wellbeing for all.

Critics of green growth argue, however, that there's 'no empirical evidence for such a decoupling currently happening'.[33] Cleaner technologies may generate more goods without carbon emissions but they may also lead to increased consumption of other natural resources. Carbon emissions aren't our only problem. New technologies such as nuclear fission could be used in ways that ruin the ecosystem even more. In other words, energy efficiency gains may well be offset by increases in the scale of resource depletion.[34]

Most writers in this field maintain that a dramatic shift in public policy and political economy is needed, away from economic efficiency and towards human sufficiency. The wealthy can cut their consumption and enjoy better wellbeing by reducing anxiety about gaining things no one needs, like excessively large homes and private jets, and collectively we could reduce the inequality that causes social unrest. We must stop ruining the planet and learn to live a better quality of life, in reciprocity with our environments, with other species and with one another – the rich with less unnecessary stuff and the poor with a fairer share of essentials. If we don't make these changes, then undesirable changes will be forced on us anyway by natural disasters.

The more radical alternative is *degrowth*: abandoning economic growth and purposefully reducing material and energy usage to levels that balance with the planet's capacities to supply resources and absorb waste and pollution. It's the obsession with economic growth that's responsible for polluting the environment, cutting public services and widening inequality.[35] We can't use economic growth to buy our way out of ecologically unsustainable activities. We should instead forget about economic growth and think of wellbeing, or thriving, as 'renegade' economist Kate Raworth[36] puts it, within limits the planet can sustain.

Many degrowth advocates call for participatory democracy through people's assemblies and referendums, including the democratisation of international agencies such as the International Monetary Fund and World Bank. They often say we should dismantle state hierarchies, ban undemocratic lobbying and political finance and return control of resources to the people. They would redirect industry, deal equitably with the social dislocation, and reduce consumption to meet human needs. This assumes people would democratically choose this pathway. But would the wealthy and those who aspire to wealth happily agree to curtail their lifestyles and ambitions? Or would a degrowth policy need to be imposed by a dictator? Degrowth calls for a stronger state to reduce inequality and eradicate poverty. But how would states address poverty when economies and budgets are cut? Moreover, degrowth needs a global commitment, but it can't guarantee that the necessary international agreement would work. Some states would evade the regulations and take advantage of their competitors' self-imposed penury.

The degrowth model rightly questions GDP (economic output) as an indicator of policy success, but we don't have accurate figures of all resources extracted and consumed globally. Measures of material throughput are less accurate even than GDP, and, as there's no precise model of how the variables interact, we can't estimate the trade-offs under any specified degrowth trajectory.[37] Degrowth would require strong governmental actions to restructure industrial activities, restrict consumption to basic needs and then deal with social change and even unrest.[38] But, so far, it lacks robust policy rationales for doing so.

The global bonanza produced by burning oil, gas and coal has enabled exponential population growth and higher living standards, but the outcomes are socially unjust and harmful to ecosystems. More people consuming more resources per person isn't viable if we want to avoid further disasters. The warnings of *Limits to Growth* (see Chapter 2, 'Making predictions')[39] weren't heeded, and the consequences are becoming apparent. But present policymaking is premised on – if not addicted to – unsustainable growth. Degrowth doesn't presently look achievable, however, as an alternative. And, while green growth may be more palatable, it appears that it may be recommending too little change, given the scale of the problems, and it may be too late to prevent disaster. Nevertheless, governments must take action on this.

New media

Information and communication technologies (ICTs) have produced profound changes in how government is organised, how its services are delivered and how it communicates with us. Tax returns and passport renewals, for example, can be done online, and, aside from classified information, it's easy to find out what governments are planning and doing and to engage in public consultation processes. More efficient and open government, meaning greater transparency and hence higher trust, are general benefits of e-government. For example, tenders to deliver services can be tracked online, giving assurance that applications are being processed in a timely manner. If used effectively with the aim of delivering public value (meeting people's needs and expectations) then e-government can boost political trust. The traditional public bureau was hierarchical and paper-based, so the adoption of ICTs has flattened organisational structures, changed the skills requirements of governmental agencies and altered the ways in which they interact with the public. The implementation is costly, however, and failures are common. If innovation is treated as a purely technical exercise, ignoring the needs of users, then people may lose confidence in digital services and in their government. The results of e-government are less promising so far in developing countries, among communities that lack efficient internet services and for people who are unfamiliar with working online or who lack trust.[40]

There are also political concerns about abuses of ICTs. Governments of all kinds engage in digital surveillance, indiscriminately collecting metadata; while oppressive governments shut down or restrict the internet and social media in order to control unrest and stifle dissent.[41] On the other hand, there are many dangerous groups that recruit, plan and operate online, and that genuinely deserve close monitoring. Groups as various as Islamic State (see Chapter 6, 'Quasi-states') and violent white-supremacist skinheads use the internet and social media to access and spread content, to recruit and induct newcomers, to network with like-minded people and to incite and coordinate violent actions.[42] So the internet connects people who, in the pre-digital world, wouldn't have become aware of, or would have lost touch with, one another. As we know from personal experiences, this digital connectivity can be beneficial, but it also enables toxic politics and real-world violence among the minority who are predisposed to that.

Online extremism is a global issue that calls for control. The genocidal violence and ethnic cleansing in Myanmar in 2017, the mass murder in two mosques in Christchurch, New Zealand, in 2019, and the uses of Facebook on both occasions, illustrate the problems here. Arising from the live-streaming of the latter attack was the Christchurch Call to Action to Eliminate Terrorist and Violent Extremist Content Online, led by France and New Zealand and supported by 58 governments and 12 online service providers, including the big

Silicon Valley brands. This international agreement isn't binding or enforceable but it supports numerous activities to ensure a free, open and secure internet, respect freedom of expression and yet to eliminate violent and terrorist content. The kind of content targeted here should be limited to that which is potentially harmful or deadly. The production and consumption of content that threatens, inspires or records violence neither arises from nor serves any meaningful enjoyment of liberty. On the contrary, its aim is the deprivation of life and liberty. Hence the call to action seeks in principle reasonable limitations to online expression. Concerns have been expressed that it represents a threat to freedom of speech, but one can't sit by and allow people who intend to cause harm to operate online with impunity. Vigilance around civil liberties is always warranted, of course.[43] And international efforts to control online extremism may not be effective, some say. That remains to be seen, but, in matters that affect public safety, the possibility of ineffectiveness gives no licence for inaction.

Whether harmful or not, social media create a perception that content is being shared by a community to which users can or do belong, rather than just being out there in the public domain. Machine learning means that users get exposed to selections of content, voices and opinions based on what they've already viewed, liked and shared, and this draws them towards like-minded others and into online communities.[44] This can be beneficial, but not if an online community advocates hatred and discrimination or, worse still, plans and coordinates real violence. But, while platforms such as Telegram have facilitated such things, there was plenty of political polarisation, propaganda and violence before there were social media, and only a minority of people adopt extreme views or conspiracy theories arising from time spent online. Social media aren't solely to blame, then, but engagement in them can nudge or attract some people towards extreme ideas that they may already have begun to entertain but hadn't previously shared. Once enough people are drawn in, social media use can reinforce extreme political beliefs through a sense of belonging. This doesn't always lead to violent actions, as there are plenty of internet warriors who don't take any real action, but in some cases it does. The social media platforms have been complicit in the spread of hate, as they put profits before people and, in effect, collude with authoritarian governments.[45] Political pressure needs to be applied to them, and to the corporations that advertise on their platforms.

Every person who anonymously writes or shares online messages that incite discrimination or violence is also a person located somewhere who could be more constructively engaged in their community. A global problem may have some local solutions, then. The promising conclusion is that things that may look impossible – controlling hateful and violent online content – can be addressed by governments when they're determined to collaborate internationally as well as return to their roots locally. A concern, on the other hand, is that malicious actors may use Artificial Intelligence (AI) to flood the internet with misinformation and deep fakes, causing confusion and discord and making open and fair political debate even more difficult. Or machine learning will go off on its own tangent and make itself unstoppable. AI will far exceed human capabilities, and programmers are unaware of how these models arrive at their answers, so no one can confidently state what AI *can't* do in future. There have been concerted efforts to develop regulations, but AI will change the political environment and alter the scope of what governments do.

Conclusion

The best kinds of government are those that can work with uncertainty and disagreement because, in the real political world, there's nowhere to rest and we're always in the thick of fast-moving contested situations with unpredictable futures. One shouldn't say that, if we only had better government, everything would be sorted. But we do need to think about improvements. The aim of this book has been to inquire into how we can restore political trust and get better government and public administration, based on efforts to understand the past and the present, including those aspects that we may not like and may not go away. As my main concern is government in general, as a complex set of practices, I haven't looked at particular policies, other than as examples of underlying principles.

To get better government, we need to be clear about aims and purposes. A basic aim is to regulate events and make our communities, commerce and public conduct predictable – or less unpredictable – and hence to enable people to live prosperous and safe lives. Another aim is to deal with adversaries, emergencies or threats. By means of government, we aim to care for our fellow human beings – a quality that's been neglected recently by many states, though for a time there was significant innovation in welfare states. There's sense still in the Lockean maxim that government is instituted for the safety and security of those who are governed, and we would also look beyond that towards the people's wellbeing: the common weal, or commonwealth, in the older meanings of those words.

We must now add the care of the planet, arising from our collective responsibility for polluting it. And societies need a government of AI, but not *by* AI, so that new apps and devices super-powered by machine learning don't become our masters. How will we live a fully (or even fuller) human life once machines that recollect much more and work much faster than us become part of everything we do?

That's already a big to-do list! To do it well under present circumstances requires reimagining the state and its institutions and how we're governed. This question of how to get better government is common, but diverse in its particular national circumstances; there are many different forms of these problematic institutions and practices that we call 'government'. We face significant disagreements about how to govern and administer, let alone about particular policy goals.

Good government begins from two basic premises: those who govern are discouraged by their institutions' norms and rules from self-serving behaviour, and they're encouraged to work for a vision of the common good that they can defend in the face of disagreement; while those who are governed have a reasonable degree of confidence that the system is generally working for them, in spite of complaints (justifiable or not) about particular failures or inconveniences. Perfection, utopia or a steady state shouldn't be a goal. We need to consider constitutional and systemic changes, and ways to improve the conduct of individual actors within the system. This includes reviving the notion of public service, as a calling and a set of duties, in the administrative branches of government as well as in society's leaders.

The arts of government are pragmatic and purposeful and hence they're strategic. Faced with internal and external rivals, a competent leader summarises realistically the present situation, expresses shared values and shows a pathway forward. A major change in strategy implies change in structures. But institutional or constitutional change isn't easily achieved, and profound or revolutionary changes are often misdirected or destructive. To get better government, we begin with the institutions that we have, and these differ greatly from place to place. Gradual change generally works better than revolution. This means that progress can be frustratingly slow, but it's better to accept that we're in for patient and steady work that brings the people affected into the process as participants rather than as passive audiences – or as victims. This also requires clarity about the aims and scope of government, and hence knowing what's best left up to people to decide for themselves, or knowing how and when to intervene.

Too often, people have wished for charismatic and transformational leadership as a supposed solution, and too often this has proven to be disappointing or even disastrous. The way out of our problems involves patient collective work with trusted leaders, not a redeemer. We need to focus on building and improving basic public services, especially in developing countries, but also in those developed countries that have neglected them. This will mean facing facts about the levels of taxation or international assistance needed to fund them. Tackling corruption is an essential component of this.

One thing that countries have in common is a need for government and public administration – which comes with the general problems considered in Chapter 3. These problems have endured precisely because they're intractable: they don't get solved, but they must be addressed. For moral and practical reasons, we can't stop governing, nor can we refuse to be governed. Claiming to be a law unto oneself, or that the rules don't apply to oneself, is not a morally acceptable option, although one can of course question particular laws and rules. The critical challenge is how to govern a state or a community *better* on the assumptions that there's no singular best way and there's no use in starting another war over whose model is best. 'Autocracies versus democracies' is a bad way to frame the global situation, especially given that there are problems under all regimes. Some leaders in the western world are setting very poor examples, though not as bad perhaps as some autocrats. The trouble is that, for the purposes of political trust – or trustworthy government – our 'broken' systems of government have to fix themselves somehow. Leaders and followers all need to reflect on themselves and strive to do better. No one can force others to change, but the means for nurturing better leaders are within reach, and we can see how people throughout the ages have approached it. Getting better government isn't a one-off achievement, then: it's a perpetual obligation.

Political leaders and administrators need to pay heed to people locally but also to think and operate globally. Borderless problems call for borderless solutions, and hence for something like a 'green Bretton Woods': an international agreement that regulates trade, permits countries to set their own goals, and yet aims to achieve sustainable consumption and reduce carbon emissions, backed by a global institution that assists economies that struggle to adjust. Many people sensibly call for better multilateral cooperation, but many of us have also lost confidence in what it means to govern, and radically different types of government and policy regimes are competing for advantage.

We must reimagine government to achieve two distinct, but not incompatible, sets of tasks: to collaborate globally and to enhance popular participation and rational deliberation. Citizens' assemblies, for example, have proven to be useful for generating public understanding and consent. A deliberative process could then produce well-informed and clear recommendations to parliaments or propositions for referendums, put forward by people who aren't seeking election. Democratic government, in practice, however, is often marred by delays, indecision and political polarisation, leading to a sense of powerlessness and being bogged down in planning and consultation. Authoritarian leadership may acquire an appeal, as an alternative, but that style of government has its well-known downfalls: a resistance to self-correction in response to failure or inefficiency, and a tendency to do harm to those who disagree.

Numerous books lately have raised the alarm about threats to democracy, but I've questioned just how democratic representative government is, or ever was, and I've endeavoured to be more constructive about the diversity of forms of government. While I favour democratic culture and norms, it's unrealistic and weak to argue, 'Democracy is in danger so we need more democracy.' No matter where we live, we need better leadership and more constructive collaboration across different kinds of governments and through multiple levels of administration – not all of which will be done democratically. There are good reasons and recommendations for improving the democratic quality of decision-making, especially in local government and around defined problems or controversies. Policymaking processes should at least pay heed to the rights and needs of all affected. But democratisation is not a universal or inexorable trend, and some global policy problems won't get addressed democratically. Centralised decision-making and international agreements negotiated among elites will continue to be common. In many circumstances, the focus may need to be less on democracy, however we may style that, and more on non-corrupt and effective administration and delivery of public services.

The countries that get the best outcomes for their people tend to be smaller ones that are better able to hear and respond to people's needs and opinions. The great powers get the greatest media attention globally, but they're not the best governed. All countries struggle with similar technically complex and fiscally costly policy issues, nonetheless. Governments need to reinvigorate public participation as far as possible, to support the quality and legitimacy of what they do. Before anyone begins a journey of political leadership, then, they could keep in mind the maxim that 'all politics is local politics'. We all came from somewhere, and all leaders rely on those localities and communities that supported them. Addressing global problems begins and ends with our understanding of, and connections with, the local communities to which we belong and which bear the consequences of high-level political decisions. Connection with people reminds us of our interdependence and mutual obligations which in turn form the basis for learning trustworthy behaviour.

Have we solved the problem of government yet? We haven't, and a premise of this book is that no one ever has, so no one ever will. To govern well is to grapple with a set of intractable and recurring problems in constantly changing circumstances. What this book contributes to that obligatory and endless endeavour is to clarify the nature of these problems – to take them apart and put them back together again – and hence to encourage readers to reflect more deeply and lower the heat of political debate. This means acknowledging our responsibilities to one another, across our political divisions and rivalries, assuming an attitude of empathetic realism, and undertaking patient work as we assess and respond to the many perplexing problems of government and public administration. Better government is needed more than ever, especially to tackle borderless problems. It requires hard work that can't be put off. It's all up to us and it's within reach.

Notes

1 Heiss, Claudia. 2021. 'Latin America Erupts: Re-founding Chile'. *Journal of Democracy* 32 (3): 33–47, URL: https://muse.jhu.edu/article/797784 (accessed 23 October 2022).
2 Vergara, Camila. 9 September 2022. 'Chile's Rejection'. *Sidecar*, URL: https://newleftreview.org/sidecar/posts/chiles-rejection?pc=1469 (accessed 23 October 2022).

3 Pasquino, Gianfranco. 2020. *Italian Democracy: How It Works*. London: Routledge. See p. 15.

4 Newell, James L. 2020. 'Political Parties, Politicians and the September Constitutional Referendum: The Politics of Frivolity'. *Contemporary Italian Politics* 12(4): 391–93, URL: https://doi.org/10.1080/23248823.2020.1854527 (accessed 4 October 2022).

5 Pasquino [note 3]. See p. 121.

6 'The Proud Boys is an authoritarian, ultranationalist group … one of the largest far-right extremist groups in the United States. They claim they do not define national belonging by race, and that they simply want to preserve Western culture. But, for the Proud Boys, Western culture is European, Christian, and governed by strict adherence to "traditional" notions of gender.' Southern Poverty Law Centre. 8 April 2022. 'Statement to the Select Committee to Investigate the January 6th Attack on the United States Capitol', URL: https://www.splcenter.org/sites/default/files/splc-statement-january-6-select-committee-proud-boys.pdf (accessed 22 September 2022).

7 'Oath Keepers believe the [US] government is secretly planning, along with foreign countries and the United Nations, to impose martial law, seize all Americans' guns, force resisters into concentration camps and install a one-world totalitarian government known as the "New World Order".' Southern Poverty Law Centre. No date. 'Oath Keepers', URL: https://www.splcenter.org/fighting-hate/extremist-files/group/oath-keepers (accessed 22 September 2022).

8 Greenberg, Jon. 16 June 2022. 'Most Republicans Still Falsely Believe Trump's Stolen Election Claims.' Poynter, URL: https://www.poynter.org/fact-checking/2022/70-percent-republicans-falsely-believe-stolen-election-trump/ (accessed 26 July 2023).

9 Miele, Frank. 28 March 2022. 'What History Teaches Us About Stolen Elections'. Real Clear Politics, URL: https://www.realclearpolitics.com/articles/2022/03/28/what_history_teaches_us_about_stolen_elections_147388.html (accessed 26 July 2023).

10 Brennan Center for Justice. 2023. 'Voting Laws Roundup: June 2023', URL: https://www.brennancenter.org/our-work/research-reports/voting-laws-roundup-june-2023 (accessed 2 July 2023).

11 In a 2018 survey, '61% say "significant changes" are needed in the fundamental "design and structure" of American government to make it work for current times. [And] a majority (55%) supports changing the way presidents are elected so that the candidate who receives the most total votes nationwide – rather than a majority in the Electoral College – wins the presidency.' Pew Research Center. 2018. 'The Public, the Political System and American Democracy', URL: https://www.pewresearch.org/politics/2018/04/26/the-public-the-political-system-and-american-democracy/ (accessed 26 July 2023).

12 Convention of States Action, URL: https://conventionofstates.com/ (accessed 20 October 2022).

13 'Republican presidents add more to deficits than their Democratic counterparts.' White, Taylor. 2020. 'Which Party Adds More to Deficits?' Towards Data Science, URL: https://towardsdatascience.com/which-party-adds-more-to-deficits-a6422c6b00d7 (accessed 26 July 2023).

14 Lepore, Jill. 26 October 2022. 'The United States' Unamendable Constitution'. *The New Yorker*, URL: https://www.newyorker.com/culture/annals-of-inquiry/the-united-states-unamendable-constitution (accessed 28 October 2022).

15 Pipes, Richard. 1995. *Russia Under the Old Regime* (second edition). London: Penguin.

16 Election Study Center, National Chengchi University. No date. 'Taiwan Independence vs. Unification with the Mainland', URL: https://esc.nccu.edu.tw/PageDoc/Detail?fid=7801&id=6963 (accessed 26 July 2023).

17 Statement by the Ministry of Foreign Affairs of the People's Republic of China. 2 August 2022, URL: https://www.fmprc.gov.cn/eng/zxxx_662805/202208/t20220802_10732293.html (accessed 26 July 2023).

18 Tsang, Steve & Olivia Cheung. 2022. 'Has Xi Jinping Made China's Political System More Resilient and Enduring?' *Third World Quarterly* 43 (1): 225–43, URL: https://doi.org/10.1080/01436597.2021.2000857 (accessed 27 October 2022). See p. 235.

19 'Western policy preferences will prevail less, the quest for harmonization across economies that defined the era of hyperglobalization will be attenuated, and each country will have to be granted greater leeway in managing its economy, society, and political system. International institutions such as the World Trade Organization and the International Monetary Fund will have to adapt to that reality.' Rodrik, Dani & Stephen M. Walt. 2022. 'How to Build a Better Order'. *Foreign Affairs* 101 (5): 142–55: (e-version).

20 'West' refers here to wealthy capitalist countries with competitive multi-party representative government, regardless of the hemisphere in which they're located.

21 Sempill, Julian. 2020. 'The Rule of Law and the Rule of Men: History, Legacy, Obscurity'. *Hague Journal on the Rule of Law* 12 (3): 511–40.

22 The Nolan Principles, or seven principles of public life, summarised these ethical standards. GOV.UK, URL: https://www.gov.uk/government/publications/the-7-principles-of-public-life/the-7-principles-of-public-life--2 (accessed 31 October 2022).

23 On the mirror of princes traditions, see: Perret, Noëlle-Laetitia & Stéphane Péquignot. 2023. *A Critical Companion to the 'Mirrors for Princes' Literature.* Leiden: Brill, URL: https://doi.org/10.1163/9789004523067 (accessed 18 December 2022). On contemporary leadership theory, see: Lussier, Robert N. & Christopher F. Achua. 2023. *Leadership: Theory, Application, and Skill Development* (seventh edition). Thousand Oaks, CA: Sage.

24 Ministerial Code 2022. GOV.UK, URL: https://www.gov.uk/government/publications/ministerial-code (accessed 31 October 2022).

25 House of Commons Committee of Privileges. 2023. 'Matter referred on 21 April 2022 (conduct of Rt Hon Boris Johnson): Final Report. Fifth Report of Session 2022–23'. London: House of Commons.

26 Altman, David, Patrick Flavin & Benjamin Radcliff. 2017. 'Democratic Institutions and Subjective Well-Being'. *Political Studies.* 65 (3): 685–704; Lee, Seung Jong. 2022. *Public Happiness: Community, Quality-of-Life and Well-Being.* Cham: Springer, URL: https://link.springer.com/content/pdf/10.1007/978-3-030-89643-0.pdf

27 Wilson, Woodrow. 2002 [1908]. *Constitutional Government in the United States.* New York: Routledge. See p. 19.

28 Engster, Daniel. 2007. *The Heart of Justice.* Oxford: Oxford University Press. See pp. 80–1.

29 'Americans' unhappiness with government has long coexisted with their continued support for government having a substantial role in many realms. And when asked how much the federal government does to address the concerns of various groups in the United States, there is a widespread belief that it does *too little* on issues affecting many of the groups asked about, including middle-income people (69%), those with lower incomes (66%) and retired people (65%).' (Original italics.) Sixty-nine percent agreed that federal government should play a major role in ensuring access to health care. Pew Research Center. 2022. 'Americans' Views of Government: Decades of Distrust, Enduring Support for Its Role', URL: https://www.pewresearch.org/politics/2022/06/06/americans-views-of-government-decades-of-distrust-enduring-support-for-its-role/ (accessed 14 October 2022).

30 This is supported empirically by social surveys, even though I've questioned the way that surveys define and measure trust. For an in-depth analysis, see: Duncan, Grant. 2019. *The Problem of Political Trust*. London: Routledge.
31 Timperley, Jocelyn. 2021. 'Why Fossil Fuel Subsidies Are So Hard To Kill'. *Nature* 598: 403–5, URL: https://doi.org/10.1038/d41586-021-02847-2 (accessed 8 September 2022).
32 Pollin, Robert. 2018. 'De-growth vs a Green New Deal'. *New Left Review* 112: 5–25. See p. 10.
33 Parrique, T., J. Barth, F. Briens, C. Kerschner, A. Kraus-Polk, A. Kuokkanen & J.H. Spangenberg. 2019. 'Decoupling Debunked: Evidence and Arguments Against Green Growth as a Sole Strategy for Sustainability'. European Environmental Bureau, URL: https://eeb.org/library/decoupling-debunked/ (accessed 8 September 2022).
34 Vadén, Tere, Ville Lähde, Antti Majava, Paavo Järvensivu, Tero Toivanen, Emma Hakala & J. T. Eronen. 2020. 'Decoupling for Ecological Sustainability: A Categorisation and Review of Research Literature'. *Environmental Science & Policy* 112: 236–44.
35 Hickel, Jason. 2021. *Less is More*. London: Penguin Random House.
36 Raworth, Kate. 2023. Exploring Donut Economics, URL: https://www.kateraworth.com/ (accessed 4 July 2023).
37 Tsuda, Kenta. 2021. 'Naïve Questions on Degrowth'. *New Left Review* 128: 111–30.
38 Fitzpatrick, Nick, Tim Parrique & Inês Cosme. 2022. 'Exploring Degrowth Policy Proposals: A Systematic Mapping with Thematic Synthesis'. *Journal of Cleaner Production* 365: 132764.
39 Meadows, D. H., D. L. Meadows, J. Randers & W. W. Behrens. 1972. *The Limits to Growth*. New York: Universe Books.
40 Malodia, Suresh, Amandeep Dhir, Mahima Mishra & Zeeshan Ahmed Bhatti. 2021. 'Future of e-Government: An Integrated Conceptual Framework'. *Technological Forecasting and Social Change* 173: 121102, URL: https://doi.org/10.1016/j.techfore.2021.121102; Twizeyimana, Jean Damascene & Annika Andersson. 2019. 'The Public Value of E-Government – A Literature Review'. *Government Information Quarterly* 36 (2): 167–78, URL: https://doi.org/10.1016/j.giq.2019.01.001 (both accessed 10 October 2022).
41 Internet shutdowns are documented by Access Now, URL: https://www.accessnow.org/
42 Gaudette, Tiana, Ryan Scrivens & Vivek Venkatesh. 2022. 'The Role of the Internet in Facilitating Violent Extremism: Insights from Former Right-Wing Extremists'. *Terrorism and Political Violence* 34 (7): 1339–56, URL: https://doi.org/10.1080/09546553.2020.1784147; Lowe, David. 2022. 'Far-Right Extremism: Is it Legitimate Freedom of Expression, Hate Crime, or Terrorism?' *Terrorism and Political Violence* 34 (7): 1433–53, URL: https://doi.org/10.1080/09546553.2020.1789111 (both accessed 10 October 2022).
43 For example, following a warning from the FBI about misinformation that could have affected the US election in 2020, the suppression of news about Hunter Biden's laptop by Facebook and Twitter fuelled concerns about unwarranted censorship for political ends – although others said it wasn't censored enough. Molloy, David. 26 August 2022. 'Zuckerberg tells Rogan FBI Warning Prompted Biden LaptopStoryCensorship'. BBC, URL:https://www.bbc.com/news/world-us-canada-62688532 (accessed 26 July 2023).
44 Fisher, Max. 2022. *The Chaos Machine: The Inside Story of How Social Media Rewired Our Minds and Our World*. New York: Little, Brown.
45 Banaji, Shakuntala & Ramnath Bhat. 2021. *Social Media and Hate*. London: Routledge, URL: https://doi.org/10.4324/9781003083078 (accessed 7 November 2022).

INDEX

Printed in the United States
by Baker & Taylor Publisher Services